The life of Mahler

Musical lives

The books in this series will each provide
an account of the life of a major composer,
considering both the private and the public
figure. The main thread will be biographical
and discussion of the music will be integral
to the narrative. Each book thus presents an
organic view of the composer, the music,
and the circumstances in which he or she
lived and wrote.

Published titles

The life of Bellini
JOHN ROSSELLI

The life of Mahler
PETER FRANKLIN

The life of Mahler

PETER FRANKLIN

Published by the Press Syndicate of the University of Cambridge
The Pitt Building, Trumpington Street, Cambridge CB2 IRP
40 West 20th Street, New York, NY 10011–4211, USA
10 Stamford Road, Oakleigh, Melbourne 3166, Australia

© Cambridge University Press 1997

First published 1997

Printed in Great Britain at the University Press, Cambridge

A catalogue record for this book is available from the British Library

Library of Congress cataloguing in publication data

Franklin, Peter.
    The life of Mahler / Peter Franklin.
        p. cm. – (Musical lives)
    Includes bibliographical references and index.
    ISBN 0 521 46199 5 (hardback)
    ISBN 0 521 46761 6 (paperback)
    1. Mahler, Gustav, 1860–1911.   2. Composers – Austria –
Biography.   I. Title.   II. Series.
ML410.M23F69   1997
780'.92–dc20
    [B]   96–25105   CIP   MN

ISBN 0 521 46199 5 hardback
ISBN 0 521 46761 6 paperback

CONTENTS

ILLUSTRATIONS

Grateful acknowledgement is made for the use of illustrations from the following sources:
Okresní Archiv, Jihlava (2); Österreichischer Nationalbibliothek, Bild-Archiv

vii

(3, 4, 6, 10, 13, 16); Mahler-Rosé Collection, Ontario (5); Arthur Spiegler, Vienna (8); Internationale Gustav Mahler Gesellschaft, Vienna (9); Bibliothèque Gustav Mahler, Paris (14); Lowin Collection (15); Dr K. Sherlock (11b). Other photographs are by the author.

ACKNOWLEDGEMENTS

My offers of thanks must begin with those essential Mahler authors whose work has literally been at my elbow or at my feet throughout the writing of this book: to Henry-Louis de La Grange, for all the volumes, in English and French, of his remarkable biography of Mahler; to Knud Blaukopf, for his irreplaceable 1976 *Mahler. A Documentary Study* (and the more recent version of its texted part); to Herta Blaukopf, for her editorial work on Mahler's letters; to Knud Martner for his invaluable *Gustav Mahler im Konzertsaal* and important annotations, with Donald Mitchell, to the latest, 1990 edition of Alma Mahler's memoir. Donald Mitchell's enthusiasm and personal encouragement over many years deserves particular mention in these acknowledgements; the splendid volume he produced for the 1995 Amsterdam Mahler Festival – *Gustav Mahler: The World Listens* – has been another valued companion.

Many friends and students have also played their part. Special thanks must go to David Cooper, Diana Douglas, Barbara Engh, Keith Sherlock, Christopher Morris and Rachel Segal, all of whom put me on to things I did not previously know or came up with suggestions, information or simply encouragement when it was needed. Even more special thanks must go to Ann Tilley, who suffered the heat and traffic around the Attersee with no less fortitude than the Maiernigg car-park or the drive to Toblach. Finally, at Cambridge University Press, Michael Black and Penny Souster were searching and supportive editors.

Introduction

. . . a person should remain a 'person' and not be frozen into a legend, turned into an insufferable plaster-bust.

(Alma Mahler-Werfel: *Mein Leben*)

. . . there is the supreme gratification of finding oneself related in destiny and sufferings with those whose habitat is on the heights . . . Outside space and time there is a select company of solitary persons who are drawn to share an all the more intense life together.
(Gustav Mahler to Alma, July 1904)[1]

These contrasting statements introduce two major preoccupations of this biography which is, on principle, uneasy about its purpose. The contrast itself points to the first of these: the tension generated by love and mutual incomprehension between Mahler and his wife. Beyond that lies a knot of wider, interrelated issues concerning notions about 'art' and 'genius' and the ways in which they were mediated in individual experience and in public creative activity in nineteenth-century Europe. In ways, that is, that have become the subject of critical scrutiny in our more nervous, sceptical world that has inherited its products. Mahler might well be central to our understanding of such matters. It is for this reason that his life is worth re-examining, even at a time when other accounts of it proliferate.

Foremost among them is the grandly authoritative and detailed multi-volume study by Henry-Louis de La Grange. All subsequent Mahler biographies, this included, must to some extent be reliant on, and derivative of, that work, complete in a three-volume French edition and due to appear over the next decade in an expanded and revised English translation. It remains, in a sense, the most important biographical product of the 1960s Mahler 'boom', in which the pioneering work of the composer's friends and early critical supporters was first significantly extended. By then, crucial source studies of the 1920s, like Natalie Bauer-Lechner's posthumous *Recollections of Gustav Mahler* and Alma Mahler's edition of her husband's letters (published in 1924, the same year as the fascimile of his sketches for the Tenth Symphony) had been absorbed and interpreted by writers like Dika Newlin, Hans Redlich, Donald Mitchell and Deryck Cooke, all of whom were able to draw upon the first, specifically Mahler-orientated, volume of Alma's own autobiographical memoirs (*Gustav Mahler. Memories and Letters*, 1940). Particularly in its abridged English version, this played its own part in the increasing popularization of Mahler which would fuel major recording projects and a small industry of publications, and continues to produce collections of unpublished letters, Donald Mitchell's ongoing series of books on Mahler's music and the important documentary and biographical work of Kurt and Herta Blaukopf, Knud Martner and Zoltan Roman.[2]

The paradox is that this work has coincided with a decline in support for artistic biography. It has become a suspect means of engaging with works of art, precisely because it comes 'between' us and them. It may also unthinkingly participate in the kind of proselytizing that ignores questioning voices. In 1988 Hans Lenneberg traced musicological suspicion of the genre back to an 1885 essay by Guido Adler. Adler (1855–1941) was one of the fathers of modern European musicology and also a close friend and early biographer of Mahler – one who wished to avoid recording personal dealings with his subject so as to view him, as he put it, 'from a higher plane'. He sought to establish the model for an integrated and technically informed study of a composer's life and works, with the accent on the works. In 1916 Adler lamented the rarity of such an approach as indicating 'an altogether monstrous cancer on our scholarship'.[3] The implication was that popular artistic biography dealt in anecdotes, gossip and stories that had little to do with any serious historical or critical enterprise.

It is worth pondering Lenneberg's attempt to rehabilitate musical biography, both scholarly and popular, as worthy of study. One of his central themes is that all texts about composers, from the fanciful romance to the sober collection of facts, can acquire the status and influence of historical documents. Much depends upon how they are read and what questions are asked of them. For what purpose were they written? Lenneberg finds the history of European musical biography to have been relatively short. The transformation of music's conceptual status from that of a practised craft to that of a contemplated, historically located and developing 'art' was what gave rise to modern musical biography, he suggests, in the mid-eighteenth century. He relates the nineteenth-century explosion of biographical writing about musicians to what Adler, on the first page of his Mahler study, described as 'the continuing growth of individualism from the Renaissance up to our own day, . . . the spread of subjectivism in the music of the nineteenth century'. Lenneberg does not, however, widen beyond music his account of the battle between scholarly endeavour and the popular tendency 'to turn artists into romantic heroes'. Are the anecdotes and myths of nineteenth-century musical biography specific to that genre, or did it perhaps inherit them, ready made, from a rich existing tradition of non-musical artistic biography? Other studies tell us more about the history of the inclination to see artists as mysteriously gifted prodigies.

In a remarkable book, published in German in 1934 and translated in 1979 as *Legend, Myth and Magic in the Image of the Artist*,[4] Ernst Kris and Otto Kurz traced the history of biographical writing about visual artists back through Vasari to the earliest recorded anecdotes. Observing the same tendency for those anecdotes to become the sources of subsequent 'history', Kris and Kurz stressed that the word anecdote, in Greek, had signified an 'episode from the secret life of the hero'. Regarding the stereotyped anecdote as the '"primitive cell" of biography', they were led to the conclusion that

> even in the histories of comparatively modern artists we find biographical themes that can be traced back, point by point, to the god- and hero-filled world before the dawn of history. These themes can be demonstrated to occur again and again even outside the orbit that links our Western tradition with ancient Greece.

Relevant themes of this type are that the subject will be of lowly birth, perhaps a shepherd youth who naively draws his sheep; that his embryonic talent will be 'discovered' by a connoisseur who then sponsors his training; that his genius subsequently becomes widely famed.

Real historical circumstances may, of course, have given birth to a subsequently mythic formula. Similarly, well-intentioned biographers have believed that they were recording the truth about real artists while pouring their data into an unconsciously adopted mould that ensured the prominence of some facts at the expense of others. Nor is autobiography exempt from the process. It is not merely late nineteenth-century sentimentality that preserves from Mahler's shadowy childhood years the picture of the poor Jewish boy, given to daydreams, found improvising on an old piano in his grandmother's attic. Nor is it without relevance to the process of 'enacted biography' (described by Kris and Kurz as identification with the culturally inherited formula) that the composer himself was occasionally led to exaggerate the mythical poverty of his own childhood and to see himself, as others did, as a Dostoyevskian figure, troubled by the evil and injustice of the world, while being 'related in destiny and sufferings with those whose habitat is on the heights'. Certain questions thus confront the student of biographical writing. What *were* the facts? What is the extent and source of the mythical dress in which they may have been presented? What was the aim of the biographer? The presentation of Mahler as the direct manifestation of a mythic type (the 'pupil of Bruckner', the embodied Romantic Hero, the ascetic scorner of fashionable taste) indicates propagandistic praise in Bruno Walter, while it implies denigration in the 'modern' Alma Mahler-Werfel, with her insistence on her husband's psychological and sexual weaknesses.

Some of the earliest Mahler-biographies rather deliberately appropriated the mythic hero model. It was familiarly associated with the canonic masters of a German tradition whose spokesmen often sought to exclude Mahler: as a first-rate conductor who was a second-rate composer, as a faker of symphonic monumentality who depended on knowledge and technique rather than the authentic inspiration of genius. The extension of that line of criticism by fascist ideologues of the Nazi period (antisemitism had played its part all along) seemed retrospectively to validate the heroic status constructed and celebrated by Mahler's early biographers. It certainly spoke to the excitement of those discovering him for the first time in the 1960s, on the basis of no special preconceptions or prejudice. That enthusiasm was to carve out for Mahler a firm place in the pantheon of a newly extended Tradition. The arty woman's 'Wouldn't you just *die* without Mahler?' in the 1983 film of Willy Russell's *Educating Rita* marked a significant stage in his popular canonization. To become canonic (what major symphony orchestra would now avoid him?) is to move back into the firing-line of Change, or to become just another plaster bust in the museum.

The biography of Mahler the tyrannical entrepreneur and ruthlessly effective mover of musical mountains – what the Eighth Symphony's original promoter, Emil Gutmann, called 'Gustav Mahler as Organiser' – was certainly not what most interested his early twentieth-century supporters, particularly the younger ones. Their allegiances were likely to be with the modernists, with Schoenberg and the Second Viennese School. Their Mahler was the composer of the structurally complex, purely instrumental symphonies no. 5, 6 and 7 and of the late works, in which the nineteenth-century symphony orchestra seemed ready to throw off its robes of power and glory to reveal sinuous polyphony and timbral mobiles constructed out of solo lines. Here too might be found a Mahler who seemed subversively to mock grandiloquence, to question fantasized romantic visions and, by embracing darkness, speak directly to a more knowing and modern kind of consciousness, as a contemporary of Freud and Kafka rather than the mythical 'pupil of Bruckner' and subsequent Royal and Imperial Court Opera Director.

This is the Mahler whose 'musical physiognomy' was boldly drawn by Theodor Adorno in his remarkable book of 1960;[5] it is also the Mahler who speaks to Pierre Boulez:

> The 'hyperdimensional' character of his music has very little of the typical *fin de siècle* turgidity, the gigantism and megalomania, the delight in sheer size for its own sake. More relevant is the anxiety of an artist creating a new world that proliferates beyond his rational control.

With complicated backhanded ingenuity of the kind that also marks Schoenberg's 1912 lecture on the composer, Boulez thus contrives to include in his appreciation a measure of criticism of Mahler's stylistic shortcomings. In his preface to the first volume of de La Grange's biography, in the complete French edition, Boulez additionally maintains an ambivalent insistence on the personal, 'biographical' or 'patchwork novel' element in Mahler's symphonic narratives. What is most interesting in Boulez's Mahler is what it possibly reveals of a Mahlerian Boulez: worrying obsessively, tastefully, about the composer's need to avoid personal confidences, the subjective, the historical, while accepting that music, by its very nature, may indiscreetly 'betray' him.

The relationship between Mahler's life and his art was not, I would suggest, crudely pathological. It was, however, an intimate and ceaselessly dynamic one whose precise nature was often obscured by the richly allusive language of his explanations, steeped in German Romantic idealism and touched (as often in his letters to Alma) by the manner of the schoolmaster. He may at times quite literally have believed that in the act of creating music, of 'expressing himself' musically, he was most intensely alive as a spiritual, moral being; that music was for him the one sure route to some Absolute, or to a form of spiritual self-realization. He certainly theorized his self-consciously Beethoven-like need to gain artistic inspiration from long walks in the countryside as a matter of spiritual exercise ('the purpose – to forget one's body', he told Bruno Walter in 1908, having recently been prevented from walking by his newly discovered heart condition). But where does that idealized and spiritualized nineteenth-century Mahler meet the modernists' Mahler, or Adorno's Mahler, whose music is interpreted as transcending the conceit of 'self-expression' to the end not of rarefied mystical revelation (as Schoenberg thought) but of a multi-voiced expression of the many. The tramping feet of the downtrodden that Adorno heard in 'Revelge' certainly seemed painfully audible to those critics who discounted Mahler's attempts to achieve the ideal while dreading and detesting his ability to resound the real.

This biography is intended to silence none of those voices, either within Mahler's music or in the unfolding tradition of attempts to interpret his life. The more clearly his works appear to exemplify German symphonic form as ideology, the more impressive becomes the extent to which that clarity (registered in the profusion of directions in the scores) represented a progressively realized threat to the form's inherited self-confidence. Perhaps it is in the moments where the hubbub of conflicting impulses and interpretations seems at its height that we find ourselves closest to understanding, in the context of the world in which he lived, the meaning of Mahler's music and the reason why we have still to listen to it.

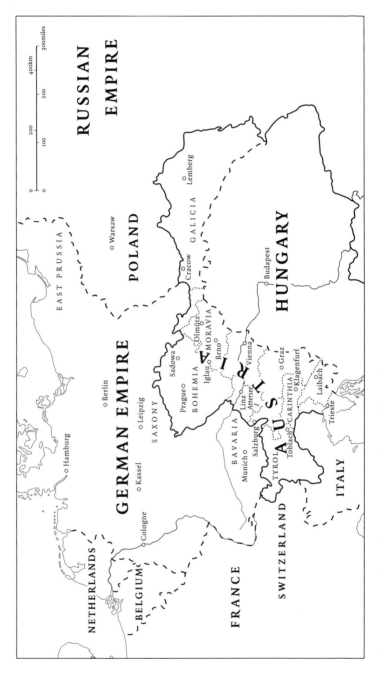

RUSSIAN EMPIRE

EAST PRUSSIA

o Warsaw

POLAND

o Berlin

GERMAN EMPIRE

o Leipzig

SAXONY

o Kassel

o Hamburg

o Cologne

NETHERLANDS

BELGIUM

FRANCE

SWITZERLAND

ITALY

o Lemberg

GALICIA

o Cracow

Sadowa

Prague o

BOHEMIA

Olmütz

Iglau MORAVIA

Brno

Linz

Attersee

Salzburg

Munich o

BAVARIA

TYROL

Toblach

Vienna

AUSTRIA

STIRIA

o Graz

CARINTHIA

o Klagenfurt

Laibach

Trieste

Budapest

HUNGARY

400km

300miles

200

200

100

0

0

The Austro-Hungarian and German Empires during Mahler's lifetime

1 Mahler's world

We first catch sight of Mahler's face and hear his voice in crowds. In Iglau, the pleasant country town in Moravia where he grew up, crowds would rarely be ethnically uniform; his own features, as a child, might have led to his being recognizable as a member of its minority Jewish community. To be thus recognized was not necessarily to be ridiculed or discriminated against. German-speaking Jews were better tolerated by the Catholic majority there than in other parts of that region of the Austro-Hungarian Empire. More than one language and many dialects would have been heard in Iglau's busy market-place, although the town was essentially an enclave of German-speaking culture, a centre of the cloth trade linked to Vienna in the south and the Bohemian but German-dominated city of Prague to the north-west. You would not need to travel far out of the city gates into the wooded surrounding countryside, however, to find yourself amongst a Czech-speaking rural peasantry. The contrasting Germanness of Iglau was marked not only by its predominant language and general cultural affinities but also by a 'mastersinger' tradition of great antiquity; Guido Adler (whose family left for Vienna in 1864, when Mahler was four years old), remembered a Hans-Sachs-like cobbler who still sang as he plied his trade in the town.

Mahler's own infant voice might first have been noticed creating a commotion in the relatively new Iglau synagogue (established in

1   An 1897 book illustration, by Hugo Charlemont, of the Iglau Stadtplatz

1861). The scene no doubt embarrassed his mother and may have angered her husband, although he would have been sitting apart from them in the customary, gender-segregated fashion; he certainly cherished his hard-won and advancing position in both the Jewish and the wider civic community of the town. The year might have been 1863 or 1864. The toddler was crying and shouting in protest at what he heard going on around him. Some of the worshippers stopped singing and were astonished to hear the Mahlers' boy piping up with a song of his own: a popular Moravian-Czech street-song called 'Ať se pinkl házi' ('Let the knapsack rock'). The least salacious version of its text seems to have run:

> A wanderer,
> a wayfarer
> went through Hungary to Moravia
> and there, in the first inn,

danced as if on water.
He danced like a madman
and his knapsack rocked with him.
Whether it rocks or not,
the devil won't take it away.[1]

The story seems almost too apt to be true and yet it passed into the family's private folklore. Mahler himself was later happy to recall it as it had been told to him. Could his first public performance really have taken the form of a rudely secular intervention in a solemn act of worship?

Public music of many kinds – folksongs, dances like the Moravian *Hatschô* and, above all, military-band music – seems later to have acted like a magnet to the dreamy, slightly disorganized and easily distracted boy. The story, and others like it, suggests that he was good at picking up and remembering songs he heard in and around the family home above his father's distillery and liquor-shop. Itinerant fiddlers and Bohemian folk-bands would frequently pass through the town and were often encountered in the outlying villages. A still richer source of freely available public music was within easy reach. Throughout his childhood Mahler had only to turn left out of the house and walk a little way up the sloping Pirnitzergasse to reach Iglau's unusually broad and spacious square, with its shops, its Neptune fountain and a statue of the Virgin Mary raised on a column. Here he must have had some of his formative early encounters with military-band music.

The Iglau Stadtplatz, or 'Stadtring', might have been made for music, and certainly of a grander kind than the town's small string dance-band could muster, or the part-amateur, part-professional classical orchestra that registered Iglau's civic pride in its German culture. Another family memory of his early infancy that Mahler later recounted was of one day wandering out of the house to follow a military band that had marched onto the square. Dressed in little more than a shirt, he had followed the band, carrying his favourite toy accordion (perhaps a concertina) on which he could play many tunes that he had picked up by ear. He was discovered in the market by some neighbours who promised to take him home if he would play them something from the band's repertoire. This he did without difficulty, having first been lifted onto a fruit stall to entertain an amused group of townspeople. On a later occasion Mahler recalled a more obsessive fixation on band music in the Iglau square. He claimed to have become so absorbed by the music he encountered on his way home from school one day that he had failed to relieve himself when necessary and suffered embarrassing accidental consequences.

A report in the *Mährischer Grenzbote* of 24 April 1873 stresses the role played by military bands in Iglau on high days and holidays – on this occasion uniting the town's Jewish and German communities in a weekend-long ecumenical celebration of the Archduchess Gisela's marriage to Prince Leopold of Bavaria. The twelve-year-old Mahler was already known as something of a prodigy in Iglau, where he had first appeared in public in 1870 and recently scored a considerable success in an 1872 concert commemorating the birth of Schiller. Just approaching what should have been his bar mitzvah, Mahler played a part in the celebration of the royal marriage, peforming Thalberg's *Fantasia on Themes from 'Norma'* in a gala concert in the Municipal Theatre. Its varied programme had 'opened with Westmeyer's Kaiser Overture, performed by the Imperial-Royal military band'. Mahler may have arranged to complete his practice on the previous day (albeit the sabbath) so as to enjoy the spectacle of the same regimental band as it 'beat Retreat in full dress and played through the streets'.[2]

Military-band music is mentioned often enough in records of public life in Iglau to reinforce anecdotal accounts of an infantry regiment having been stationed there in Mahler's early childhood. Some have nevertheless suggested that that it might be a literary fiction that, in his infancy, Mahler absorbed the daily trumpet- and bugle-calls referred to by Guido Adler. Like Theodor Fischer, of whom more later, Adler had lived in Iglau and mentions the barracks as having been 'next to' the Catholic church in a corner of the Stadtring; the changing garrison, he observed, brightened the town's life, its young officers regularly setting hearts aflutter. Ernst Křenek, however, subsequently recalled the testimony of an uncle who knew Iglau and discounted the idea that there ever *were* barracks there, at least before 1866. He was clearly wrong. Even if Adler's memory of Iglau before 1864 had played him false, the year 1866 was significant. It was the year of the 'seven-week' Prussian–Austrian war, whose gruesome climax was the battle of Königgrätz/Sadowa (now Hradec Králové), fought less than 70 miles north of Iglau. Křenek's uncle admitted that Prussian soldiers might well have been seen in Iglau following the Austrians' defeat, as they made their way south towards Vienna. It is equally likely that Austrian troops would have been seen making their way to the battle, still in the celebrated white uniforms of the Empire's heyday. Over 44,000 of them died there. Men from Iglau must have been among them; the market-place and family meal-tables would have buzzed with tales from travellers and salesmen who had seen and heard more than the newspapers admitted.

The war plays no part in Mahler's recorded reminiscences, and yet at the age of five – the age at which he had his first photograph taken, nervously mastering his fear of the camera – he would have been able to pick up exciting, perhaps terrifying fragments of stories he only half understood. If it *was* only after the military reorganization of the subsequently split, 'dual' monarchy of Austria-Hungary that Iglau acquired its garrison, that would still have brought the bugles into Mahler's life at a significantly formative and receptive stage.[3] All such influences would have been coloured by his early developed passion for literature. It had been awakened, perhaps, by songs and tales he had heard from maidservants and the older friends with whom he played in the Pirnitzergasse or in the courtyards behind the family house and that of his friend Theodor Fischer. Mahler would soon begin to weave elaborate stories around pieces of classical music for the entertainment of his family. Soldiers, funerals, country-dances and travelling minstrels all had their melodies. Music not only took part in, but could also recreate in its own terms the stories in which they figured. Interestingly, one of his earliest childhood compositions seems to have been a polka prefaced by a funeral march; no doubt it told its own idiosyncratic tale.

Theodor Fischer provided his friend with another route into the world of music. Fischer's father was one of the leading figures of Iglau's musical life, and was to play a significant role in Mahler's early musical training. Theodor himself left an invaluable memoir which not only illuminates the progress of that training, but also mentions the many books to be found in the Mahler household. In this he played a part in raising doubts about the opening chapter of the most popular mythic version of Mahler's life-story, the one the composer himself recounted in influential recorded conversations with Natalie Bauer-Lechner and his wife, Alma, who embroidered and elaborated upon it in her turn.

It runs as follows. He was born on 7 July 1860 in Kaliště (Kalischt in German), just on the Bohemian side of the Bohemian–Moravian border. His parents were an ill-matched Jewish couple: the ambitious, womanizing and often bad-tempered Bernhard and the slightly lame, long-suffering Marie who probably had a minor heart condition that was exacerbated by frequent child-bearing. The more or less arranged marriage between the carter and salesman, with his sights set on a business of his own (Bernhard's mother had supposedly hawked goods from door to door in her eighties), and the daughter of a status-conscious soap-maker from Ledec generated domestic discord amidst the poverty in which they lived. Mahler later stressed the difference of character between his parents and, indeed, the modesty of the one-storey house in which he had been born, with its unglazed windows and unhealthy nearby pond.

In fact the marriage was of a kind common amongst the Jewish communities of that part of the Empire. Many years later Mahler's sister Justine would still complain to her absent brother that matchmakers and gossips were appearing at their house preparing to settle an arranged marriage for her. Marie ('gentleness itself', as Mahler recalled her) and her rather older husband ('all stubbornness') thus seem to offer themselves as protagonists in the German-Jewish version of a Dickensian childhood riven by parental discord and paternal brutality. The earliest surviving photographs of them support this image: the squat, rather well-turned-out but sullen-looking Bernhard with his top-hat, contrasting with the nervously forbearing, barely smiling Marie, lost in a voluminous dark crinoline or virtually entombed in the elaborate outdoor rig-out in which she appears in another picture. Marie was probably as saintly as her children believed her to be. Gustav, her eldest surviving son, clearly had a close and devoted relationship with her. He would hide behind her bed and pray when she had a headache or other ailments; she in turn fussed about his often messy and disorganized ways but would protect him from his father's anger when she could.

Bernhard was not, as far as we can tell, altogether the monster portrayed by Alma Mahler ('[he] ran after every servant, domineered over his delicate wife and flogged the children'). He was in some respects a bright example of the newly mobile Jewish 'wayfarer' of the 1860s[4] – seeking if not his fortune then at least a decent living and a place in the world: first as a kind of delivery-man, then settling down to follow his father into the publican's trade and start a family. He was modestly successful. The move to Iglau after Gustav's birth (their first son Isidor had died in some mysterious infantile accident in Kaliště) was a good one. He was initially denied permission to open up a hostelry like his own father's, where drinks could be sold by the glass, but he probably did so later; one witness of the period recalled his shop as an unassuming 'Schnaps-Butik' used by coachmen. His various bottled concoctions seem in the end to have served him and the people of Iglau rather well and he opened more than one branch of his business. By 1886 the family notepaper was proudly headed 'B. MAHLER OF IGLAU / Manufacturer of liqueurs, rum, rosolio, punch, essences and vinegar'. Becoming a prominent member of the town's Jewish community, he also cherished his certificate of citizenship which, in 1873, had granted him the status of full equality with its German burghers. His relations with them had not always been straightforward. In his early years in Iglau he had been fined for minor offences in connection with his business. In 1866 he was found to have prostitutes on his premises; in 1869 his crime was using insulting language to the local police captain.

For all the tales of his violent temper, there is reason to believe that he respected and loved his children. His intolerance of untidiness, his authoritarian manner and aspirations for his offspring were not untypical of the *petit-bourgeois* paterfamilias. He was anxious that Gustav, musical ability aside, should receive a full and 'proper' education. When the inevitable conflict arose, Bernhard maintained his insistence that his son complete his *Gymnasium* education, but was easy to persuade when the extent of Gustav's real passion, given his obvious pianistic talent, became clear. He seems to have developed an undemonstrative but deep-seated pride in his eldest son's musical gifts. Bernhard appreciated that they might open doors that had been closed to him, for all his attempts to 'better himself' through reading and teaching himself what he could.

While the family's mythical 'poverty' has undoubtedly been exaggerated – not least by the composer himself – the number of children would have affected its day-to-day well-being in two important respects, medical and financial. Neither was peculiar to the Mahlers; they would have been shared by countless families of the period. Bearing Bernhard fourteen children between 1858 and 1879, Marie was pregnant in almost every year of Gustav's childhood betwen the ages of three and thirteen. This could explain why he recalled his mother as long-suffering and constantly 'ailing'. Many of her children died in the first year of their lives. The household would have been familiar with the associated grief and mourning. Gustav seems at no stage to have had more than five surviving siblings, but six young mouths to feed and bodies to clothe clearly stretched Marie's resources and resourcefulness during the first ten years of the family's residence in the first-floor apartment in the

Pirnitzergasse. Bernhard's business nevertheless flourished and developed to the point where, in 1872, he was able to buy and move his family into the next-door house. They seem to have had servants from their first arrival in Iglau; if one of the maids did, as Alma suggests, receive more than professional attention from Bernhard, that may have occasioned the rows with Marie. Gentle, by nature unworldly, her modest and thrifty ways persisted even when their material circumstances improved. As late as 1886 she was writing to Mahler in Prague, just before his move to Leipzig, asking him to let her know exactly when he was coming and adding: 'Bring home *all* your old things and clothes – perhaps I can use some of them (for the children).'

As the eldest son, Gustav's special share in the task of helping his parents look after the younger children seems to have strengthened his attachment to his mother. It would have been common for such a relationship to entail an Oedipal distancing from his father. This might unconsciously have expressed itself as a protective idealization of his mother at the expense of his father's 'brutal' sexual threat to her well-being. A disturbing incident at the Grünfelds' house in Prague possibly sheds light on that relationship. In 1871 the eleven-year-old Mahler had reluctantly lodged there while attending the Neustädter Gymnasium (his father had sent him there to improve on the poor grades he had been getting in Iglau). He had been rather scornfully treated, perhaps even bullied, by some of the Grünfelds' numerous children but had suffered apparently deeper psychological scarring as a result of having attempted to 'save' one of the family's maidservants, whom he had accidentally witnessed having sex with the nineteen-year-old Alfred Grünfeld. His embarrassment and confusion, heightened by the pair's angry demands that he swear to tell no one what he had seen, seems to have remained vividly enough in his memory for him to recall them many years later in conversation with his wife.

Bernhard's rapid retrieval of his son from Prague when he heard what was going on suggests sensitivity to his son's feelings and well-

2   Mahler c.1871

being. He appears to have taken the distressed and undernourished boy to a restaurant and then returned alone to the Grünfeld house to collect his possessions. The home that Bernhard and Marie created in Iglau reflected some of that sensitivity and advertised their aspirations to *petit-bourgeois* status. Theodor Fischer claimed that the Mahlers had only 'a large kitchen, a hall and two rooms' at number 265 Pirnitzergasse, although the available space presumably increased when they later moved into the equivalent apartment of the next-door house. His description of what he appears to have called their 'salon', in one version of his story, is nevertheless revealing:

> The large room was furnished as a sitting-room in the sober style of the time, with the standard rep coverings [a corded fabric]; there in a frame under glass hung his father's certificate as a freeman of Iglau, there stood a glass case with porcelain and glass and all kinds of unusual objects, a bookcase filled with the works of classical and contemporary authors which Gustav Mahler read at an early age, and there too stood the Vopaterny grand piano on which Gustav Mahler practised and studied as soon as he had piano lessons.[5]

By this account, the Mahlers were able to affect a style of life closer to gentility than anything resembling real 'poverty' before their eldest son reached his twelfth year, back in his beloved Iglau.

He had returned to the German *Gymnasium* behind the Church of St Ignatius, which he reached by crossing the full length of the Stadtplatz. The problem with his previous progress at the *Gymnasium* is demonstrated in a surviving report from 1870 where a modest string of 'Adequate' and 'Satisfactory' assessments is broken by a single 'Excellent' – significantly enough for Mosaic Religion – and a 'Praiseworthy' for Gymnastics. It was another six years before he finally completed his *Matura* (or *Abitur* – the examinations formally concluding high-school education), and then he had to re-sit papers in Greek, German, Geography and Physics. By that time (1877) he had already completed his second academic year at the Vienna Conservatory, where he had begun to win prizes that demonstrated the strength and commitment of his real educational preoccupation, conceived long ago in Iglau.

Encompassing military bands, folk-dances and popular songs, the music that Mahler loved, of course, was more broadly constituted than the category accepted by his formal 'music' teachers, the earliest of whom seem to have been performers from the town orchestra who gave him piano lessons, initially inspired, perhaps, by his mother's (or even his father's?) inclination towards 'improving' culture. One of these teachers, Franz Viktorin, was connected with the world of professional high culture, being Kapellmeister of the Iglau Stadttheater. Most of its productions were plays, but his passable opera company regularly staged works by such composers as Auber, Meyerbeer, Flotow, Bellini (*Norma*) and Mozart (*Don Giovanni*).

Some of Mahler's early teachers introduced him to the study of harmony and counterpoint; this he seems to have devoured with as much relish as the music he played on the piano. Influential was the Iglau musician Heinrich Fischer, father of Theodor, who taught him some music theory and may have given Mahler his first formal harmony lessons. He also provided a next-door 'second home' for him, one that was inevitably filled with music and talk about music. It may have been Heinrich Fischer who arranged some of the young Mahler's early appearances in Iglau as a local prodigy; Fischer did some turns of duty as Kapellmeister at the Stadttheater following Viktorin's departure and was for years the director of the Iglau male-voice choir. It was as choirmaster of the Catholic Jakobskirche, however, that he performed his most solemn role in the town's musical life.

Guido Adler's recollections testify to the atmosphere of tolerance that existed between Iglau's Jewish community, led by Rabbi Unger, and the majority German Catholic one, whose Church of Sankt Jakob, standing a little way back from the east side of the Stadtplatz, was a local landmark, its unequal towers rising above a high point of the gently undulating hill on which the town had been built. Here Mahler had more frequent documented encounters with Catholicism than he seems to have done with Judaism in Iglau, although we must assume that he attended the synagogue with his parents and that his mother would have encouraged him to do so (not least as an example to his younger brothers and sisters). After his return from Prague in 1871, however, Mahler certainly joined his friend Theodor, singing under his father's direction, in the choir of the Jakobskirche when it performed large-scale works like Beethoven's *Christus am Ölberg* and the Mozart *Requiem*.

In a world whose only mechanical means of sound reproduction were the barrel-organ and devices like carillons and musical boxes, live music was part of every sphere of life: from civic ceremony and celebration, religious worship in Catholic church or synagogue to country outings and secular festivals, to the privacy of bourgeois domestic life. It could even reach into the deepest recesses of an individual's subjective experience if, like Mahler, one played the piano and associated musical with literary stimulation. Both could provide means of imaginative escape from the constraints of daily life – be they a dry and demanding schoolteacher or the pressures of an overcrowded family apartment in which domestic rows and children's squabbles, rages and beatings were regular occurrences. Many who knew Mahler as a child testified to his tendency to daydream. At times his dreaminess invaded his music. During his student years he could easily 'lose himself' while accompanying a mediocre performer in a work that had ceased to interest him. Intense mental activity – emotional, imaginative or philosophical – could on occasion interrupt or halt the flow of music, or internalize it as something heard only in his head. The implications of the most fully idealized music being inaudible beyond the realm of individual subjectivity has mystical and ironic implications, neither of which were lost on the adult Mahler. One of his most telling childhood recollections concerned a striking negative image of music's relation to emotional experience. Fleeing from a scene between his parents, he had run into the street. Instead of finding the calm that would allow him to re-establish a more harmonious inner state, he had found himself confronted by a barrel-organ churning out the popular song-tune 'Ach, du lieber Augustin'. His own interpretation of the effect of that conjunction was that it hampered his subsequent ability to disentangle 'high tragedy' from 'light amusement'. We will return to the implications of that self-assessment, offered many years later to Sigmund Freud.

No such theoretical discrimination was available to Mahler during his Iglau childhood and adolescence, rich in confusingly intense experiences; to the boy who liked to be alone when he practised the piano and who would escape onto rooftops to read his favourite books. The stories he made up, often inspired by music, were rooted solidly in the world of real experience, with all its discord. He later claimed, in conversation with Natalie Bauer-Lechner, that he was moved to tears by some of his own 'musical' stories – like the one he invented for Beethoven's Op. 121a Variations on Wenzel Müller's 'Ich bin der Schneider Kakadu' ('I am the tailor Kakadu'). It followed the events of the tailor's troubled life, ending with his burial and 'a parody of a funeral march – which to him [Mahler] conveyed the meaning: "Now this poor beggar is the same as any king . . ." '.

The Mahler family, as we have seen, was frequently visited by death. Children in the first year of their life were particularly vulnerable. In December 1865 Mahler's baby brother Karl had died, in 1866 his brother Rudolf. Arnold (just approaching his second birthday) and Friedrich (born in April 1871) had both died in December 1871 of scarlet fever; Alfred just survived the first year of his life before dying in May 1873, not long after his brother had consolidated his reputation as the Iglau 'Wunderkind' by playing Thalberg at the royal wedding celebration concert. In 1875[6] there occurred what has always been regarded as Mahler's most traumatic early experience of death, when his brother Ernst, just a year younger than himself, succumbed to a long illness. Mahler claimed to have spent hours beside his sickbed, telling him stories. Perhaps it was this death that encouraged Mahler's sister Justine, then six years old, to 'play dead' herself, having placed candles around her bed – was it in the hope that someone would come and tell her stories?

Ernst was Mahler's favourite brother, the companion of his games, with a ready ear for his musical stories. That Mahler not only confronted more serious issues with him but also seems to have defined his most intimate family circle as consisting of himself, Ernst and their mother is indicated by an extraordinary dream he recalled from around the age of eight. In it, the three of them had been standing at the window of their first-floor sitting-room when their mother had suddenly exclaimed 'God, what's happening?' as the sky filled with sulphureous mist in a kind of apolcalypse. Then Mahler found himself alone in the market-place. Through swirling vapour he glimpsed the fearful figure of the Eternal Jew (*Ewige Jude*), his coat billowing in the wind in such a way as to suggest a huge hump on his back. Carrying a staff topped with a golden cross, he pursued the fleeing boy and tried to give *him* the staff before he had awoken with a cry. Mahler interpreted the staff as a symbol of restless wandering – perhaps we should link this story with his childhood assertion, to the question of a relative about what he would do when he grew up, that he wanted to be 'a martyr'.

This earliest significant memory of Mahler's giving evidence of a problematized conceptualization of what it meant to be a Jew (in a dream in which the Christian cross also appeared) is striking in that it included Ernst as a necessary bystander or spectator. Some commentators have attempted to weave psychological theories around Mahler's sense of loss when Ernst died. Their relationship was close, and although the most orthodox Jewish mourning rites could entail abstention from music and theatre for up to a year, Mahler may have come to terms with the loss by turning his brother into the hero of one of his most ambitious early compositional projects: an opera based (it is assumed) on Uhland's 1818 play *Herzog Ernst von Schwaben*. He possibly played excerpts from it in 1874 or 1875 to the manager of a country estate, Gustav Schwarz, who had summoned Mahler, on the advice of a friend, to help him assess some musical manuscripts that had been discovered in an attic. Schwarz subsequently interceded with Bernhard Mahler on his son's behalf, recommending that he be permitted to continue his musical training in Vienna, in spite of Bernhard's fears about the effects of the Royal and Imperial metropolis on his morals and on the proper completion of his *Gymnasium* education.

The death of Ernst was a symbolic psychological turning-point in Mahler's life. With that loss he seems to have begun to see himself in a new, somewhat tragic light, as an apprentice adult whose task was to master the art that had already made him something of a local celebrity. He had begun to give piano lessons, although his impatience and a tendency to slap his charges when they made mistakes did little to increase his circle of pupils. At the same time he would have to find a way of accommodating the demands of public performance with the rich imaginative life of a notorious and self-confessed dreamer of considerable intellectual and emotional complexity: the child who, when left sitting in the woods outside Iglau by his father, remained in the same spot, lost in thought, for hours before his father remembered him, as night was falling.

That image of the future composer, pensive amidst the impersonal sounds of nature, is romantically attractive. Yet just as an experience of family tension had precipitated him into a street jangling with the sound of a barrel-organ, so it is appropriate to close the story of the young Mahler of Iglau by putting him back into one of the crowds in which we first encountered him – here, appropriately enough, as evoked in someone else's story. Joseph Roth's novel *The Radetzky March* (1932) chronicles the decline of the Habsburg Empire through the experience of a single family, three generations of which serve Emperor Franz Joseph, from the battle of Solferino (1859) to his death in the middle of the First World War in 1916. Relevant to our present story is Roth's picture of what he calls 'the little Moravian country town of W.', whose infantry regiment boasts a particularly fine band which gives an open-air concert every Sunday in the town square:

> Its bandmaster upheld the tradition of that race of Austrian military composers whose precise memories, ever alert to variations of old themes, enabled them to compose a new march every month. These marches were identical as soldiers. Most began with a roll of drums, contained a tattoo accelerating to march time, and ended with a threatening roll of thunder from the kettle-drums – that cheerful, brief storm of military music.[7]

It would not take much imagination to turn 'W.' into Iglau itself and to place Bernhard Mahler's eldest son amongst the admirers of Roth's vigorously conscientious bandmaster Nechwal:

The slackness of other bandmasters, who allowed a drum major
to conduct the first march, and waited for the second item before
deigning to raise the baton, struck Nechwal as an indication of
the decadence of the Austrian monarchy. As soon as the band had
arranged itself in the prescribed circle . . . the bandmaster stood
ready among his musicians, his ebony baton with its silver knob
discreetly raised. These open-air concerts . . . all began with the
Radetzky March. Although the march was so familiar to the
members of the band that any one of them could have played
it in his sleep without a conductor, their bandmaster nevertheless
considered it essential to follow every note of the score. With a
burst of musical and military zeal, as though they were trying it
out for the first time, he would raise his head, his eye, his baton,
and every Sunday direct their full force into those segments of the
circle (he stood in the centre) which might need his direction. The
bluff drums rolled, the sweet flutes piped, clear cymbals crashed.
Pleased and pensive smiles spread over the faces of his audience.
Though they stood still, the blood tingling in their legs made them
feel that they were marching. The younger girls held their breath,
lips parted. The maturer men bent their heads and remembered
manoeuvres. The elderly ladies sat in the neighbouring park with
their little gray heads trembling. And it was summer.

2 Becoming a musician in Vienna

Roth describes the hero of *The Radetzky March*, young Carl Joseph von Trotta, as being inspired with patriotic fervour by Bandmaster Nechwal's concerts. He imagines himself marching into some future battle in which, sword flashing, he might one day die for his Emperor and for the sake of the great Empire whose honour Radetzky had helped to save in 1848. That, Roth subtly implies, was the ideological function of such music. Nechwal's public image as a conductor and score-follower, staving off the collapse of the world as he knew it with his zealously attentive baton, nevertheless acquires a darker, more mysterious dimension at close quarters. After the Sunday concerts, the bandmaster would call on Carl Joseph's father, the District Commissioner before whose official residence he had performed. Listening to his conversation about the current Lehár operetta in Vienna, Carl Joseph suspects that 'hidden in the depths of Herr Nechwal's soul lurked many secrets of the great nocturnal underworld'.

Another Austrian Jewish writer of the period, Stefan Zweig, has illustrated how the multifaceted meaning of music might have been refocused in the mind of a young Jew, seen by his parents as the family's best hope of acquiring the cultural status that was associated with intellectual universality ('longing to resolve the merely Jewish – through flight into the intellectual – into humanity at large'). Having suggested that Austrian Jews, however humble, were peculiarly sensitive to levels and nuances of social distinction, Zweig (born in 1881) explains the cultural dynamics and social structure of Vienna, the imperial capital city in which he grew up, through a series of deliberately theatrical and musical metaphors. These express something deeper than the usual tourist evocations of the city of Mozart, Beethoven, Schubert and the Strauss family. It was, he suggests, a city fanatically devoted to 'art' as a means for the public preservation and processing of shared illusion – specifically theatrical and musical art. The cosmopolitan, multinational city had rapidly expanded into a metropolitan centre of modernity. Yet it was still marked by its visible containment within a readily accessible surrounding landscape – 'One hardly sensed where nature began and where the city: one melted into the other without opposition, without contradictions.' At the centre of the new, late nineteenth-century Vienna were the Royal and Imperial Court Opera and the great *Burgtheater*, where the humblest member of the audience 'virtually became a guest in the Imperial household'. Vienna, he suggests, was indeed a 'wonderfully orchestrated city':

> The palace was the centre, not only in a spatial sense but also in a cultural sense, of the supernationality of the monarchy. The palaces of the Austrian, the Polish, the Czech, and the Hungarian nobility formed as it were a second enclosure around the Imperial palace. Then came 'good society', consisting of the lesser nobility, the higher officials, industry, and the 'old families', then the petty bourgeoisie and the proletariat. Each of these social strata lived in its own circle, and even in its own district . . . But everyone met in the theatre and at the great festivals such as the flower Parade in the Prater, where three hundred thousand people enthusiastically applauded the 'upper ten thousand' in their beautifully decorated carriages. In Vienna everything – religious processions such as the one on the feast of Corpus Christi, the military parades, the 'Burg' music – was made the occasion for celebration, so far as colour and music were concerned. Even funerals found enthusiastic audiences and it was the ambition of every true Viennese to make a 'lovely corpse', with a majestic procession and many followers; even his

3   The Court Opera House in Vienna

death converted the genuine Viennese into a spectacle for others.
In this receptivity for all that was colourful, festive and resounding,
in their pleasure in the theatrical, whether it was on the stage or in
reality, both as theatre and as a mirror of life, the whole city was at
one.[1]

Zweig's autobiography, The World of Yesterday, clarifies how Mahler
might have found the musically animated life of Iglau writ large in
the imperial capital to which the steam railway carried him more

than once in the early autumn of 1875. The last trip had taken the fifteen-year-old boy off to his first term as a student at the Conservatory of the Friends of Music. This was partly as a result of the sympathetic encouragement given to his parents by Gustav Schwarz, manager of the Morowan Estate on which Mahler had spent part of that summer with his friend Joseph Steiner. Schwarz himself, in early September, took Mahler to play to Julius Epstein (Professor of Piano at the Conservatory) at his house in Baden, just south of Vienna. Epstein subsequently recalled what was possibly a slightly later visit at which Bernhard Mahler came with his son to hear for himself what the professor had to say about his abilities, particularly as a composer.

The remarkable thing is that the teenager seems not only to have taken this favourable estimate of his potential in a matter-of-fact, unsurprised way, but also to have coped with the move to Vienna with similar equanimity. Close as Mahler's ties to his home and family were, and would remain, there is little evidence of nervous fragility or any tendency to homesickness. A few of his Iglau friends no doubt went to study in Vienna at the same time; one Iglau classmate, Emil Freund, we will encounter there later, along with Theodor Fischer. The family he left behind now comprised his father and mother (the latter in an advanced state of pregnancy, Emma being born that October), his sisters Leopoldine and Justine (aged twelve and seven respectively) and his brothers Alois and Otto (aged eight and two). In Vienna he was to find himself in close daily proximity with the Empire's social and cultural élite, the latter including Brahms and the celebrated *Neue Freie Presse* music-critic and University Professor Eduard Hanslick. Elderly people could still be found who were able to describe Beethoven and Schubert from personal recollection.

It might, perhaps should, have been daunting and awe-inspiring but music, although still a growth industry at that time, was a highly competitive profession and to be successful one had to get on with it, acquiring a hard skin and a degree of ruthlessness. The bookish

Mahler may have heeded the warning of Wackenroder and Tieck's celebrated *Outpourings of an Art-Loving Friar* (1796), which had closed with Wackenroder's Romantic moral-tale 'The Remarkable Musical Life of the Tone-Poet Joseph Berglinger'. Berglinger is the son of a large, poor family (his father a doctor who had fallen on hard times) who finds in music an ideal source of inspiring escapism. He leaves home to study it: first finding his idealism crushed by the repressive rules of technical musical training, then being disillusioned by the indifference of audiences to the works of his mature genius. The narrator ends his tale with a series of rhetorical questions that might have been carved over the entrances to most of the Conservatories and art-schools of Europe during the latter half of the nineteenth century:

> Should I say that he was perhaps born to enjoy art rather than to practice it? Are there men perhaps of happier constitution in whom art works silently and secretly like a veiled spirit, never disrupting their daily affairs? Or must the man of unfailing inspiration perhaps anchor his exalted visions boldly and firmly in this earthly life if he is to become a genuine artist?[2]

Mahler, unlike Berglinger, seems to have felt that his Iglau teachers, like Heinrich Fischer, had given him sufficient access to musical techniques for him to be at his least diligent in Conservatory classes on harmony, counterpoint and form. Their rules and methods were intended to help define and police the boundaries of style that distinguished Music as a high art from mere 'music' of the kind that could be heard in cafés and dance-halls or at parades on the Prater. This would not have been a problem if he had been set on becoming another Bandmaster Nechwal, a composer of marches or popular songs. The difficulty for Mahler was that he had already internalized the Romantic idealism of Joseph Berglinger without really needing to suffer the constraints of a technical training whose subsidiary function was a socializing one, its aim the imparting of an ideologically charged 'taste'. That was something Mahler would have to struggle to acquire later, in his own way and for his own reasons.

The more mundane and materialistic struggle to pay his Conservatory fees and to keep body and soul together was what the fifteen-year-old had first to confront. Much of his life revolved around pianos. There were the pianos he rented for the various rooms in which he lodged and on which he gave lessons (like many students, Mahler had to earn money to keep himself afloat; occasional small allowances from home were quickly spent). It was at the piano that he acquainted himself with new scores and tried out his own compositions. Above all, the piano was his instrument, his major study at the Conservatory, where he was to become a star member of Julius Epstein's class. It was as a pianist that he first began to win prizes. However, the compositions of his own that he had played to Epstein in his initial audition had led to his also being accepted from the start, rather unusually, into the composition class of Franz Krenn. This extremely traditional organist may have had reasons to chide his new pupil for a lack of proper attention to the rules, but agreed to Mahler's being awarded a first prize for excellence in composition, following the one he had already achieved for piano, at the end of his first academic year (in July 1876), the prize work being the first movement of a piano quintet.

Whatever the privations of his material existence in Vienna, stories of his early developed reputation for arrogance, eccentricity and forgetfulness, stemming from his tendency to obsessive involvement in matters of art and the mind, need to be balanced by careful attention to evidence of the sociability and *savoir-faire* that enabled him to make the very most of his life in the still developing capital city. On the 'Ringstrasse' – the broad encircling thoroughfare where the city walls had once stood – two of the great buildings with which Mahler was to become associated were as new as their architectural style was traditional, celebrating an appropriated past with eclectic grandiloquence. The Court Opera House by van der Nüll and Siccardsburg had opened in 1869, the 'Musikverein' building of the *Gesellschaft der Musikfreunde* (Society of the Friends of Music), in which the Conservatory was housed, in 1870. The compromise between modernity and tradition that these buildings proclaimed would exasperate artists and designers of the next generation. In the 1870s that compromise was appropriate to the musical culture whose aspiring leaders were being educated within them.

Men like Guido Adler (also from Iglau, of course) and Felix Mottl were already on the brink of success in their chosen careers when Mahler arrived in 1875 (the one as a pioneering historical musicologist, the other as an influential conductor). Amongst his contemporaries were some talented musicians known to us now mostly through their friendship with him – Rudolf Krzyzanowski, Anton Krisper and Hans Rott in particular. One of Mahler's friends, Hugo Wolf, was nevertheless to become the most celebrated song composer of his age, but he too acquired a further historical role as a player in the drama of Mahler's own advancing career. Younger musicians Mahler was to encounter at the Conservatory included the violinist Arnold Rosé, subsequently leader of the Vienna Philharmonic (and Mahler's brother-in-law) and Franz Schalk, later his assistant Kapellmeister in Vienna.

All the races that made up the ethnically diverse, 'multinational' Habsburg Empire were represented by Mahler's contemporaries at the Conservatory. The aim of their teachers was to make them all executants and officials of a traditional musical culture whose special value was defined by its universality and its transcendence of the popular, the ephemeral, the ethnic, the worldly. The 'mastery' of the greatest works was taken to be synonymous with their structural articulation as models of a theoretical 'organic unity'. In them, the boundary between what was artificial and what seemed natural was intended to be as indistinguishable as that between the city of Vienna and its wooded, surrounding hills to the youthful eye of Stefan Zweig.

Mahler's nascent deviancy with respect to official musical taste found support in the company of a forceful group of students and young intellectuals, not all of whom were musicians. Their interests were linked by a then fashionable desire to bring about a wider and more dynamic union of Germanic and German-speaking peoples than that encompassed and affirmed by the Austro-Hungarian Empire of Franz Joseph I. This they sought to achieve in the name of both Wagner and the anti-Wagnerian philosopher Nietzsche, and in the spirit of an idealistic and even iconoclastic socialism. To understand the path by which Mahler found his way into the sphere of influence of Vienna's 'Reading Society of German Students' in 1878, we must build up a more systematic picture of his response to cultural life in the capital of a multi-ethnic Empire that faced both the threat and the challenge of powerful German states, recently unified under Prussia, beyond its borders. Wagner's is the easiest influence to deal with. The ageing German master of Bayreuth captured the imagination of Mahler's generation like no other living composer, partly *because* the great critic Hanslick disapproved of him. So, too, did most of Mahler's teachers at the Conservatory, not least for the reason that his insistently and specifically German 'total work of art' (*Gesamtkunstwerk*) seemed set on undermining the supranationality of truly great music (meaning, that is, music in the Austrian and specifically Viennese tradition).

Although we cannot be sure when Mahler first encountered Wagner's music, we know that Julius Epstein claimed to have detected 'Wagnerism' in the compositions that his future student had played to him in 1875. What is certain is that Mahler would have rapidly found himself swept up in the youthful tide of Wagner-mania that engulfed Vienna's music-students in the winter of 1875–6, when Wagner himself was resident in Vienna for two separate periods. During the first he stayed at the Imperial Hotel for six weeks, including the whole of November 1875, supervising and attending the performances of *Tannhäuser* and *Lohengrin* conducted by Hans Richter at the *Hofoper*. During the second visit (March 1876) he himself conducted a performance of *Lohengrin* (2 March). He had, in fact, conducted some of his music in Vienna earlier in 1875, before Mahler arrived, including the first ever performance of the closing scene of *Götterdämmerung*; he had been welcomed with enthusiasm and solemnity by youthful members of the Wagner Society, which Wolf and Mahler were to join in 1877.

The only anecdote linking Mahler directly with Wagner involves an attack of shyness, later much regretted by Mahler, that prevented him from helping the Master on with his coat when the opportunity presented itself in the foyer of the Opera. Hugo Wolf was far bolder, becoming a regular 'hanger-on' and engineering a number of direct encounters with Wagner. Wolf recorded his almost delirious enthusiasm in his diary and in letters home. It appears from these that before hearing *Tannhäuser* in the composer's presence in 1875 (Wolf was nearly crushed in the queue for the gallery) he had never heard any of Wagner's music. With his friends Mahler and Rudolf Krzyzanowski – at one stage all three shared lodgings – Wolf devoured *Götterdämmerung* at the keyboard; when they took to singing the parts the landlady evicted them.

Once again music and everyday life came into conflict in Mahler's experience. On this occasion his angrily heightened idealism may have been further inflamed by a strong sense of the implications of Wagner's mostly negative reception by older-generation Viennese critics and music-lovers. Wagner had directed some harsh words at the Vienna Court Opera in the newly extended version of his notorious, originally anonymous, essay 'Das Judentum in der Musik' ('Judaism in Music') when it had been republished under his name in 1869. His bitterness concerned supposed Viennese machinations against *Die Meistersinger* (eventually presented there in 1870, and again in 1874). He was explicit in his denunciation of Eduard Hanslick – caricatured in the opera's character Beckmesser – whose hostility Wagner explained as a manifestation of the anti-German spirit of someone who was part Jewish. Over the next few years Mahler, like many other young Jewish Wagnerites in antisemitic Vienna (Joseph Hellmesberger, Director of the Conservatory, made no bones about it) must have struggled with this more personal area of conflict against the background of increasingly politicized cultural division over the issue of Wagner. Many were wary of his supposed German nationalization of music, and conservatives could not ignore the taint of revolutionary radicalism that he still carried from 1848, when he had become a political exile, losing his job as a Kapellmeister to the King of Saxony.

One cannot simply assert that Wagner's antisemitism inspired some form of the partly mythical, and now discredited, 'Jewish self-hatred' in Mahler; there is evidence that he came to regard many of Wagner's ideas with scepticism while continuing to admire his music dramas.[3] But some of Wagner's ideas exercised a demonstrable grip on the imagination of Mahler and his contemporaries in the late 1870s. It must be assumed that antisemitism from him, of all people, played its part in defining the path towards 'assimilation' that Bernhard Mahler had perhaps long ago envisaged for his son – one that eventually led Mahler to convert to Roman Catholicism some twenty years later. The official state religion of the Empire was also the faith, held with humble conviction and almost childlike sincerity, of the first major Viennese composer of the older generation with whom Mahler came into close contact. Significantly, he too had been branded a Wagnerian (as indeed he was) and suffered all that it was possible to suffer in Vienna at that time as a result. That was Anton Bruckner.

In 1875 Bruckner was still struggling to find a platform for either of his as yet unperformed Second and Third Symphonies, the latter dedicated to Wagner with his enthusiastic consent. He taught at the Conservatory and had finally succeeded in gaining enough support to overcome Hanslick's opposition to his being appointed to an honorary lectureship at the University towards the end of November that year, during Wagner's stay in Vienna. Mahler never formally studied with Bruckner, but before coming into direct contact with him around the time of the ill-received first performance of his Third Symphony in 1877, would have heard tales about the 51-year-old organist, with his shabbily rustic clothes, his Upper Austrian dialect, and his tendency to fall on his knees in the middle of a class if he heard an angelus bell. The critic Max Graf recalled just such an event in a lecture he had attended some years later. It inspired more than the anticipated student giggles:

> I have never seen anyone pray as Bruckner did. He seemed to be transfixed, illuminated from within. His old peasant face, with the countless wrinkles covering it like furrows in a field, became the face of a priest.[4]

While Mahler's childhood years in Iglau were marked by an ability to move with relative ease between the synagogue and the Catholic Church of Sankt Jakob, greater tension might have attended such passage in Vienna, even in the 1870s. Close connections with his home town would nevertheless have helped shield him from the full implications of that tension at first. On occasions Bernhard Mahler would visit him in Vienna, perhaps bringing a food parcel that his son would rapidly consume with his friends. At Christmas (finances permitting) and during the summer vacations, Mahler returned to Iglau, continuing former friendships and being fêted by his younger brothers and sisters (at Christmas 1875 he had a new baby sister, Emma, to become acquainted with). It is significant that Mahler frequently invited Conservatory friends there, suggesting that he was far from being ashamed of his home and family. Towards the end of the first summer vacation of his Conservatory period (1876) he invited Rudolf Krzyzanowski to stay; admittedly he took him off to Ledetsch to visit an aunt on his mother's side – always considered the more pretentious branch of the family by his father – but they were joined in Iglau by two other Conservatory friends for a concert they were all to give on 12 September. Mahler had arranged for it to take place in the Czap Hotel, the proceeds going to his old school. The concert was well received by the local critic who wrote admiringly of the works by Krzyzanowski and Mahler (a Violin Sonata and what was probably the surviving Piano Quartet movement). They were in a programme including works by Vieuxtemps, Alard and two solo piano items played by Mahler: Schubert's 'Wanderer' Fantasy and a Chopin Ballade.

Mahler's second Conservatory year, 1876–7, was somewhat more stormy than the first. Following a breach of discipline, Wolf was thrown out by Hellmesberger in March 1877, and Mahler seems to have survived bouts of temperamental insubordination and discourtesy only through the good offices of Julius Epstein, who continued to keep an eye on his impecunious star pupil. It was a year no less rich in musical experiences (did Mahler attend the third performance of Brahms's First Symphony?) and ambitious composition projects, including an opera called *Die Argonauten*. With Krzyzanowski and Hugo Wolf, Mahler also joined the Academic Wagner Society of Vienna, two of whose founder members were Guido Adler and Felix Mottl. This enlarged his circle of friends, bringing him into contact with literature and philosophy students as well as other musicians. Bruckner was a member of the Society, and Mahler was certainly among his student 'followers' by the time of the Third Symphony's disastrous première in December 1877. Bruckner came to enjoy his company. Mahler's first publication (1880) was a piano duet version of that symphony, completed at the composer's request with the aid of Ferdinand Löwe.

Before that Bruckner première Mahler suffered the indignity of needing two attempts to pass his high-school *Matura* back in Iglau, after which he was eligible to register for university courses. Once again his work in religion was considered the best; remaining fragments of his two failing essays from 1877 (he eventually passed in September) give us a fascinating insight into Mahler's mind around the age of seventeen. His piece 'On the motives that brought about Wallenstein's decline' was deemed to have wandered from the actual subject, but his musings on the dreams and poetic fantasy of the solitary individual, who is in greatest danger when he fails to distinguish the real from the imagined, are revealing. Even more remarkable is an uncompleted German essay from earlier in the year (handed in, with a rough draft, after 1½ hours) on 'The influence of the Orient on German literature'. It starts promisingly enough with a paragraph on the 'productive influence' on a nation of knowledge of other

peoples (the Chinese exclusion of foreign influences cited as a cautionary example of self-inflicted isolation). What follows is introduced as a 'brief digression on the origins of poetry' and develops
into a meditation on the 'otherness' of cultures physically and
climatically separated from one's own:

> And yet we find an attraction in what is strange. Let us now recall
> our opening words: 'What is most productive for a people is the
> knowledge of the literature of other peoples . . .'
>   It is above all the German mind which aspires to a
> comprehensive outlook; through the assimilation of the products
> of different nations there emerges, with regard to ideas of form . . .[5]

There the essay had broken off. Notions picked up from student
'pan-Germanists' in Vienna had got him thus far; but how might he,
a Jew, do justice to what emerged from that process of implicitly
imperialist assimilation, which tended also to imply subjection and
control? The pan-Germanists wanted a unification of all the German
peoples currently scattered across two empires, the German and the
Austrian-Hungarian. Implicit in that unification was an inevitable
threat to Austria-Hungary as it was then rather precariously constituted; absorption into expansionist Prussia and the marginalization
of non-Germanic races were central goals of pan-German politics.
Given Mahler's developing perception of himself as a theoretically
stateless Jew (in pan-Germanic terms), standard formulations about
universalism or supranationalism seem predictably not to have
worked for him. For Mahler 'Assimilation' would come increasingly
to mean assimilation into *German* culture.

Back in Vienna, in that autumn of 1877, he resumed his Conservatory studies and was now, at last, eligible to enrol for classes at the
University. This he did, choosing the Philosophy Faculty and signing
up for the History of Ancient German Literature, the philological
study of Middle High German, the History of Greek Art and Art Criticism. Mahler seems also to have attended some of Bruckner's
Harmony lectures and a general history course of some sort, but

must have dropped these subjects at an early stage, as they are deleted from his student record. At the Conservatory he also dropped out of Epstein's piano class to devote himself to music history and composition (which now became his major study). It was, however, the expansion of his social and intellectual horizons, resulting from his membership of the University, that constituted the central event of the academic year 1877–8. Series of events would perhaps be more appropriate. He later confessed that his attendance at lectures was poor, but it was everything else that flowed from his new status as a university student that counted.

The social and intellectual organization of student life outside lecture-halls could be intimidating and was apparently designed to clarify 'insider' and 'outsider' status. The still largely male student body was dominated by a number of powerful fraternities, or *Burschenschaften*; one joined at the invitation of existing members, but might then wear the relevant fraternity's colourful cap, attend its meetings and form close bonds that would often last throughout its members' adult professional lives. Many of the fraternities were little more than drinking or duelling societies with brutal and often self-destructive codes of ethics. Some of them were already actively excluding Jews by the late 1870s. Other fraternities had more intellectual or political interests. One of the most ambitious student organizations at that time was not, properly speaking, a fraternity at all but an intellectual debating club called the 'Reading Society of Vienna's German Students' (*Leseverein der deutschen Studenten Wiens*). At its heart in 1878 were members of a circle that had formed around two men who were to become influential left-wing Austrian politicians: Engelbert Pernerstorfer (1855–1918) and Victor Adler (1852–1918), the latter a Jew who later became the first leader of the Austrian Social Democratic Party. Other members of the circle included the historian Heinrich Friedjung, Adler's brother-in-law Heinrich Braun and the young poet Siegfried Lipiner, a disciple of Gustav Fechner and an early advocate of the philosophical ideas of Friedrich Nietzsche. Most importantly, the *Leseverein*, whose membership included a number of parliamentary deputies by this time, was to a significant degree a political organization – so threatingly political, in fact, that it was closed down by government decree on 19 December, 1878. On the following day its members took to the streets in protest, singing an old song – 'Wir hatten gebauet ein stattliches Haus' ('We had built a stately house') – whose words had been written in 1819 by August von Binzer, the leading member of a democratically inclined and German-nationalistic *deutsche Burschenschaft* that had been dissolved at the instigation of Austria's future Chancellor: the diplomat and jealous guardian of the Empire, Prince Metternich.[6]

In order to understand why the *Leseverein* was similarly dissolved in 1878, why its members had sung a German-nationalistic song and how its aims linked socialism with Nietzscheanism, we must consider the history of Austrian liberalism. Prior to the Empire's defeat by Prussia in 1866, Austria's 'old liberals' had relied on the eighteenth-century Enlightenment and the philosophical ideas of Immanuel Kant for their concept of a post-feudal state in which the power of the aristocracy was curbed in favour of that of the monarch, as 'enlightened despot'. The introduction of German as the official administrative language of the Habsburg Empire in 1784 without an aggressive policy of 'Germanization' was characteristic of that ideal of harmonized diversity in which the new middle-class entrepreneur flourished at the expense of the old landowners. The historian William J. McGrath has suggested, however, that the reactionary and anti-liberal character of Metternich's regime, following the Napoleonic wars, had helped to foment a new, more revolutionary liberalism. It erupted briefly in 1848 but then had to come to terms, as 'new liberalism', with the effects of the war of 1866 and the *Ausgleich* ('compromise'): a split Empire with both Hungarian and Austrian focuses of power, and in which the German-speakers felt newly deprived of any hope they might have had for a specifically German unity or a thoroughly Germanized state. This new liberalism of the 1870s coincided with the economic 'boom' of the so-called *Gründerzeit* and the consolidation of a bureaucratized Imperial administration that came to be characterized by legalistic pedantry. All this was what the *Leseverein* members objected to. Sub-groups within it formulated policies which sought to replace the 'liberalism' of a fat-cat bourgeoisie, relying on an underprivileged and under-paid industrial working class, with a form of socialism in which the decaying and increasingly unreal Empire of Franz Joseph I was to be replaced by an egalitarian union of all the German peoples. An inspirational anti-Enlightenment philosophy was needed, they believed, along with a shared experience of German culture, language and mythology, to replace the decaying culture of Catholicism and the idealistic supranationalism of the old Empire. It was in this often complex, ideologically volatile mixture of aims and ideas that Nietzscheanism, Wagnerism, liberal Catholicism and socialism played their part in animating the student milieu into which Mahler fully entered in 1877.

He did not join the *Leseverein*, but seems at once to have participated in an Iglau students' small-scale version of it: a literary debating group that included his old friend Theodor Fischer, his former classmate and future legal adviser Emil Freund and his cousin Gustav Frank. Fischer would recall their discussions of 'literary and current concerns' ending in walks around the moonlit city in which they became 'totally abandoned to romantic enthusiasms'. Still more important was the extension of his circle and interests in the two years following his graduation from the Conservatory in the summer of 1878 (he gained a first prize for composition, but without any commendation of 'excellence', on the strength of a submitted Scherzo for piano quintet). During second-semester University courses in Classical Sculpture, the History of Dutch Painting and Philosophical Historiography Mahler continued his student existence in Vienna, earning what he could by teaching. He may well have been back in Iglau when the dissolution of the *Leseverein* took place in December 1878, but would soon have heard about it at first hand. In 1878–9 he was taken up by Victor Adler and his wife Emma, whose brother Heinrich Braun became a friend of Mahler's at around the same time. He also became acquainted with the wealthy, non-practising doctor Albert Spiegler and his wife Nina (or 'Nanna'), both friends of Adler. The young *Leseverein* star Siegfried Lipiner was a member of the same group and became a kind of intellectual leader or 'guru' in that circle, some of whose members remained Mahler's closest friends for the rest of his life.

By the time he had forged these new relationships he had completed (in 1878) the poetic text of his first major work: a fairy-tale cantata deriving from one of the *Nursery and Household Tales* of the Brothers Grimm. Set in an archaic world of knights and minstrels, it concerns a crime of fratricide whose outcome is the dramatic collapse of the murderer's world. *Das klagende Lied* was fully completed and orchestrated in 1880; that it alone survived from Mahler's youthful music-dramatic projects, rather than the operas *Herzog Ernst von Schwaben*, *Die Argonauten* or *Rübezahl* (of which only Mahler's fairy-tale libretto remains) might, it has been suggested, be a function of its psychological involvement with his feelings about the death of his brother Ernst. Should we see Ernst in the murdered brother whose sad story is only heard when the minstrel plays upon a flute made out of one of his bones? But perhaps the work's symbolism is of a different order. The two brothers who set out to find the flower that will win the hand of the proud Queen could equally be representatives of a split German people. Is the fate of the Habsburg Empire foretold in that quintessential Mahlerian moment when the song of the disinherited outsider intervenes in and thoroughly wrecks the wedding-banquet that is attended, off-stage, by marching-bands from the Iglau town square? Each reading is as valid or as far-fetched as the other; much depends upon what stories the interpreter intends, or indeed *permits* music to tell. That problem would return to haunt Mahler, like the 'plaintive song' of the singing bone.

3   Playing the artist – the beginnings of a career

> Wasn't I half-unconsciously playing a part for my own benefit
> and for that of others, in this case the aspiring poet?[1]

Arthur Schnitzler, the Jewish Viennese writer and dramatist, asks
this question of himself in a section of his autobiography dealing
with his youthful development in the period around 1878. Although
he was a close contemporary of Mahler's (just two years younger),
Schnitzler's background was more securely middle class. But much
in his recollections corroborates and extends Zweig's analysis of the
peculiarly theatrical nature of Viennese life in ways that are applica-
ble to Mahler. Did he, too, 'play the part' of the poet, of the Romantic
composer during those years in which the audience for his works
was largely restricted to himself and a close circle of his friends and
loved-ones? Perhaps it was necessary to act the role in which you
wanted the world to cast you.

I am not speaking here of sham or deception so much as of the
way in which culture reproduces itself and evolves in the subjective
consciousness of its participants. For Mahler and Schnitzler, in their
slightly different ways, acting the poet was an essential stage in their
development as modern artists: inheritors of the Romantic world of
artistic illusion who came to see it for what it was, without quite
being able to renounce what it ideally promised. In worldly terms,
when you were young, art offered a career, a route out of financial

hardship, social disadvantage or marginalization. On the 'higher' plane, it promised truth, revelation, passion, fulfilment; the gifts you sought which were also yours to give. Mahler, who was much admired by Schnitzler, possibly more fully dramatized the tensions and contradictions within the art-ideology of his age precisely *because* of the central place that Music held within it.

Such tensions and contradictions manifested themselves in spiritual and emotional immediacy, but also reflected social and political circumstances. For Mahler, as a Jew and as a student associate of members of the Pernerstorfer and *Leseverein* circles, the philosophical, the religious and the political were inextricably linked. While all that his culture taught him about music might have distanced it from politics, his early struggles with art and ideas were often as much political as they were religious in implication and imagery. Zweig's picture of the Vienna of his youth translated the tension between artistic inwardness and worldly pressures into one between reconciling nature and the noisily fragmented city. Versions of that duality were part of the whole tradition of Romanticism and its sometimes idealized, sometimes overtly politicized antipathy to 'the world'. They might take us back once more to Wackenroder's story of the ill-fated composer Joseph Berglinger, who eventually makes the following admission in a letter to his father:

> How much nearer I was to my ideal in the innocence of my
> youth, in quiet and solitude, when I merely enjoyed art instead
> of practising it as I do now in the dazzle of fashionable society,
> surrounded on all sides by the most cultivated and discriminating
> of men! You must wonder what I would really like most to do. I
> would like to turn my back on all this culture and flee to my simple
> Swiss herdsman in his mountains, and join him in his Alpine songs
> for which he feels homesick no matter where he may roam.

It would be naive to accuse Mahler of posturing when in 1879, at the age of nineteen, he wrote a long and often tortured letter to his friend Joseph Steiner, the librettist of the abandoned opera *Herzog*

Ernst von Schwaben. It covered a period of three days while he was working as a summer-vacation music-tutor on the estate of a Hungarian family. In it the youthful idealist adopted the tone and subject-matter of Wackenroder's troubled composer and the long line of Romantic heroes to which he belonged:

> I can't go on like this much longer! When the abominable tyranny of our modern hypocrisy and mendacity has driven me to the point of dishonouring myself, when the inextricable web of conditions in art and life has filled my heart with disgust for all that is sacred to me – art, love, religion – what way out is there but self-annihilation? Wildly I wrench at the bonds that chain me to the loathsome, insipid swamp of this life . . .
>
> . . .
>
> What a strange destiny, sweeping me along on the waves of my yearning, now hurling me this way and that in the gale, now wafting me along merrily in smiling sunshine. What I fear is that in such a gale I shall some day be shattered against a reef – such as my keel has often grazed!
>
> It is six o'clock in the morning! I have been out on the heath, sitting with Fárkas the shepherd, listening to the sound of his shawm. Ah, how mournful it sounded, and yet how full of rapturous delight – that folk-tune he played! The flowers growing at his feet trembled in the dreamy glow of his dark eyes, and his brown hair fluttered around his sun-tanned cheeks . . . the tranquil happiness all around me is tiptoeing into my heart too, as the sun of early spring lights up the wintry fields. Is spring awakening now in my own breast? . . .

It is an extraordinary document, rising to an early climax in a fist-shaking denunciation of a deceiving, mocking deity, the source of mankind's 'unspeakable misery', who rules from 'cold and lonely heights'. Anti-authoritarianism would manifest itself in many areas of Mahler's later life; here it arises from real personal anguish, characterized by wild mood swings from suicidal despair to joy in nature. The letter is, of course, a self-consciously literary performance in which Mahler is both expressing himself and watching himself doing it, relishing every occasion for allusion to novels, fairy-tales and his own creative projects – including their abandoned opera (linked explicitly here with a memory of his dead brother Ernst). There is also a reference to a girl he had been attracted to, a year or two previously, during one of his Moravian summers on Gustav Schwarz's estate, when Steiner had probably been his companion. Later, details from some fateful chain of events linked to that blossoming love-affair are linked in a surreal montage that anticipates the style and subject-matter of his childhood dream about Ahasuerus, the 'Eternal Jew'. Again the mixture of Catholic and Christian imagery is striking (the 'Melion' referred to was a teacher at the Iglau *Gymnasium* with whom Mahler remained on terms of close friendship for some years):

Suddenly a table rises out of the ground, and behind it stands a spiritual figure veiled in blue clouds: It is Melion hymning the 'Great Spirit', at the same time censing him with genuine Three Kings tobacco! And beside him the two of us sit like altar-boys [Ministranten] about to assist him in his Holy Office for the first time.

And behind us a grinning goblin hovers, decked out in piquet cards, and he has Buxbaum's face and calls out to us in a terrible voice, to the melody of Bertini's Etudes: 'Bow down! for this glory too shall turn to dust!' A cascade of smoke from Melion covers the whole scene, the clouds become ever denser, and then suddenly, as in Raphael's painting of the Madonna, a little angel's head peers out from among these clouds, and below it stands Ahasuerus in all his sufferings, longing to ascend to him, to enter into the presence of all that means bliss and redemption, but the angel floats away on high, laughing, and vanishes, and Ahasuerus gazes after him in immeasurable grief, then takes up his staff and resumes his wanderings, tearless, eternal, immortal.

O earth, my beloved earth, when, ah when will you give refuge to him who is forsaken, receiving him back into your womb? Behold! Mankind has cast him out, and he flees from its cold and heartless bosom, he flees to you, to you alone! O take him in eternal, all-embracing mother, give a resting-place to him who is without friends and without rest![2]

Quite a scene. The 'genuine Three Kings tobacco', with its Nativity-scene allusion concealed in a trade name, even suggests an element of parody. The letter has justifiably been read as providing an invaluable insight into the creative and emotional sources of much of Mahler's later artistic output and his characteristic mixture of the sardonic and the emotionally surcharged. The manner in which it is staged is also revealing. Devices like the swirling clouds seem to be lifted directly from the scene-change directions in Das Rheingold and the whole sequence is brought to life by a powerfully visual imagination, schooled in Romantic dream-sequences like those of 'Jean Paul' Richter, one of Mahler's favourite writers. Already we sense the future opera director stage-managing the theatre of his own inner life. In his evocation of the orchestrated city that was fin-de-siècle Vienna Zweig had omitted only to mention the similarly dramatized representations of inner life in its relation to the cultural construction of the whole.

But a shared theatre, even an inner one, with shared settings and characters is not necessarily a fully determined one that 'writes itself'. At least not for an aspiring composer like Mahler. He failed to win a coveted 'Beethoven Prize' for composition both in 1878 (with his now lost overture Die Argonauten) and 1881 (Das klagende Lied) on the grounds, no doubt, that his music was all too self-willed and lacking in that timeless correctness of manner and form which marked 'great' works, supportively modelling the status quo. In the theatre of Mahler's mind and works what was obvious and correct was always re-negotiated, re-staged in ways that clarified ever more sharply the underlying problematics of the norm.

Art, love, religion . . . all that was 'sacred' to Mahler; in each of these areas of experience he became the focus of tensions that troubled his generation in its attempt to discover the truth behind the parts that they were all playing, the drama in which they were participating. Mahler was already negotiating for himself the position of an outsider in the area of religion. This we know from another letter he wrote in August 1879 from the Baumgarten family's estate outside Nagytétény, near Budapest. Announcing to Albert Spiegler his imminent arrival in Vienna, en route for Iglau, he continued:

> how I yearn to see human beings again, and how I long once again to hear the sound of the organ and the peal of the bells. A breeze as of heavenly wings flows through me when I see the peasants in their finery at church. They kneel in prayer before the altar, and their songs of praise mingle with the sound of drums and trumpets. – Ah it is long since there was any altar left for me: only, mute and high, God's temple arches over me, the wide sky. – I cannot rise to it and would so gladly pray. Instead of chorales and hymns it is thunder that roars, and instead of candles it is lightning that flickers . . .[3]

If, as seems to be the implication, Mahler was still attending Christian church services as an 'observer', the sense of confusion and spiritual homelessness that they brought on was reinforced by the geographical rootlessness of his life as a young conductor, moving from post to post from 1880 onwards.

In the period 1880–8 Mahler served his apprenticeship as a 'Kapellmeister'. The term was familiarly used to designate the person responsible for the music in a theatre: the conductor of the orchestra who would also, depending on the size and importance of the house, be an orchestrator, an arranger, even a producer of operas and operettas that were constantly being cut and pasted into shapes that fitted the resident company, small or large. His first job, for the summer season at a modest 'spa' theatre, presented itself in 1880 at a time when his spirits were generally low – partly on account of the unhappy experience of an unfulfilled love-affair in Iglau.

This was the year in which his acquaintance with former *Leseverein* members deepened, along with his Wagnerism. The publication, in the *Bayreuther Blätter*, of Wagner's essay 'Religion and Art' – on the

4   Mahler in 1881

redeeming social power of vegetarianism – had an immediate impact on the basement café set which Mahler, now sporting a full beard, tended to frequent. Heinrich Braun, Victor Adler, Hermann Bahr, Siegfried Lipiner, Hugo Wolf, Friedrich Eckstein and future political leaders Michael Hainisch and Thomas Masaryk, were all regular members of the same group, whose discussions turned upon politics, Wagner, Ibsen, Shelley and a range of scientific topics. By the end of the year more than one of them, Mahler included, had turned vegetarian. The beard that he had grown should not be taken, as it might have been half a century later, as an outward sign of the bohemian and somewhat impoverished 'alternative' lifestyle that he had undoubtedly adopted at that time. Zweig notes that Vienna's was then a totally adult-orientated culture:

> The newspapers recommended preparations which hastened the growth of the beard, and twenty-four- and twenty-five-year-old doctors, who had just finished their examinations, wore mighty beards and gold spectacles even if their eyes did not need them, so that they could make an impression of 'experience' upon their first patients.[4]

What impression such accoutrements made in 1880 on the small troupe of singing actors and musicians in Bad Hall, south of Linz, is not clear. But the job effectively sealed Mahler's fate, giving him some formative experience as a theatre-conductor, albeit of operettas by Offenbach, the younger Johann Strauss and Suppé.

There was nothing idealistic about that job in the little 200-seat wooden theatre, where performances had to begin at 5.00 p.m. so that they could be completed in daylight (it was too dangerous to use candles or gas-lights). But Mahler had actively been seeking a job since beginning that semester's University courses in Archaeology and History (of Ancient Philosophy, Europe at the time of Napoleon, and the 'History of Music since the death of Beethoven' taught by Hanslick). Poverty may have played the largest part in his efforts to mobilize all his influential friends, including Guido Adler, to help him find a post. He signed a five-year contract with the agent-impresario Gustav Lewy (or Löwy) and soon accepted the Bad Hall job, against the advice of his parents, but at the prompting of Professor Epstein, who saw that it would provide useful experience.

Thus Mahler began his career as an entertainer of well-to-do holiday-makers and iodine-bath 'cure'-seekers from Vienna and Linz. He later claimed that he had had to put the music on the stands and wheel the pram of Director Zwerenz's baby daughter in the intervals. Because of the special place of music and musicians in Austrian culture of the period, however, his position in no way hindered his being taken up by an elegant group of young men associated with the fashionable, forty-year-old painter Heinrich von Angeli. Alma Mahler would later claim that an excursion with this group had caused Mahler to miss the beginning of a performance and Zwerenz to sack him. But Zwerenz was willing to take Mahler with him to his next post as director of the theatre in, of all places, Iglau. That, Mahler told impresario Lewy, was not possible 'because of my family'. The job of assistant conductor still lacked the status that might have persuaded his parents that their former budding concert-pianist son was really 'making good'; just the previous year he had played a Schubert sonata in an Iglau concert celebrating the Emperor's twenty-fifth wedding anniversary.

So Mahler returned to Vienna and his life as a student who also composed music. *Das klagende Lied* was nearing completion while the opera *Rübezahl*, whose libretto Mahler had given to Lipiner for an opinion, remained more dream than reality. The calling of Art in that period was, of course, all about making dreams real, and where Mahler was generally, even painfully able to distinguish the one from the other (although he claimed to have had a nightmarish 'Doppelgänger' experience while working that autumn on *Das klagende Lied*), others of his friends were not. 'Madness' of one kind or another lurked in many a garret in that city of dreams. Mahler himself would lay many of his own later miseries at the door of the Beethoven Prize jury – including Brahms, Hanslick and Joseph Hellmesberger – which twice refused him the coveted 500-guilder prize. His friend Hans Rott seems to have been driven insane by anger and disappointment at his failure to win a prize in 1880. However exaggerated the partisan differences between Brahms and the young Viennese modernists influenced by Wagner and Bruckner may have become, there is evidence that Brahms could be cuttingly unkind to aspiring composers. It was almost certainly after Rott had played his extraordinary symphony to Brahms that he had advised Rott to give up music altogether.[5] Rott's grasp on reality snapped on the train taking him to his new job as a choral conductor in Alsace. He warned a fellow traveller, about to light a cigar, that Brahms had filled the train with dynamite. He descended rapidly into insanity, dying in an institution in 1884.

The whole episode, and similar fears about his Conservatory friend Anton Krisper, affected Mahler at a vulnerable time in his life. 'If you know one happy person on this earth', he had written to Emil Freund, with whose family in Seelau he spent part of the summer of 1881, 'tell me his name quickly, before I lose the last of what courage remains in me.' But his energy and appetite for new ventures remained strong; it must have been in the early part of 1881 that he was associated with another invention of members of the Pernerstorfer circle: a so-called 'Saga Society', devoted to the renewal of culture through creative and imaginative absorption in the world of Germanic mythology. Mahler was the group's musician, on one occasion playing them the overture to *Die Meistersinger* (as he had formerly accompanied the Pernerstorfer circle in a rendering of 'Deutschland, Deutschland über alles'). Given the fragility of his emotional state, it was probably as well that by the time *Das klagende Lied* followed Rott's symphony into the Beethoven Prize panel's 'reject' pile (December 1881), he was busy in his second job: as principal conductor at the Provincial Theatre in what is now Slovenian Ljubljana; then it was Laibach in Carniola, in the far south of the Austrian part of the Empire.

Conditions in the Laibach theatre were not greatly better than those in Bad Hall; again it was a rather shoe-string affair, directed by a comic actor whose wife ran the box-office. It had an eighteen-piece orchestra (enlarged a little for opera) and a small troupe of singing actors who had to perform in plays, operettas and operas. But the eighteenth-century building itself, though small, was comparatively solid and had a touch of style, an echo of the grandeur of larger municipal and court theatres elsewhere. Its repertoire was significantly broader than that in Bad Hall. During the six-month season he spent there, from September 1881 to the beginning of April 1882, Mahler conducted around fifty performances of works that ranged from the usual operettas through plays with incidental music (including Beethoven's for *Egmont* and Mendelssohn's for *A Midsummer Night's Dream*) to operas by Donizetti, Rossini, Verdi (*Ernani* and *Il Trovatore*), Weber (*Der Freischütz*) and Mozart (*Die Zauberflöte*). Learning his trade and, often, the operas as he went along, the 21-year-old asserted himself gamely, shooting piercing and sometimes effectively intimidating glances at the musicians through his horn-rimmed spectacles and generally receiving appreciative reviews in both German and Slovenian newspapers. Mahler owed much to that southern outpost of the Empire in which he first conducted Beethoven, Mozart and Verdi and gave his last public performance as a solo pianist.

Returning to his student life in Vienna via Trieste (where he first saw the sea), Mahler might well have had occasion to admire the Empire's expanding railway network, which linked its important business, administrative and military establishments – and also its theatres. At most major and many minor stations you could alight from the train and very soon find your way to a theatre. Operas generally reinforcing the *status quo* (idealistic subjectivity and folksy community generally won over the mad, the bad and the revolutionary) and operettas 'safely' satirizing it played there to brightly fading aristocrats and earnestly blooming members of the bourgeoisie. These musically enacted stories were richly meaningful even when outwardly frivolous. Even Hanslick, who might have sought to extricate the 'music' from such stories in the University course Mahler had begun with him in 1880, was well known as a man who

> loved the facile sensuousness of Italian arias, the wit of the French *opéra comique*, the melodious stream of Strauss's waltzes and Offenbach's operettas, just as the careless, pleasure-seeking, brilliant and elegant society of Vienna did. From the viewpoint

of Viennese optimism he regarded Wagner, Liszt and Bruckner as rude intruders into a world of pleasure, sensuality and easy wit.

And what Hanslick disapproved of could be a matter of some moment when his 'feuilleton' reviews began on the front page of Vienna's leading liberal newspaper, the *Neue Freie Presse*.

It was by tackling seriously works in all styles that Mahler began in his way to 'intrude' in the world of musical theatre in the 1880s. Not that there was anything controversial in his one performance at the Iglau Stadttheater in September 1882, when he conducted Suppé's *Boccaccio*, perhaps to oblige Zwerenz; his parents must have been present. Things soon changed. His next brief appointment at the Royal Municipal Theatre in the east-Moravian town of Olmütz (Olomouc), from January to March 1883, was formative both for himself and the mediocre company, slightly larger than the one in Laibach. He was hardly in the best of spirits there. His vegetarianism was incomprehensible to the local restaurateurs and in his lodgings he was plagued by the noise of pianos and the lack of books to read. He judiciously manoeuvred Mozart and Wagner out of the repertoire and found that he could achieve his best results with a work like Méhul's *Joseph in Aegypten*. He wrote revealingly about it to his new Viennese friend, the future archaeologist Fritz Löhr, with whom he spent part of the following summer:

> this time they have tried somewhat harder – though I'm afraid it's only a way of showing they're sorry for this 'idealist' – a very contemptuous epithet, this. For the idea that an artist can become utterly absorbed in a work of art is quite beyond them. At times, when I'm all on fire with enthusiasm, when I'm trying to sweep them along with me, give them some impetus, I see these people's faces, see how surprised they are, how knowingly they smile at each other – and then my boiling blood cools down and all I want is to run away and never go back. Only the feeling that I am suffering for my masters' sake, and that some day perhaps I shall kindle a spark in these poor wretches' souls, fortifies me, and in some of my better hours I vow to endure with love and understanding –

even in the face of their scorn. – You will smile at the dramatic tone in which I speak of these trivialities. – But isn't this actually the prototype of our relationship to the world?

One of the 'poor wretches' in that company left a bemused but admiring account of Mahler's time there. 'He was not liked, but they learned to fear him' was his estimate of Mahler's effect on the people and performers of Olmütz. The writer also recalled encountering Mahler 'running demented, weeping loudly, through the streets'. He assumed that his recently ailing father had died. In fact it was the death of Wagner that Mahler was mourning in that February of 1883.[6]

He had been working in Laibach when others of his Viennese friends had attended the first performance of *Parsifal* at Bayreuth the previous year, but he was to hear it there in July that year: 'the greatest, most painful thing . . . I should have it with me in all its sanctity for the rest of my life'. He had made the journey on the proceeds of a trial week he had spent working at the Royal Theatre in Kassel, still further north in the heart of the German Empire, where he was to find himself in a new post that August. It was to be his longest engagement thus far (August 1883 to April 1885) and certainly the most prestigious. By October 1883 he had officially been given the position of 'Royal Musical and Choral Director', although he was subordinate to the Kapellmeister (Wilhelm Treiber) and the Intendant – the official, appointed from Berlin, whose responsibility it was to manage the theatre in a manner appropriate to its status as a 'royal' institution. Intendant Adolph Freiherr von und zu Gilsa was a Prussian Officer with a string of medals, including the Iron Cross, who managed young Mahler with the aid of a lengthy list of contractual obligations. The style of his administration can be gauged from records indicating that Mahler was fined twice in September 1883 alone: once for 'walking noisily on the heels of his boots during rehearsals and performances', once for occasioning 'peals of laughter' among some of the women of the chorus.

In spite of the almost inevitable tension that developed between the 23-year-old (who had claimed to be 25 when he signed the contract in 1883) and his superiors, Mahler had some success in Kassel, not only with such operas as he was allowed to conduct but also, for the first time, as a composer. In June 1884 he quickly wrote a complete suite of incidental music for the main item in a charity evening of operatic extracts. This was for a series of 'tableaux vivants' based on Scheffel's popular narrative poem *Der Trompeter von Säkkingen*; it inspired a number of works around this time, including a rather trite opera by Victor Nessler. Mahler's music was much applauded, but that he later disowned (and apparently destroyed) it may be due less to his music than to the conservative subject-matter of the piece, about the quelling of a peasant uprising and the ennoblement by the Pope of Werner, suitor to the Baron's daughter and the 'trumpeter' of the title. Having become a 'Ritter', a knight, the former humble musician now wins his heart's desire. Mahler would hardly have wished to face his socialist friends with that to his name.

In fact some of its music did survive for a time in the subsequently discarded (but not destroyed) 'Blumine' movement of the First Symphony which did not take shape, however, until after Mahler had left Kassel. He had started to plan his move as early as January 1884, when the great Hans von Bülow had brought his famous Meiningen Court Orchestra to Kassel for two concerts. Mahler had been bowled over, and after failing to gain entry to von Bülow's hotel had written to him, offering his services as a pupil-apprentice ('I am ready for anything you have in mind'). In correct, but crushing, Prussian fashion Bülow quickly returned the letter to Kapellmeister Treiber, whereupon it went into Mahler's official file. His final triumph in Kassel, following the cancellation of his contract in April 1885, would nevertheless put Treiber firmly in his place.

With his relations with Baron von Gilsa in tatters, his name repeatedly in the punishment book, Mahler was busy with preparations for a music festival that was partly designed to celebrate the patriotic feeling that was then, as he put it in a letter, the 'fashion' in Kassel (which was also a centre of German folklore; the brothers Grimm had worked there and Arnim and Brentano's *Des Knaben Wunderhorn* was first published there). In spite of the involvement of the opera orchestra, Mahler, as director of the Münden Mixed Choral Society, had been chosen by the committee over his superior, Treiber, to conduct the main festival event: a performance of Mendelssohn's *St Paul*. Loyal to Treiber, the orchestra withdrew, and the three local choirs had to be accompanied by a mixed orchestra, including players from a number of other establishments and the band of an infantry regiment. The Moravian bandmaster in Mahler rose to the occasion, and he pulled off a resounding success in the performance in a huge infantry drill-hall in Kassel, impetuously conducting nearly 500 performers with a long stick visible to all. He clearly relished every moment of it and reports of the concert circulated widely.

He who had faithfully served his 'masters' was now becoming one himself, in a way that strikingly mobilized all the associated meanings that the term has in German, as in English. The implications were to shadow and throw into sharper relief the uncompromising nature of his idealism, both as a conductor and as a composer, right up to the first performance of his Eighth Symphony in the last full year of his life (1910). Even at this early stage in his career he had come to realize that artistic mastery meant little without an attendant mastery over people and the ways of the world. While the situation in Kassel had been deteriorating, Mahler had gone on sending letters in every direction, aiming to secure a better position. Two such letters were to bear fruit. The first was to Max Staegemann, director of the Leipzig Opera, with whom a six-year contract was soon being arranged; Mahler would be appointed as junior conductor alongside the already celebrated Arthur Nikisch (five years Mahler's senior). Then, providentially filling the gap between his departure from Kassel and the beginning of the Leipzig contract in 1886, there finally came an invitation from the famous opera director and Wagner-impresario Angelo Neumann, who had just taken over direction of the German Theatre in Prague.

From impending disaster in Kassel, Mahler suddenly found himself embarked on a career that was moving forward rapidly and excitingly. He spent a year in Prague (August 1885 to July 1886), conducting a wide repertoire of works, including Mozart and, perhaps most importantly, Wagner (Rienzi, Tannhäuser, Lohengrin, Der fliegende Holländer, Die Meistersinger, Das Rheingold and Die Walküre). Then he moved to Leipzig where he began by standing in for Nikisch in the magnificent, 2,000-seat Municipal Theatre. He set the seal on his fame as an opera conductor in a matter of two years there (1886–8). During that period he completed a successful performing version of Weber's posthumous opera Die Drei Pintos and composed his First Symphony and the first movement of the Second (as Todtenfeier); he was also to fall scandalously in love with the wife of Weber's grandson, who had entrusted him with the sketches for Die Drei Pintos.

Mahler had exclaimed in 1879 to Joseph Steiner that 'art, love, religion' were all that was most sacred to him. Art and religious feeling inevitably fed upon his youthful love-life, which was intimately bound up with his earliest significant compositions. Here the mediation between private and public realms demonstrated revealing tensions and contradictions that require judicious interpretation. Were his works, in the language soon to be developed by Freud, 'sublimations' of unfulfilled sexual desire or cryptically polite allusions to secret passion? Life and art merged here in a very particular way; the life is essentially no more easy to 'read' from surviving letters, gossip and anecdotes than the art. Was Mahler really as inexperienced in sexual matters as he would claim, at the age of forty, in the course of his affair with Alma Schindler? The modern consensus is that he cannot have been. Biographers like Gartenberg and de La Grange take their cue from Zweig, who makes it clear that public prudery in Vienna, at least for young men, was matched by private licence in the company of the prostitutes or lower-class girls who seemed to smile obligingly from any number of back-street windows in that city of easy pleasures.

By his thirties, Mahler had acquired a reputation as something of a womanizer, although some stories reinforce the suspicion that he might have been rather the reverse, and that intense, unconsciously homoerotic relationships with close male friends like Anton Krisper were complemented by equally intense ideal-izing friendships with women. Mahler may have been prone to forming 'elective affinities' that tended towards yet failed quite to reach direct sexual expression. He also had a pronounced puritan-ical streak. Alma Mahler (dare we trust her in this, of all topics?) relates the story of his having lectured a singer in Laibach on the subject of her 'loose morals':

> whereupon she swung herself on to the piano and slapping her thighs informed him that the purity of his own morals aroused her utter contempt.

It is not improbable that Mahler might, had he visited prostitutes in the company of Hugo Wolf or one of his other student acquain-tances, have behaved like Arthur Schnitzler's friend Adolf, 'who after bestowing his favours on such a lady would follow it up by reproach-ing her, with unctuous lectures, for her profligate way of life'.[7]

It is both difficult and dangerous to come to any dogmatic conclu-sion about Mahler's youthful sexual experiences. Their traces are comprehensively covered by the public manner of the gallantly ideal-istic, easily hurt Romantic Lover that we encounter in letters to, about and from the women in his life – as in the poetry and music that attended all the relevant hopes and disappointments. In 1879–80 it had been Josephine, daughter of I. Poisl, the postmaster in Iglau. Mahler appears to have started writing about her to Anton Krisper in September 1879 ('A new name is now inscribed in my heart alongside yours . . .'), but by Easter the following year he was writing directly to his 'passionately beloved' Josephine:

> just at a time when I am closer than ever to the goal of my desires – when that which we (oh, would I could say – *we both*) so ardently longed for, would soon be fulfilled.

> I have never humbled myself before anyone. Look, I kneel
> before you!

In June 1880 her father wrote to Mahler, warning him that 'there
never was and there *never* will be any serious affection on her part'. By
then Mahler had already been writing love poems, three of which,
dedicated to her, he later set to music. All of them, like another poem
about the affair that he sent to Anton Krisper, adopt the manner of
the Romantic lyric with its often deliberate evocation of the folk-like
tone of those idyllic innocents, like Fárkas the shepherd or Wackenroder's Swiss herdsman, who were 'at one' with themselves, each
other and Nature. These early poems are marked by their juxtaposition of what Schiller called 'naive' and the 'sentimental' modes, with
not a hint of anything directly sensual or erotic. All *that* is displaced
to a distant realm of longing towards which the broken-hearted
dreamer must ever toil. The last two stanzas (of four) of the first song
'Dedicated to Josephine' present the complex with great clarity. The
sentimental lover is encouraged to abandon himself to a naive
absorption in nature, but his rational alienation refuses to permit it
(the music of the second stanza draws on a sad, solemn line from *Das
klagende Lied*):

> The sun looks down on you so amiably.
> How can you have sorrow or regret?
> Throw away your burdens, you sorrowful man,
> And rejoice in the sun and the sky.

> 'No sun, no sky gives me any delight,
> Yet I love the Spring;
> Ah! She whom I wish above all to see,
> She lingers long, far away,'

The 'happiest' of the three completed songs ('Hans und Grete')
seems to have been lifted from the libretto of *Rübezahl* and narrates, as
from an idealized distance, the story of a Hans who finds his Grete in a
dance that would later contribute something to the Scherzo of the
First Symphony, in 1888. That symphony, written in the full flood of

emotion released by the love-affair with Frau Marion von Weber in Leipzig, was to take the form of a grandly dramatized version of the same sense of a rift between Nature and the lost or wandering Self that had become an institutionalized opposition within Romanticism. It would first be cogently explored in the four *Songs of a Wayfarer*, the *Lieder eines fahrenden Gesellen*, which form the basis of the symphony and which had been written out of the experience of his second major love-affair. This was with Johanna Richter in Kassel. She had ended it in her rooms in the closing hours of 1884, sending Mahler out alone into 1885, where he was greeted by bells and a New Year chorale: 'it was just as if the great world stage-manager had wanted to make it all artistically perfect. I wept all through the night in my dreams.'[8]

In his early twenties Mahler was 'playing the artist' for real. While privately performing the part of the Romantic Lover as defined by the literary manners of a discreetly administered culture, marked by public repression and denial, he was gathering a full drawer of 'works'. These helped to clarify the cultural nature of the 'subjectivity' on which his passionate experience relied. Music had always told stories to Mahler. It was in the progressive elucidation of the story that his own music told that he began to find his way as a symphonist; in the medium, that is, in which his world celebrated the reconciliation of the public with the private in a manner more complex even than in opera. Appropriately enough, the poles of mood and emotion represented by the works that he had amassed by the end of his time in Leipzig were, on the one hand, a form of Romantic Agony, and, on the other, heroic optimism. The *Lieder eines fahrenden Gesellen* gave voice to the former and resolved the conflict between Innocence and Experience in a decidedly tragic absorption in Nature (symbolized by sleep beneath a lime tree (*Lindenbaum*)) and in music that closed with the echo of a funeral march. In the symphony, however, resolution came in an extrovert triumphal march, derived from its opening evocation of 'Nature' but now depending on the thrillingly regimented precision of a great body of orchestral players, leaping to the command of Mahler's youthful baton.

4 The 'devil' in the wings

My grateful thanks to all – the Adlers, Pernerstorfer and Bondi – for
the New Year greeting. *Perhaps via Friedjung it would be possible to get
an announcement* of my new appointment published *in the Viennese
press*. If possible with a 'short obituary [*Nekrolog*]' as well. It could
be helpful for my future, although I do not have many rungs left to
climb now. But my final goal is and must remain Vienna – I can
never really feel at home anywhere else.[1]

Mahler wrote this in Kassel in January 1885, in a letter to Albert
Spiegler. In it he announced his engagement as Kapellmeister in
Leipzig for the following year. At the age of twenty-five he had learnt
how his world worked and how best to succeed in it. Through a
combination of extreme and single-minded self-confidence with
judicious self-promotion he was proving ever more effective in what
a modern journalist, echoing Zweig, might call 'orchestrating' the
progress of his own career. To do so was really no more than to
acknowledge, in a practical way, the wider ramifications of art as a
cultural institution. They extended far beyond the theatres and con-
cert-halls in which he worked. In Kassel Mahler had battled like an
'unruly schoolboy' (as he later admitted to von Gilsa) with Prussian
authority, communicated via the officially appointed Intendant to a
hierarchically organized and strictly disciplined theatre management, mirroring that of the state. He began to acquire more author-

ity and power of his own as he moved up the rungs of a ladder of increasingly prestigious appointments that ended with the directorship of the Vienna Court Opera in 1897. The point repeatedly stressed by his friends and early biographers was that his metamorphosis into a somewhat tyrannical, often feared and sometimes hated orchestral and operatic conductor-manager was driven by aesthetic idealism; by the almost fanatical urge to rescue Art from 'slovenly Tradition' (as he called it). Yet if that idealism was an ideological component of the traditionally constituted culture which it served, then Mahler, the upwardly mobile Kapellmeister, might be seen as an ever more effective functionary of that culture, his idealism an intensification and not a subversion of its essential character.

From his earliest appearances as a pianist 'Wunderkind' in Iglau, Mahler was involved with public and official uses of art. His music-making had been associated with the celebration of royal weddings and anniversaries, the honouring of a great German poet and charity fund-raising (for the Iglau *Gymnasium* or the victims of the earthquake in Ischia). Such events oiled the wheels of the humanely liberal constitutional monarchy that Franz Joseph I and his most loyal subjects so dearly wished to preserve. Already at Laibach, however, Mahler was providing music for official occasions whose brilliance was often deliberately designed to dispel worrying political shadows. One of these had been a gala evening marking the opening of the Diet of the Duchy of Carniola. Laibach was its capital, its population composed of 40 per cent Slovenes to 60 per cent Germans and military personnel. Several members of the Diet, along with 'the Imperial-Royal Provincial President and his family' heard Mahler conduct Beethoven's *Egmont* overture as a curtain-raiser to Bauernfeld's aptly named and politically innocuous comedy *Bürgerlich und Romantisch* (literally *Bourgeois and Romantic*, but *Homely and Romantic* might be a more idiomatic translation).

In Prague, in 1885, the situation was more complex still. There Mahler's appointment was at the Royal German Theatre, whose fortunes had been declining in inverse proportion to those of the flourishing Czech National Theatre, where Smetana, Dvořák and the Russians were played. Mahler visited the Czech theatre frequently and would have had reason to feel divided loyalties, given his own Bohemian and Moravian roots in that city where Czechs out-numbered Germans by three to two. An article of 1888 on 'The national significance of the German theatre in Prague', quoted by Blaukopf, notes that originally, before the National Theatre was built, plays in Czech had been staged

> on two or three afternoons a week for the lower classes, until the Czechs built a small temporary theatre. After twenty years of economy and hard work it was replaced by the magnificent National Theatre which is their pride and joy.

The 'lower classes' are revealed to be Czechs only when they acquire their own theatre! The article had gone on to explain that the Germans had started to desert their own theatre for that of the Czechs, until

> Angelo Neumann was called in to save it from disaster, and at a stroke the German public was back. He engaged an entirely new company and embarked on a period of great activity. Drama and opera filled the house every evening, and the performances of Wagner's *Ring* acted as a magnet to the whole theatre-going public of Prague.[2]

Mahler had a fine time there, even as representative of an embattled official German culture. He was given free rein by Neumann, who was prepared to gamble on his youthful enthusiasm and determination. It paid off richly. Although illness prevented Mahler's mother from making the journey, we must assume that some of his brothers and sisters would have responded to his invitations to come to see him conduct. His Prague triumphs included *Das Rheingold* and *Die Walküre*, a memorable production of *Don Giovanni* (in the city in which it had its première) and a remarkable concert in February 1886 in which he had conducted extracts from *Götterdämmerung*, *Parsifal* (the Act I 'transformation' music and the closing scene) and Beethoven's Ninth (from memory). In spite of unpleasant childhood memories and a typical concluding 'scene' with Neumann, he would happily have stayed in Prague, had his contract with Leipzig not been binding. But the theatrical life of that beautiful city was certainly more than just an arena in which a bright young conductor might flourish. The politics of nationalism and imperialism played a significant part, which Mahler had every reason to understand; he would surely recall it when he subsequently chose Smetana's *Dalibor* for his first new production at the Vienna Court Opera, at a time of increasing tension over the issue of Czech nationalism.

In fact Mahler continued to flourish in far-away Leipzig, in spite of the fact that his position subordinate to Nikisch led to a bitter sense of rivalry and frustration. Busy as his own schedule was, some of his most cherished performances were those where he had taken over when Nikisch was indisposed, like the performance of *Die Walküre* in February 1887. More importantly still, his character and personality as a public figure with a mysterious, slightly daemonic private life (largely devoted to books and, it was rumoured, composition) found their mature form. They also found one of their first, fascinated chroniclers in his friend Max Steinitzer (who wrote criticism as 'Sikkus' and was later better known as the friend and biographer of Richard Strauss):

> As a young man Mahler was the incarnation of Man as Expression among so many for whom only Man as Form exists. He had the best intentions of being polite, but whenever anybody made some shallow or commonplace remark (which may have been exactly what the moment required), his glance became far too piercing . . .
> . . . Mahler could be so like Hoffmann's description of 'Kapellmeister Kreisler' in *Kater Murr* that it was quite uncanny.[3]

Steinitzer would occasionally meet Mahler in his favourite café, the Café Français, from which they could gaze across to the broad façade of the mid-nineteenth-century 'New Theatre'. No rival establishment here eclipsed the brilliance of Saxon Leipzig's fore-most temple of art, with its huge auditorium and first-rate company. Standing in the centre of the town and facing the Augustusplatz, it had been designed to have, at the rear, its own attached piece of Romantic 'Nature'. While industrial chimneys smoked in the city's suburbs, opera-goers and promenading townsfolk might descend from the terrace at the back of the theatre to an oval lake with foun-tains, benches and a fringe of trees.

Just as Mahler's character and personality assumed their typical form in Leipzig (increasing self-assurance had led him to shave off his beard, leaving a broad moustache), so too did many features of the daily routine that he would follow during opera seasons for many years to come. Rising early to work or read, he would then leave for his relentlessly exacting and often orchestra-inflaming morning rehearsals (like others after it, the relatively conservative Leipzig *Gewandhaus* orchestra, devoted to Nikisch and its kindly concert-conductor Karl Reinecke, respected but heartily disliked Mahler, on one occasion complaining to the city council about his temper and unusual strictures). The early afternoon would be spent in the café. There would invariably be a long walk at some point, then more work and the evening opera-performance, followed by dinner in the com-pany of friends like Director Max Staegemann or the Weber family.

His friendship with the Webers came to dominate most of his last year in Leipzig. It was Carl von Weber, the composer's grandson, who entrusted Mahler with the sketches for his grandfather's unfin-ished comic opera, *Die Drei Pintos*, and thus played a key role in what was, in effect, to be Mahler's first major success as a composer. It was in the company of the Webers' three children that Mahler later claimed (not altogether convincingly) to have first 'discovered' Arnim and Brentano's Romantic collection of folk song and verse: *Des Knaben Wunderhorn*. He certainly began setting some of them at that time (1887). Frau Marion von Weber began by taking an almost motherly interest in their brilliant young friend, but was to inspire in him a grand and potentially destructive passion. It seems to have reached a stage where the possibility of their attempting to run away together drew ever closer, perhaps during the latter part of 1887, following Mahler's summer vacation travels (Iglau, Vienna with Fritz Löhr, Alpine walking with the Krzyzanowski brothers).

Whatever the truth about the 'affair' with Marion von Weber, the *Pintos* was a remarkable product of his close relationship with her and her husband. It was compiled and completed from a mixture of dedicated sketches, items from Weber's *Nachlass* and some delicious inventions of Mahler's own (like the Intermezzo opening Act II). *Die Drei Pintos* was, above all, a testimony to the care with which Mahler had mastered the craft, and the repertoire, of the theatrical Kapellmeister in the 1880s. The piece was in every respect as conservative as it was charming: a 'Singspiel' in which mistaken identity and threatened duels lead to the inevitable conclusion, with the young lovers united and the pranksters routed. Its first performance under Mahler in January 1888 was reviewed by all the major critics, Hanslick included, and attended by many impresarios and opera directors, a number of whom would stage the much-discussed work in their own theatres the following season. Tchaikovsky had been in Leipzig at the time and attended the first performance with some pleasure. Richard Strauss (four years younger than Mahler) saw the material when he came to conduct in Leipzig in the autumn of 1887, first making Mahler's acquaintance at that time and subsequently writing enthusiastically about the *Pintos* to his mentor, Hans von Bülow. However threateningly the storm-clouds might have been gathering in his private life and in his relations with the Leipzig stage-manager, however cool Cosima Wagner's response to his performance of *Lohengrin* might have been when she visited her husband's birthplace in November 1887, Mahler's name was soon to be known throughout Europe as the Leipzig conductor who had completed *Die Drei Pintos*.

It was perhaps as a result of the chemistry of private passion and public success that Mahler felt fully justified in standing his ground

in the wake of the public altercation with Chief Stage-Manager Gold-
berg that led to his resignation from Leipzig in May 1888. It is equally likely that that same chemistry, aided by the ten-day public
'mourning' holiday following the death of the Kaiser Wilhelm I in
March, played its part in opening the inner 'flood-gates' (as Mahler
called them in a letter to Fritz Löhr) and inspiring him to complete
his First Symphony. Not all of his friends greeted the news with
excitement. Whatever the merits of *Die Drei Pintos*, Max Steinitzer was
clear that he had more faith in Mahler's literary talent than his
promise as a composer at that time – that is until he actually saw and
heard sketches for the symphony. Mahler also played it on the piano
to the Webers and the Staegemanns, to their amazement and
delight. While he was writing it, Steinitzer recalled Mahler often
saying goodbye, after a walk or a meal, 'with a half-expectant, half-
worried look' and the comment 'Perhaps today the *devil* will come!':

> This was the name he gave to the mood from which the first motif
> of the finale of the First Symphony and the first movement of the
> Second originated, and which gave to his features at that time his
> almost constant expression.

Before either piece of musical devilry was to be heard in performance, Mahler was faced with the problem of finding himself a
new appointment after Leipzig. In spite of their parting quarrel
(Mahler had, as often before and on many occasions to come,
refused to back down when his artistic judgement was overruled by a
superior), Angelo Neumann invited him back to Prague to conduct
five performances of the *Pintos* in August 1888, prior to a German
tour of the production with Cornelius's *Barbier von Bagdad*. The first
was again a great success, but during rehearsals for the second
Mahler had another row with Neumann and, in spite of his growing
fame, was firmly put in his place and summarily dismissed.
Fortunately, diplomatic and professional wheels were turning elsewhere. When he arrived late (he had been composing in a café) for a
lunch engagement with David Popper – the celebrated cellist and

professor at the Budapest Academy of Music – Mahler may have been unaware that Guido Adler had already been in correspondence with Popper, recommending him as an outstanding candidate for the technically vacant post of Director of the Royal Hungarian Opera in Budapest. Popper was sufficiently impressed by Mahler to go back with a strong recommendation that he was indeed the man for the job. Other candidates, such as Felix Mottl, had been considered, and further negotiations had to be completed, but by mid-October Mahler had signed a contract and moved to Budapest to take up his most prestigious post yet. It was one in which the peculiar politics of theatrical life in the Dual Monarchy were to embroil him more directly even than they had in Prague.

Governmental and cultural politics became almost indistinguishable from each other in the Royal Hungarian Opera. Its failing artistic and economic health reflected the anachronistic situation in Hungary. This was closely related to what was going on in the Empire as a whole, threatened by the conflicting interests of its constituent nationalities. Hungary had seized the opportunity of the Compromise (Ausgleich) of 1867, following Austria's defeat by Prussia. As a result, it had acquired greater autonomy, or rather the Magyar aristocrats had. They had managed to hold on to the reins of power even while losing their old land holdings at an alarming rate to the middle-class magnates who represented economic modernity. The imperial fantasy was played out in Hungary on the back of multiple contradictions, of which the economic one was by no means the most significant. Assuming the role of Hungarian nationalists, theoretically a threat to the multinational unity of the Empire and yet empowered by the new 'Dualism' of Austria-Hungary, the Magyars were obsessed with the suppression of other nationalisms generated by their own ethnic minorities – such as the Slovaks but, most fatally of course, the Serbs, Croats and Slovenes: the 'Slav' and other peoples whose forced unification and bitter rivalries have so bloodily stained the history of modern Europe.

Mahler almost inevitably found himself joining the many other

Germans and Jews who sided with the traditionalist but powerful Magyars. Many of these were liberal admirers of German culture, like Count Albert Apponyi – the subsequent promoter of the Magyar-izing Education Law of 1907 and later Hungarian representative at the League of Nations. He was an admirer (and former acquaintance) of Wagner, as was one of Mahler's other great friends and supporters in Budapest: the composer and Director of the Budapest Academy, Ödön von Mihalovich. At the opposite end of the political spectrum were the forces of internal nationalist disruption, most unpleasantly represented by Catholic, Slovak-sympathizing anti-semites.

Mahler's task was to reconstruct the Royal Opera in the wake of a period in which it had been dominated by the leading composer of Hungarian national opera, Ferenc Erkel, and his conductor sons Alexander and Gyula. Both of them were employed by the Opera, but it was Alexander (Sándor) who had carried out the duties of director until Mahler's 'surprise' appointment by State Secretary Ferenc von Beniczky. Beniczky was the government commissioner whose job was to oversee the management of Budapest's theatres and who later assumed the role of 'Intendant' (the former holder of the office had been relieved of his duties in January 1888). Disappointed by Sándor Erkel's lackadaisical and artistically unexciting ways as director, Beniczky hoped that the fiery young Mahler would bring audience numbers back to an economically viable level and – this was the difficult part – turn the house into a fully Magyarized, 'Hungarian' national opera at the same time.

The fact that Mahler chose for his delayed first appearance on the rostrum, in January 1889, a half Ring-cycle (Das Rheingold and Die Walküre), sung for the first time in Hungarian, only emphasizes the cultural and political complexity of the task as he saw it. Insisting that tickets be sold only in pairs, for both operas seen in their correct order, the now youthfully clean-shaven Mahler (first pictured in Budapest with a moustache and vestigial goatee beard) scored a resounding success in translating German art into Hungarian. For a time his, and the theatre's, star was in the ascendant. Ludwig Karpath, later a significant Viennese critic, then an aspiring singer, recalled Mahler's appointment as having the effect of a 'bombshell' on the Budapest opera audience, dominated as it still was by the aristocracy and leading financiers and including only a minority of intellectuals and members of the so-called 'liberal' professions:

> Let it not be forgotten that Mahler was at that time still a Jew . . . and this fact alone was such as to cause a sensation. Just as great a commotion was raised over the salary, by the standards of the time exorbitantly high, of ten thousand florins per annum for a period of ten years.

Nevertheless, the Wagner performances were greeted with wide acclaim that drowned for a time the rumblings of antisemites and the partisan bitterness of supporters of Sándor and Gyula Erkel (the latter was dismissed from his conducting duties by Beniczky in March that year).

When Fritz Löhr visited Mahler in Budapest at Easter, he found his old friend judiciously building a circle of interesting and influential friends, for some of whom, on Easter Saturday, Mahler gave 'an authentically Magyar dinner, in truly princely style'.[4] Not all was well, however. Mahler's father had died, and hurried journeys between Budapest and Iglau were adding to the tensions of his highly public and often contentious professional life in the Hungarian capital. Perhaps these played their part in exacerbating the bowel troubles that were to plague him throughout his life and which caused painful haemorrhoids that were even more painfully operated on in Munich that July. His summer travels afforded little respite that year. In the course of them he had to deal by letter with problems arising from Sándor Erkel's attempts to leave Budapest (feeling himself demoted to a position embarrassingly subordinate to Mahler's). Two visits to Iglau also failed to convince him, as head of the family now, that his mother's health was likely to improve.

She died in early October that year (1889). Although Mahler had managed to spend some days at her bedside in September, he had soon had to leave his sister Justine to cope, with occasional assistance from Fritz Löhr (his sixteen-year-old brother Otto was already lodging with the Löhrs, now that he was studying at the Conservatory in Vienna). Returning to Budapest, where the last of three *Lohengrin* performances was due on 9 October, Mahler first heard that his married sister Leopoldine had died in Vienna at the age of twenty-six, either from meningitis or some sort of cerebral tumour that had caused her great pain. Still suffering from his own 'subterranean troubles', to the extent that he had to take morphine to get through the performance, he went on to conduct *Lohengrin*, having just received a telegram to say that his mother's condition had worsened. She died two days later. He soon moved his remaining two sisters out of the Pirnitzergasse house in Iglau for the last time (his brother Alois was doing military service and thus taken care of for the time being). Löhr took both Mahler sisters back to Vienna; Emma stayed there with her brother Otto, while Justine, tired and ailing after the better part of a year spent as nurse to their mother and manager of the family, went on to join Mahler in Budapest. She later took up residence with him there for a time.

In such circumstances, it is remarkable and not a little sad that Mahler presented at this time the first really significant and critically discussed performances of any of his own works. Little over two weeks after his mother's death, Mahler was to be found, on 13 November 1889, accompanying the young singer Bianca Bianchi in some of his own songs, inserted into a string quartet concert (marriage-rumours linked him with the singer in Budapest gossip). Loewe's 'The fisherman' completes a group that included first performances of Mahler's 'Frühlingsmorgen' and 'Erinnerung', to texts by Leander, and 'Scheiden und Meiden' – the first of his settings from *Des Knaben Wunderhorn* to be heard in public. Songs and performers were both applauded; one critic judged Mahler 'the hero of the evening', although another criticized the 'overly pretentious' art-

5 Mahler (second row, third from right) with his sister Justine (to his right) and members of the Budapest Opera orchestra (detail)

fulness of 'Scheiden und Meiden' as going beyond the bounds of the folksong style that it invoked. The attempt at 'Germanizing' himself that may have played a part in the conception of such songs in Leipzig, perhaps even in Kassel, nevertheless appeared to have succeeded, if the nationalist and subsequently anti-Mahler Pesti Napló was to be believed:

> German song literature is so rich, and has had such an over-abundance of genius, that only exceptional talents can still make an intense impression. The composer is one of their number.

Published on the day that this concert took place was the programme for the Philharmonic concert, one week later, on 20 November, for which Mahler may well have been laying the groundwork. It tells us much about the nature and qualities of the First Symphony, whose première, conducted by Mahler, formed the centrepiece of an otherwise unremarkable programme conducted by Sándor Erkel, that such preparation had, if anything, the reverse effect to that intended. The songs seem to have heightened the sense of strangeness and excess that assailed many influential members of the audience for that first major première of Mahler's career as a composer.

The performance of the symphony in its initial, five-movement version as a 'Symphonic Poem in Two Parts', with no overtly publicized narrative explanation or movement-titles, is generally represented as an unqualified disaster. Mahler himself subsequently claimed that his friends avoided him after it and that the reviews were uniformly hostile. In reality the response was very mixed. For players, audience and critics alike the occasion provided a focus for expectations and prejudices that were part of the ongoing cultural politics of Mahler's high-profile activities as Budapest's opera director. The very fact that Sándor Erkel conducted the Cherubini overture which preceded the symphony and the aria from The Marriage of Figaro and Bach-Abert Prelude, Chorale and Fugue which followed it turned the concert into an inevitable contest between the two men's supporters. The interest generated by the event and some extremely positive reports of the invited-audience dress-rehearsal of the symphony on 19 November ('as grandiose as it is rich in ideas and distinguished in orchestration'[5]) approached the feverish. Fritz Löhr had come from Vienna and was as moved by that preview performance as Mahler, who issued a letter to the Philharmonic, thanking the players and adding: 'today's dress-rehearsal convinced me that I shall never again have the opportunity to hear my work to such perfection'.

In the absence of any extended first-hand account of the concert on 20 November, we have to rely on indications from the reviews that, while some members of the audience made a point of vociferously welcoming the return of Sándor Erkel to conduct the last two items on the programme, still others had contributed to 'a storm of applause' after each movement of the symphony. The most hostile review in the German press had been by Viktor von Herzfeld, a Vienna Conservatory colleague of Mahler's who had won the coveted Beethoven Prize in 1884. Although a supporter of Mahler's work at the Opera, his review took the form of what would become a standard put-down of the talented conductor who dared also to compose:

> Judging from the title 'symphonic poem', and from our genial Director's known predilection for the most radical advances of the 'new romanticism', one should have been prepared for extravagances of all sorts . . . Instead, we heard music which, aside from occasional eccentricities, did not rise above the level of the ordinary (at least!) in any department – melody, harmony or orchestration.

Kórnel Ábrányi junior, in the Pesti Hírlap, had more interesting things to say. He made it clear that the work was an important and interesting one whose reception reflected contradictory views of Mahler's 'exposed position . . . as Director of the Royal Hungarian Opera'. He went on to suggest that the work was nothing if not characteristic of the man:

> the same traits of knowledge and genius mixed with nervous restlessness, impulsiveness and immaturity.

Most interestingly specific is Ábrányi's judgement of the first three movements – 'a country idyll with forest murmurs . . . an Andante in noble style . . . a jovial Scherzo'; these he considered 'quite symphonically conceived'. In contrast, he found the symphony's second part confusing and disappointing. He could not make out if the funeral march was to be taken seriously or parodistically and heard in the finale a 'mad witches' dance' of crashing and squealing with, at the end, 'a wild bacchanalia'. One might argue that this was a far from irrelevant response to a symphony that so deliberately explored the familiar Romantic categories of Nature, Love and dancing Folk before strikingly interrogating and recontextualizing them in the third movement and that 'devil' of a finale. Appropriately, the urgent expressive intensity of the latter, more precisely its very beginning, had so startled one 'fashionable lady' sitting near to Fritz Löhr 'that she dropped all the things she was holding'.

It was, in short, a sufficiently brilliant and suitably scandalous first performance to have strengthened Mahler's credentials as a radical 'new romantic' and whetted adventurous appetites for more. No doubt some of his acquaintances had felt at a loss as to what they should say to him after it, and may appear to have shunned him; his friend Herzfeld had obviously hurt him. However, de La Grange's claim that the First Symphony met with a 'total lack of comprehension' in Budapest seems as excessive as Fritz Löhr's own suggestion that Herzfeld's review initiated 'a long period of suffering for Mahler in his creative life'.[6] Both surely misjudge the robust style of *fin-de-siècle* music criticism and, indeed, the overt nature of the assault on polite aesthetic conventions that was made by such prototypically 'modern' music – multifaceted though Mahler's deeper intentions may have been. The revisions, explanations and titling that marked Mahler's subsequent performances of the First Symphony from October 1893 tell a complex story, as we shall see.

His low creative productivity in the intervening four years had more to do with the success, the controversies and, indeed, the sheer grind of his busy life as an operatic conductor in that period than with disillusionment about his compositional ability. Indeed, the remaining year-and-a-half of his time in Budapest was typical of much of the rest of his operatic career in its mixture of triumphs and controversies. Meanwhile he must have struggled to maintain a fitfully satisfying private life, given the new, quasi-parental worries about his younger brothers and sisters and the high profile of his public career. Not long after the First Symphony's première in November, Mahler had aroused a rather acrimonious debate by presenting Meyerbeer's Les Huguenots with significant cuts made on the basis of what were, in effect, Wagnerian principles. His popularity began to fall somewhat as nationalist and conservative critics maintained their steady flow of negative reviews and dire warnings of the 'ruin' they claimed he was bringing upon the Opera.

Performances of Die Walküre and Halévy's La Juive were Mahler's major preoccupations in the early months of 1890. In spite of a recurring desire to hear more of his native language, particularly sung, there are indications that he was considering staying more or less permanently in Budapest, until the resignation that March of Prime Minister Tisza. The appointment of Count Gyula Szapáry as Tisza's successor signalled a move to the nationalist-conservative right that Beniczky no doubt immediately saw as signalling the beginning of the end of his own position at the Opera. In these circumstances, Mahler wisely arranged that the ageing Ferenc Erkel should conduct some of his own music in a gala concert (otherwise conducted by his son Sándor) marking the 400th anniversary of the death of King Matthias Corvinus. He may have begun to suspect that he could not long outlast Beniczky. His end-of-season preoccupation with a production of Mozart's The Marriage of Figaro nevertheless earned him renewed admiration from his most senior Hungarian supporter, Count Apponyi.

Zoltan Roman has noted that the first celebration of May Day as a workers' holiday took place in Budapest that year. A delegation of opera personnel subsequently petitioned Beniczky for better pay and conditions. Mahler was shortly to leave with Justine for an Italian tour, the primary purpose of which was to search for new operas and promising guest singers to solve the problem of a persistent dearth of suitable Hungarians. One of the two operas he brought back, Mascagni's new *Cavalleria Rusticana*, was a great success in his last season in Budapest and was to be the last work he conducted there, in March 1891. (The other new Italian opera, Franchetti's *Asrael*, was a failure, but Mahler's interest in it should not be overlooked – it concerned the Faust-like redemption of the evil spirit Asrael by the loving Nefta and ended with an angelic chorus.)

Mahler's own compositional preoccupation later that summer in Hinterbrühl (where he and his brothers and sisters were sharing a villa with the Löhr family) was with some of the *Wunderhorn* songs that appeared in Books II and III of his *Lieder und Gesänge* (1892). On his return to Budapest the cycle of controversies and successes picked up with renewed vigour. The mounting tension no doubt played its part in leading Mahler to engage in active negotiations that autumn with the director of the Hamburg Opera. Yet the new season opened memorably enough with another Mozart production: the celebrated *Don Giovanni* in which Mahler restored the usually spoken recitative dialogue to its original sung form, accompanying it himself on an upright piano in the orchestra pit. A performance of this captivated the initially sceptical Brahms when he visited Budapest that December. Mahler was clearly delighted to be able to tell Löhr, in January 1891, that Brahms, the fantasized murderer of Rott and rejecter of *Das klagende Lied*, had become his 'fiercest partisan and benefactor. He has distinguished me in a way that is quite unheard of with him, indeed treats me on terms of real friendship.'

Justine took herself back to Vienna that autumn, during which time Mahler was visited by an old Conservatory-period acquaintance, the energetic, slightly 'spinsterish' violinist and viola-player Natalie Bauer-Lechner, who had been divorced from an older husband five years previously. Mahler seems to have welcomed the replacement female companion and moved into a hotel so that she could have his apartment to herself. From her subsequent account we learn that she found him embroiled in a typical dispute with two singers, possibly party to a conspiracy against him. They claimed to feel so affronted by a reprimand from Mahler – who did not mince his words when his anger was aroused – that they had challenged him to a duel. He declined to offer them satisfaction, but the newspapers made the most of the incident and Natalie recalled that Mahler's every appearance on the streets of Budapest caused people to stop and crane their necks to catch a glimpse of him.

The press had been anticipating his departure for some months when, on 22 January 1891, Beniczky was officially replaced as Intendant by Count Géza Zichy, a one-armed pianist, erstwhile poet and composer and Magyar aristocrat of arrogantly conservative, nationalist and antisemitic persuasion. Zichy did not want Mahler to remain as director, and altered the opera's statutes in such a way as to ensure that he had the power of veto over anything that Mahler did. His hostility led to one turn of events that Mahler must rather have relished, given the fate of his own plea to Hans von Bülow from Kassel: a letter from Zichy offering the Budapest directorship to Felix Mottl was returned by Mottl directly to Mahler. The inevitable row between the two men was followed by a period of judicious public docility on Mahler's part.

He even weathered the 13 February gala charity evening, attended by the King himself. Its first half had concluded with a rather tawdry one-act comic opera by Károly Huber, many of whose jokes were antisemitic (Franz Joseph appears to have absented himself with distaste after it and not returned to the theatre). The newspapers were alive with predictions that soon came true. By the middle of March 1891 Mahler had resigned as Director of the Royal Hungarian Opera, having arranged severance pay with Zichy and a contract with Pollini in Hamburg. An audience backlash led to demonstrations during the performance of Lohengrin, no longer under Mahler's baton, on 16 March, which ended in cries of 'Viva Mahler!' and 'Down with Zichy!' But Mahler had gone. His old Leipzig rival, the Hungarian-born

Nikisch, succeeded him at twice Mahler's supposedly 'exorbitant' salary.

Twenty years later a Budapest paper carried a reminiscence, possibly by Ludwig Karpath, of Mahler's post-resignation statement to reporters (it claimed, intriguingly, that he went on to dance the csárdás with a young woman):

> Children, the Budapest Opera gave me a golden key with which to open the door to the world at large. I have money, fame, determination and freedom – I can go out into the world.

Within two weeks he was installed in his new post in Hamburg; one of the earliest reviews (1 April) of his initial appearances there, by the relatively conservative Josef Sittard, indicates just how right he had been:

> If the great reputation that preceded him led us to expect a superb achievement, then Herr Mahler exceeded even these expectations and, a thing which only happens in the rarest of cases, electrified the audience on the very first evening by his brilliant conducting. The same ovations were given to the new leading Artistic Director of our Opera yesterday after the last act of Siegfried as on the preceding Sunday at the opera Tannhäuser. Herr Mahler is a conductor who has in his command not only the notes in the score, but, what is more, the spirit of the artistic work: and he also possesses the gift of transmitting this energy to the entire cast and carrying them along with him. There is no entry that is not cued by him, no dynamic shading that remains unobserved; Herr Mahler holds the reins in his hand with an energy which binds the individual firmly to him, draws him, we might say, with magical force into his own world of thought.[7]

The boy from Iglau who used to listen to the military band in the Stadtplatz had now, at just over thirty, become a veritable general amongst European musicians. In Austria-Hungary, as in Prussia, the power of his baton was often officially equated with that of the State whose cultural forces he was drilling. Yet here, in the 'free' Hanseatic

6   Mahler in 1892

city-state of Hamburg, things were somewhat different. A vibrant
civic culture, often considered to rival that of Prussian Berlin, served
ideals that were at once more autonomous, secular and materialistic
than those policed by the Intendant in Budapest or, for that matter,
in Vienna. The administrative Director-Manager of the Hamburg
Municipal Theatres, Bernhard Pollini (born Pohl), was less the old-
fashioned state official than a modern impresario, the entrepreneur

of a high-status, but essentially popular, middle-class culture. He hired artists, temperament and all, on the grounds that they brought audiences into his theatres and kept them coming back. Mahler certainly did that, but his anti-materialist brand of Romantic idealism expressed itself once more in the warfare that was to break out between himself and Pollini (who may have tempted him with the possibility of a 'directorship' of the Opera, but in reality retained ultimate executive and administrative power himself, like Zichy). It was particularly, and most interestingly, in Hamburg that the tensions and anomalies of Mahler's position as a theatre conductor led him towards the relatively staid world of the symphony concert; in Hamburg, as in most other European cities, serious concert-life remained more traditional and conservative than that of the novelty- and pleasure-orientated opera-house. The same tensions led him into an ever more absorbed and creatively productive inner life as a composer of symphonic works and songs that simultaneously embraced and subverted the norms of the concert-tradition on which those works' continuing existence depended.

Years later Mahler would famously complain that he felt himself 'thrice homeless . . . As a native of Bohemia in Austria, as an Austrian among Germans and as a Jew in all the world. Everywhere an intruder, never welcomed.'[8] By the time he had completed his longest-yet engagement (six years) in Hamburg, he was well on the way to becoming triply homeless in more intimate and professional terms: as a conductor in the opera-house, as a conductor-composer in the concert-hall and as an increasingly acute explorer of the boundaries and possibilities of the art he practised with both prodigious assurance and self-reflexive scepticism.

In the opera-house, of course, Mahler had little left to learn, except how to get on with those in authority over him. He made a good start with Pollini, who was obliging in many ways and tried to give him the space he needed. But his nervously delayed return to Hamburg after the summer-vacation in 1892, on account of the serious cholera epidemic that had struck the city (causing over 8,000

deaths), angered Pollini. He imposed a heavy fine on his first conductor and thereby ignited the fire of Mahler's hostility; it would
smoulder and occasionally flare up throughout the next five years.
Perhaps it was the kind of productive tension he needed. He certainly sought to instil it in his orchestra, inspiring the usual range of
emotions from devoted admiration through grumbling resentment
to terror and outright hostility. Some of the brass players were occasionally so intimidated by his stabbed cues that they were unable to
produce a note. One celebrated rehearsal, in which he kept making
one of the flautists repeat a particular phrase alone, led to the player
rushing in tears from the hall, only to gather some strong-armed
friends outside. They meant to wreak immediate physical revenge on
Mahler, who survived by summoning a police escort to see him
home.

Still, more often than not, the magic worked on the night. There
were extraordinary performances, not only of standard repertoire
works, including Wagner of course, but also of subsequently
celebrated newer operas like Tchaikovsky's *Eugene Onegin*, whose
German première in 1892, conducted by Mahler, was applauded by
the composer in person. In 1894 there came Humperdinck's *Hänsel
und Gretel*, just the year after its first performance in Weimar by
Richard Strauss. A recollection by Richard Specht of his first experience of Mahler's conducting in Hamburg is typical of many similar
anecdotes from this period (one must remember that the audience
would not have known which of the theatre's conductors would be in
charge on any given night):

> 'Walküre'. The interval bell clatters; it grows quieter in the auditor-
> ium, a few people still seeking their places while others chattered.
> A whispered 'Ah, Mahler', goes through the house: a small, wiry
> man hastens through the orchestra with heavy stamping tread, a
> severe countenance, at once passionate and hard, masterfully
> resolute. He reached the stand and for a moment turned his
> flashing eye-glasses onto the stalls, then gave the signal to begin:
> the storm- and Donner-motif began to flicker like lightning in the

lower strings. But the auditorium is still not quiet. Mahler
involuntarily signals his impatience, but the noise continues. He
breaks off abruptly, stops and lays the baton down and turns calmly,
with folded arms, to the audience: 'Please, I can wait!' Dead
silence, then a storm of applause followed at once by the most
attentive silence for the quietest beginning of that painfully
beautiful work. I still remember thinking: 'He wouldn't dare
do anything like that in Vienna!'[9]

In practice, Mahler's idealism became part of his attraction, part
of the 'theatre' when he was conducting. It points to the contradictions of his position as an opera conductor at that time, particularly
in Hamburg – contradictions that were heightened by the circumstances underlying the successful guest-visit to London that he
made from late May to mid-July in 1892. He was to conduct a
Wagner and *Fidelio* season with Hamburg singers and a somewhat
'scratch' orchestra (Mahler seems at one stage to have hoped to
engage the Budapest Opera orchestra). The first complete *Ring*
cycles in both Covent Garden and Drury Lane were presented under
his baton that summer; the impresario for whom he presented
them increases the significance of the event still further. Sir Augus-
tus Harris was not only a man of the theatre in the Pollini mould, he
was more specifically a man of the *popular* theatre who considered
Das Rheingold a 'damned pantomime' and indeed divided his time
and that of his own theatre (Drury Lane) more or less equally
between grand opera and Christmas pantomimes of pre-Hollywood
splendour and, it must be said, vulgarity. He loved crowd scenes
and processions, often of a patriotic and 'historical' nature, and
would feature music-hall stars like the celebrated Dan Leno in his
extravaganzas of song, humour and spectacle. Mahler enjoyed
London and was duly admired in the grimy Victorian metropolis by
critics of the stature of Bernard Shaw, but the ironic conjunction of
Germanic idealism and the king of pantomime had implications
that were to heighten Mahler's exasperation with the theatre and
fuel his aspiration to devote more time to work in the concert-hall.

In this he was inspired once again by the example of Hans von Bülow.

Bülow was far and away the most famous musician resident in Hamburg at that time and conducted a regular series of subscription concerts there. Now in his sixties, he had notoriously lost his wife, Liszt's daughter Cosima, to Wagner, become a friend and advocate of Brahms, and maintained a reputation as one of the major Beethoven pianists and conductors of his day. He had also, we recall, cruelly spurned Mahler's youthful entreaty from Kassel. Not only did he continue practically to inspire Mahler's admiration; Bülow's idealism was of a strikingly similar nature. It was if anything even more prone than Mahler's to express itself in theatrically uncompromising ways, and he had significantly similar quarrels with opera managers like the ferocious Count Hochberg in Berlin – and, more recently, Pollini in Hamburg. For this elaborate combination of reasons, few expressions of praise from celebrated musicians of the older generation, following Brahms's congratulations for his Budapest *Don Giovanni*, can have delighted Mahler quite as much as that of Bülow, who was won over by that same early *Siegfried* of 1891 that had so impressed Josef Sittard. Before long Mahler was being treated as a favoured protégé and colleague by the great conductor, who would install him in a prominent seat close to the podium at his concerts, occasionally conversing with him *from* the podium as if the whole event were a private matter between the two of them.

The fairy-tale nature of this reversal of Mahler's fortunes was emphasized by the fact that Bülow's ill health, from the 1891–2 season onwards, and his early death in February 1894, gave Mahler his first really secure opening into the world of high-profile symphony-concert conducting: first as Bülow's 'stand-in' and then as his successor. In the 1894–5 season Mahler began to excite and scandalize the Hamburg concert audience by importing not only his tyrannical idealism but also his celebrated 'waywardness' as a theatrical conductor into the concert-hall. The most scandalous of his crimes was deemed to be his 'rescoring' of Beethoven's Ninth Symphony. In

1895 he flirted with the idea of having the Turkish March in the finale played initially by an off-stage wind band that seemed to be advancing on the hall from outside. Mahler's season lost money and was not repeated.

To understand his editing of other composers' music we have to consider his own compositions of that period: the Third Symphony, begun that year; more relevantly still, perhaps, the gigantic Second Symphony, clearly conceived as a successor to Beethoven's Ninth. Hans von Bülow had, however, failed to comprehend its first movement (then entitled 'Todtenfeier' ('Funeral Rites')) when Mahler played it to him on the piano. The finale of the Second owed its conclusion to that most celebrated moment of 'inspiration' in Mahler's career – at Bülow's own 'Todten-Feier' (as the invitation service-sheet was headed) in the florid 3,000-seat Baroque Michaeliskirche on 29 March 1894. Reduced once more to being a figure in a crowd, Mahler had been riveted by the congregational hymn – the 'Gemeinde-gesang' led by a boys' choir in one of the floating galleries, to the words from Klopstock's *Messias*: 'Aufersteh'n, ja aufersteh'n wirst du / mein Staub, nach kurzer Ruh . . .' ('Rise up, yes you will rise up / my dust, after a short rest . . .'). At least one independent eye-witness corroborates Mahler's claim to have understood at that moment how he should conclude his symphony. His friend the Czech composer Joseph Bohuslav Foerster found him at home soon afterwards working at his desk at the opening of the 'Resurrection' Symphony's choral conclusion. Bülow's passing might have inspired not only the hushed solemnity of the chorus's first entry, but also the closing paean, with its celebration of the 'wings which I have won me'. These soon helped Mahler onto the symphonic podium that Bülow had quitted; an elevation, if not quite a resurrection.

Such a complex work as the Second Symphony nevertheless demands an appropriately complex reading, and that, as Mahler would later suggest, requires a full comprehension of the symphony that had preceded it, perhaps too, the one that would follow it. The three comprised what he would come to regard as an enormous trilogy – his 'passion' trilogy, as he once called it, into which his 'life's blood' had been drained. To better contextualize this description certain features of Mahler's maturing character and personality need to be more clearly grasped. Of the many collections of anecdotes and memories of Mahler that survive from this period of his life, a remarkable account left by the Hamburg critic Ferdinand Pfohl is of particular interest.

Apparently written long after Mahler's death (his letters, published in 1924, are frequently cited), it nevertheless contains some remarkable evocations of a man Pfohl had initially found prickly and rather suspicious, but whom he had grown to love and respect during a period of close friendship. In the end he had felt painfully hurt when Mahler moved on to higher things in Vienna, discarding him like a kicked-away ladder (as Pfohl would put it). This was the period in which Natalie Bauer-Lechner would soon be recording innumerable things that Mahler said to her, particularly during the 'composing' summer holidays between 1893 and 1896. Pfohl, who had arrived in Hamburg in 1892, additionally evokes the manner in which Mahler must often have said them: 'arresting, weighty, intractable; as if they were swallowed barbs, he had to choke his words out of his mouth'. In conversation with Pfohl, the shortcomings of others frequently exercised Mahler:

> For all manner of disapproval, disagreement, disdain or scorn, he always made use of the same term: the once more widely used word of profane colloquial speech in what was Royal and Imperial Austria, now the Austrian Republic: the word 'Trottel' ['idiot' or 'fool']. There were times when he would scream it out like an Italian tenor; at others he would growl it in a low, inimitable tone of the most extreme disdain.

Pfohl had ample opportunity to enjoy the well-nigh symphonic complexity, the shifting moods and tonality of Mahler's speech on long afternoon walks around Hamburg, often to the harbour district. Mahler would hold forth on religion, and the need for some kind of faith, however ostensibly naive, and on the problem of public noise; he would pronounce upon matters intellectual, philosophical and even occasionally gastronomic. In one of his most characteristic moods, however, it was spiritual matters that seemed troublingly dominant: Mahler appeared to Pfohl as 'one who had questioned God, and been cast out of the Light and into the Darkness':

> one whose crime was Knowledge and who now sought the way back to the lost paradise – undergoing a penance of remorseful contrition in order to rise once again to Heaven, seeking to reach God and the angels, and his brethren, on the soaring bridge of music that joins this world and the hereafter.[10]

This is, of course, recollection with carefully considered hindsight, and knowledge of works that were either unperformed at that time or actually uncomposed when he first met Mahler in 1892. Nevertheless, the description of the composer's 'Lucifer'-like appearance that directly follows is exemplary in its use of imagery from German Romantic literature:

> His gaze, from darkly gleaming semitic eyes, was arrestingly sharp, the eye-lids slightly red – as with many people who do too much reading, too much work at night. To look at he was small, dainty, elegant; there was a touch of charm about him. It was as if he carried an invisible chivalric sword with a golden handle, as if he were dressed and ready for a minuet with daemonic princesses from the world of Theodor Amadeus Hoffmann.

Like Pfohl, like Max Steinitzer in Leipzig, Bruno Walter, on his first encounter with Mahler at the Hamburg Opera in 1894, also saw the celebrated conductor as a figure straight out of one of those E.T.A. Hoffmann' stories that hover tantalizingly between the supernatural and the psychological. Of particular interest in Pfohl's memoir is his claim to have been responsible for the Hoffmann-esque title for the third movement of the revised First Symphony whose second performance Mahler conducted in Hamburg on 27

October 1893. To explain his suggested formula *Funeral March in 'the manner of Callot'* (*Ein Todtenmarsch in 'Callots Manier'*), Pfohl had bought for Mahler a copy of E.T.A. Hoffmann's *Fantasiestücke in Callots Manier*, in whose introduction Hoffmann explained his own allusion to the early seventeenth-century French engraver:

> The irony which mocks man's miserable actions by placing man and beast in opposition to each other only dwells in a deep spirit, and thus Callot's grotesque figures, which are created from man and beast, reveal to the penetrating observer all the secret implications that lie hidden under the veil of the comical.[11]

The problem for Mahler at that time was not simply how to sharpen and focus the work, still in five movements, but how to help the more reactionary critics to understand the significance and implications of his allusions to, and divergences *from*, conventional symphonic manners. Perhaps for that reason, the 'story' that Mahler hinted at in the new programmatic titles was elaborately literary in its allusions to Hoffmann, 'Jean Paul' Richter and Dante:

Titan, a tone-poem in symphony-form

PART I

'From the days of youth', flower-, Fruit- and Thorn-pieces

I.   'Spring and no end' (Introduction and Allegro Comodo). The Introduction depicts the awakening of Nature from the long sleep of winter.

II. 'Blumine' (Andante)

III. 'With full sails' (Scherzo)

PART II

IV. 'Stranded!' (a funeral march in 'the manner of Callot'). The following might explain this movement: the external inspiration for the piece came to the author from a parodistic picture well-known to all children in Austria: 'The

Huntsman's Funeral', from an old children's book:
the animals of the forest accompany the dead
huntsman's bier to the grave; hares escort the little
troop, in front of them marches a group of Bohemian
musicians, accompanied by playing cats, toads, crows etc.
Stags, deer, foxes and other four-legged and
feathered animals follow the procession in comic
attitudes. In this passage the piece is intended to
have now an ironically merry, now a mysteriously
brooding mood, onto which immediately . . .

v.   'D'all Inferno' (Allegro furioso) follows, like the
suddenly erupting cry of a heart wounded to its
depths

As yet there was no reference to the *Lieder eines fahrenden Gesellen* (the
performance of the Symphony followed that of six 'Wunderhorn'
songs on 27 October) or any overtly autobiographical implications.
In the event, this rather complex and obfuscatory explanation failed
to persuade the critics, but did not deter the audience from responding warmly. That no doubt heightened the superior antipathy of the
more conservative critics not only to the work itself, but to the very
location of its performance. The Ludwig Konzerthaus, on the edge
of Hamburg's red-light district, was home to the 'popular' concerts
given by former military-band-leader Julius Laube, at which most of
his audience sat at tables, smoking and drinking (more conventional
seating was available in the balcony).

The Laube orchestra, suitably expanded, nevertheless managed
to cope with both Mahler and his First Symphony, which thus occasioned a response no less confused than the original performance
in Budapest. The supposed nature-idyll Part I was still considered
the better, less eccentric part of the symphony by traditionalist critics who remained perplexed by the funeral-march and were scornful of the finale's modelling of a chaotic 'inferno' of negativity.
Others found the last movement unsatisfactory; even Richard
Strauss later had difficulty in understanding the *repeated* break-

through to the triumphal march. Mahler responded with a homily that presented the movement as a partly cautionary internalized narrative of becoming:

> at the place in question the conclusion is merely apparent (in the full sense of a 'false conclusion'), and a change and breaking-down that reaches to the essence is needed before a true 'victory' can be won after such a struggle.
>
> My intention was to show a struggle in which victory is furthest from the protagonist just when he believes it is closest. – This is the nature of every spiritual struggle. – For there it is by no means so simple to become or to be a hero.[12]

As a totality, the symphony appears to depict a conflict in which the alienated expressive subject struggles towards Wagnerian redemption, brutally relegating to the past the idyll of the first part's youth, nature and innocence even as it achieves 'reconciliation' with it. The romantic symphonic tradition may have supplied the rationale for that doubly prepared concluding triumph, but Mahler was soon discovered by his friends to be reading Schopenhauer, Dostoyevsky and Nietzsche and worrying anew over the implications of the 'story' that his music seemed to be telling, or rather that the Symphony itself, as a cultural form, told. He was to reconceptualize that symphonic reconciliation in the Second Symphony (where the 'happy ending' formula is complicatedly reinterpreted as both external epiphany and egoistically willed 'expression') and in the Third, whose canvas would become Life itself, its material drawing upon almost everything that was 'music' in Mahler's world.

To the conservative mind, the metaphysical pretensions of such things suggested blasphemy. Their popular inclusiveness suggested republicanism, even socialism to critics with more interpretative subtlety than anti-modernist scorn. Precisely here, however, the unfolding story of Mahler's life appears to challenge simplistically politicized readings of the Second and Third Symphonies. Before the Third was heard complete, Mahler's career had contrived a possibly compromising commentary upon its ostensibly egalitarian modern-ism. In 1897, following his conversion to Roman Catholicism in the 'Kleine Michaeliskirche' in Hamburg, a series of elaborate under-cover negotiations and machinations at last reached their tri-umphant climax. By the end of the year he would be Director of the Royal and Imperial Court in Vienna. His long-cherished 'final goal' had been achieved. Heroically enough, he had become a cultural conqueror at the age of thirty-seven.

5 Imperial and royal (Nature and the city)

Another letter; this one written in Hamburg, to Fritz Löhr, in 1894 or 1895. In introspective mood, Mahler reveals that he had long envisaged the problems likely to beset him, should his dream of returning to Vienna come true. At the same time he summarizes the contradictory drives and convictions that animated the increasingly ambitious symphonic projects to which he was devoting his summers, in spite of persistent worries about his family:

> The situation in the world being what it now is, the fact that I am Jewish prevents my getting taken on in any court theatre. – Neither Vienna, nor Berlin, nor Dresden, nor Munich is open to me. In my present peculiar (by no means melancholy) state of mind it does not really upset me. – Believe me, German artistic life the way it is at present holds no more attractions for me . . . Supposing I came to Vienna, with my way of going about things? I should only need to try once to convey my interpretation of one of Beethoven's symphonies to the famous Philharmonic Orchestra, trained as it has been by honest Hans [Richter], to be involved forthwith in the most repulsive dog-fight. I had the same experience even here, where I hold undisputed sway by virtue of Brahms's and Bülow's utterly unqualified championship of me!
>
> What a storm I bring down on my head whenever I depart from normal routine and try out some idea of my own. – I have only one desire: to work amid simple, ingenuous people in some small town where there are no 'traditions' and no guardians of 'the eternal

laws of beauty', to my own satisfaction and that of a small select circle who can follow me. – If at all possible, no theatre and no 'repertoire'! But, of course, for as long as I must pant along after my precious brothers, always so daringly taking wing, and till my sisters are tolerably provided for, I have to continue my lucrative bread-winning artistic activity.

. . .

I have achieved a kind of fatalism, which finally makes me regard my own life, whatever turn it may take, with a certain 'interest' – and even enjoy it. I have come to like the world more and more! I am 'devouring' an increasing number of books! They are, after all, the only friends I keep by me! And what friends! Heavens, if I had no books! They become ever more familiar and more of a consolation to me, my real brothers and fathers and lovers.[1]

That he excludes sisters here suggests that Emma and Justine were less troublesome to him than his 'precious brothers', Alois and Otto, although Mahler did his best to provide for them all and to bring them together as a family during his cherished summer vacations. From 1892 onwards the pattern was established by which Justine, assisted by her friend Natalie Bauer-Lechner, would rent a country property that provided for her brother's inspirational walking requirements and afforded peace in which he might compose. But it had to be sufficiently accessible for a constant stream of friends and acquaintances to be able to visit them and generate in miniature that 'small town' community in which Mahler could refresh himself without the intervention of external authority. In 1891, however, he was still dividing his summer between his family, walking with old friends like the Krzyzanowski brothers and paying a courtesy call on Pollini, who was taking a cure in Bad Gastein. Mahler also found Natalie Bauer-Lechner there and took some long walks with her. That was the summer in which, following a return visit to Bayreuth, he made a rare extended trip alone, taking himself by boat from Hamburg to Copenhagen. He visited Göteborg before crossing to Norway, where he caught a glimpse of Ibsen and admired the dramatic coastal scenery as he sailed south towards Denmark and thence back to Hamburg.

The less peripatetic pattern that established itself in Berchtesgaden, in the summer of 1892 – the year of the Hamburg cholera epidemic – was continued in 1893 at Steinbach in the Austrian Salzkammergut, on the south-east shore of the Attersee, where he spent four happy and productive vacations (1893–6). Here Natalie Bauer-Lechner became ever more committed to her journal-keeping, thanks to which we have a full and intimate picture of those summers, and much else, through the eyes and ears of someone whose admiration for Mahler was growing into love. His well-publicized affair with the young Wagnerian soprano Anna von Mildenburg, during his last two years in Hamburg, must nevertheless have kept Natalie on her guard. She occasionally annoyed him, but others, his brothers not least, annoyed him more. They were reckless and unthinking in their financial affairs and inclined to make irresponsible demands. Both were to disappear altogether from Mahler's life: Alois by making his own way in the world and then emigrating to America, Otto, whom Mahler was trying to get established in a musical career (he was talented, in spite of his unimpressive performance at the Conservatory), by committing suicide. He shot himself in February 1895, in the house of his and Mahler's friend Nina Hoffmann-Matscheko. She was, with some appropriateness, a scholar and translator of Dostoyevsky. The silence in Mahler's letters and, apparently, in Natalie's journal about Otto's death no doubt reflects the shame that suicide was thought to bring upon a family, although Mahler tended always to become withdrawn in periods of grief. That year he brought Justine and Emma to live with him in Hamburg, thus making more permanent the domestic arrangements of the Steinbach summers, during which he felt most uninhibitedly 'himself'.

The day-to-day arrangements at Steinbach were managed, to the best of her ability, by Justine, who took on the role of housekeeper. But it was the open-air- and cycling-fanatic Natalie who would more often walk with him after lunch. During the course of their treks she would hear about his morning's work in the tiny 'Häuschen' – a small wooden structure that he had built for the summer of 1894 in the lakeside meadow attached to the inn in which they rented rooms. Nowadays that meadow becomes an almost impenetrable summer transit-camp of vans, tents and caravans. The Attersee was already fashionable in the 1890s. Victor Adler and Engelbert Pernerstorfer spent their summers on the opposite shore, and other Viennese notables had villas in the vicinity. The *Gasthof und Fleischhäuerei zum Höllengebirge*, on the narrow road between Weyregg and the village of Steinbach, was set apart from the larger resorts. Even so, the inn's other visitors, the occasional organ-grinder and farmyard animals and ravens had to be silenced by Natalie and Justine as best they could while Mahler worked in his little studio on the lake shore. With their connivance, it protected him well enough; it also afforded views across the broad expanse of water, with its pleasure boats and the regularly passing steamer service whose nearest landing-stage was a ten-minute walk away. Further south rose the vast and solemn cliff-face of the *Höllengebirge*, towards which they would often head in the afternoons.

Apart from all the cycling, swimming and walking, composition remained the real focus and prize of those summers – or rather of the long working mornings. During that period the First Symphony was beginning slowly to make its way in a hostile concert-world; after the Hamburg performance, Mahler had Richard Strauss to thank for another at the June 1894 festival of the forward-looking *Allgemeine Deutsche Musikverein* in Weimar (Strauss was a conductor at the Grand Ducal Theatre). In Steinbach, far from the urban bustle and from the recalcitrant players and antisemitic critics of 'German artistic life', he now found the time and surroundings in which to complete the mighty Second and Third Symphonies – whose performance and dissemination would be wholly dependent upon big-city German culture, with its orchestras, critics and crowds.

That contradiction resounds in their structure, content and epic

7 Mahler's 'Häuschen' on the shore of the Attersee (renovated; photographed in 1994)

proportions. I have suggested that the triumphant conclusion of Mahler's machinations to return to Vienna, including the judicious conversion to Christianity (to the State religion of Roman Catholicism) appears to compromise claims that his creative philosophy was essentially critical or subversive. Nevertheless, the problems that he envisaged for himself on his return to a more antisemitic, more conservative and anti-liberal Vienna than the one he had known as a student, were rapidly to materialize in nagging opposition to his work at the *Hofoper* and often scornfully dismissive reactions to his symphonies. We have to assess what was going on with care, and to listen attentively to the symphonies' contradictory voices, exasperatingly audible to his contemporaries. Given that matters of taste were always involved, resulting from the mixture of high and low styles, noble and 'banal' material, the kind of stories that his music told, both in public and in private, become ever more significant and absorbing. Here the outward events of Mahler's life were far less important than what went on in the world of his remarkable musical imagination, stocked as it was with novels, histories and books of philosophy.

The multiplicity of the stories of his music, the metamorphoses they underwent and the dialectical nature of their evolution are important keys to the secrets of that world. It has long been accepted that it is impossible to conceive of Mahler's 'programmatic' narratives uniformly as projects or plans, derived from a literary model or real-life experience, which were then presented in musical form. The unfolding of his music and the conceptualization of its meaning did not reflect his life; they *were* his life, on the level of emotional and intellectual experience at its most engaged ('Only when I experience do I "compose" [*tondichte ich*] – only when I compose do I experience!', was how he once put it). Nevertheless, the American Mahler-scholar Stephen Hefling has argued that the initially separately conceived first movement of the Second Symphony, as 'Todtenfeier', might represent a quite detailed programmatic response to part of a similarly named poetic drama – in the German translation by Mahler's old friend Siegfried Lipiner – by the nineteenth-century Polish nationalist writer Adam Mickiewicz. Mahler's own published programmes would certainly blur any straightforward 'autobiographical' significance by suggesting that the First Symphony's triumphant hero ('was it Mahler himself?', audiences might have asked) was here seen at his burial. Hence the 'Funeral Rites' (*Todtenfeier*); but the theme of Mahler's descriptive programme of the movement was not the 'rites' so much as the *questions* that their spectacle inspired in a new authorial voice:

> What is life? – and what is Death? Have we any continuing existence? Is it all an empty dream or has this life of ours, and our death, a meaning?[2]

The music itself is no set-piece funeral-march; its solemn progress is fraught with tension and angrily interrupted by outbursts and protests *against* such solemnity and all it implies. And then there is the tonally and experientially distant 'second subject'. The lyrical alternative to the first-subject material, conventional in the later nineteenth century, is here presented as an intervention of dream-like Otherness. In the massive first movement of the Third Symphony that opposition would be characterized still more boldly as between Winter and Summer, Death and Life, the forces of Chaos opposed to the unruly rabble of old Pan, who wakens from his winter sleep to rout the enemy. The battle – explicitly represented and so headed in the manuscript score – forms the focal point of Mahler's most elaborate invocation of the manner and instrumentation of the military bands he had so loved as a child, E-flat clarinets, rat-a-tat side-drums and all. It was also the movement about which he spoke to Natalie Bauer-Lechner in terms of mystical epiphany, using all the imagery of Romantic 'inspiration':

> It's frightening the way the movement seems to grow of its own accord more than anything else that I have done . . . Real horror seizes me when I see where it is leading, the path the music must follow, and that it fell to me to be the bearer of this gigantic work . . . today it came to me in a flash: Christ on the Mount of Olives, compelled to drain the cup of sorrow to the dregs – and willing it to be so . . .
>
> Whereas I could clarify and to a certain extent 'describe' in words what happens in the other movements, that is no longer possible here; you would have to plunge with me into the very depths of Nature, whose roots are grasped by music at a depth that neither art nor science can otherwise reach. And I believe that no artist suffers so much from Nature's mystic power as does the musician when he is seized by her.

The suffering that such music would cause Mahler in terms of adverse criticism was certainly not occasioned by its 'mystic power', but by its blatant and explicit use of military-band-style march tunes and military-band instrumentation ('bizarre and trivial elements', 'incomprehensible platitudes'). The first movement of the Third even appeared to quote the opening two bars of the old song by

Binzer that had been sung by the demonstrating members of the *Leseverein der deutschen Studenten Wiens* after its enforced closure in December 1878. This was what led some to hear in it the earthy and far from mystical sounds of a music whose 'cheap' and 'tasteless' presence in a German symphony (of all forms!) threatened the very fabric of society as a kind of cultural terrorism, even a demonstration of socialism. The success of the work with popular audiences would later seem to reinforce this suspicion. And then there was Nietzsche, along with singing angels from *Des Knaben Wunderhorn* and a pair of movements ('What the flowers in the meadow tell me', 'What the animals in the forest tell me') that sounded sentimental, or humorous, or both in ways that were confusing if titles were published, even more so when they were not.[3]

The Scherzos of both Second and Third Symphonies were no less unusual and programmatically protean in Mahler's descriptions of them. Their origin in settings from *Des Knaben Wunderhorn* adds a further and perhaps authoritative interpretative gloss. In each the conventional imagery of dancing 'folk' (Mahler had implicitly invoked it in the First Symphony) is replaced by descriptions of dancing *animals*. In the hierarchy of life-forms in the Third Symphony the animals acquire pathos as they listen to and attempt to imitate the sound of the 'human' post-horn, but their predecessors in the Second had been mindless fish who, in their imperviousness to St Anthony's *Wunderhorn* 'sermon', satirize human weakness. This then generates a musical 'cry of disgust' at what had gone before – at music that was pointless and spiritually unproductive: music which, in one of Mahler's descriptions, was linked to that of dancers in a ballroom, seen through a window as they move to an accompaniment that is 'inaudible' to the alienated author who is watching from outside.

Here once again the oddities of Mahler's music are reflected in even odder programmatic descriptions. Their implication is that the music was engaged in a tensely meaningful and minutely detailed critical confrontation with its inherited 'traditional' forms and implications – which explains its unsettling and even directly threatening quality. Its general character is best explained less in terms of specific literary narratives than of a particular literary genre as practised by one of Mahler's favourite writers. We have already seen him alluding, in a published programme for the First Symphony, to the extraordinary humorist, romanticist and satirist 'Jean Paul' Richter (1763–1825), author of *Titan* and the *Blumen- Frucht- und Dornstücke* (known also as *Siebenkäs*). Richter is familiar to Germanists, as he would have been to Mahler, as an innovative, experimental deployer of the so-called *Traumdichtung*: of fantastic and sometimes implicitly symbolic visions that intervene in his narratives in striking ways and at strategic moments. Their imagery and content are typically apocalyptic or elysian; indeed the two are usually linked, as J. W. Smeed has pointed out, in a two-part form. A dark and hellish evocation will be followed by a heavenly and reconciling alternative. Nowhere is the form more strikingly used than in the pair of *Traumdichtungen* that form the first and second 'flower-pieces' of *Siebenkäs*. According to Bruno Walter, this humorous account of 'the Wedded Life, Death and Marriage of Firmian Stanislaus Siebankäs, Parish Advocate in the Burgh of Kuhschnappel', was Mahler's favourite: 'he pronounced it to be Jean Paul's most perfect creation'. Its two *Traumdichtungen* read like source studies for the apocalyptic and visionary imagery which runs throughout his first three symphonies (to which the Fourth might be added, as a special case).[4]

In spite of Hefling's reading of the 'Todtenfeier', it is worth pointing out that Mahler's own single recorded allusion to Mickiewicz's drama referred to his *First Symphony*. It involved the final, devastating line of Konrad's 'Improvisation', in which anti-authoritarian anger extends into the realm of the metaphysical. Mahler called Konrad's denunciation of God – 'you are not their Father but their *Tsar!*' – a 'flaming indictment of the Creator' and went on to suggest that the same cry resounded in his own symphonies, 'for a certain period at least'. A reading of the two *Siebenkäs* visions – 'The Dead Christ proclaims that there is no God' and 'A Dream within a Dream'

– might encourage us to extend that conflation of metaphysical imagery and intellectual iconoclasm by regarding the finale of the First Symphony, and much of the following three symphonies, as musical *Traumdichtungen* in Jean Paul's sense (he believed that in dreams we gain access to higher reality, what he called the 'second world').[5] Both of the *Siebenkäs* pieces weave transcendent and apocalyptic fantasies around the image of a dead person lying on a bier. The first, often compared to the episode of the 'Grand Inquisitor' in Dostoyevsky's *The Brothers Karamazov*, depicts a kind of witches'-sabbath of dead souls; it is visited by Christ, who announces a dreadful truth:

> I have traversed the worlds, I have risen to the suns, with the milky ways I have passed athwart the great waste spaces of the sky; there is no God. And I descended to where the very shadow cast by Being dies out and ends, and I gazed out into the gulf beyond, and cried, 'Father, where art Thou?' But answer came there none, save the eternal storm which rages on, controlled by none . . . Shriek on, then, discords, shatter the shadows with your shrieking din, for HE IS NOT!

What Christ goes on to explain is, in effect, that God is a conceit of the living mind – but one whose moral value is demonstrated in the 'Dream within a Dream', whose similarly bleak apocalyptic landscape is redemptively smiled upon by the Virgin Mary. She welcomes Christ to her arms, inspiring 'bliss' in the writer as she proclaims 'None, save a mother, *knows* what it is to love.' To interpret Mahler's conversion to Roman Catholicism in the light of all this (which incidentally illuminates his protestation, recorded by Pfohl, that belief in a hereafter had an 'inner' truth to which rational argument was irrelevant) is at the same time to see how his reading of Schopenhauer, Dostoyevsky and Nietzsche might have validated even the pragmatic aspects of that conversion in a Zarathustra-like internalization of 'divine authority'. The stakes were high. To accept that an external God could have no meaningful existence, as Jean Paul had pointed out in the cautionary 'Introduction' to the first of the *Siebenkäs* dreams, was potentially to experience the collapse of the spiritual universe and the social order it supported:

> shattered and shivered, by the hand of Atheism, into innumerable glittering, quicksilver globules of individual personalities, running hither and thither at random, coalescing, and parting asunder without unity, coherence, or consistency. In all this wide universe there is none so utterly solitary and alone as a denier of God.

In 1896 the new owners of the Steinbach inn raised their prices. This effectively prevented Mahler from booking the usual suite of rooms for his party the following summer. Thanks to the railway, the lakeside- and fell-scenery of the Attersee had been accessible enough even from Hamburg to form part of that redemptively coherent-seeming realm of Nature into which (as Zweig put it) the imperial capital itself seemed to melt 'without opposition, without contradictions'. Yet, as for so many of his contemporaries, it became essential to Mahler as a surrogate 'second world', cherished precisely for its difference to that of the city. The compositions that he took with him to Vienna in 1897 – works written in, and ostensibly 'wrested from', that realm of Nature – were appropriately and noisily full of oppositions and contradictions. In them, the social and ideological components of the pseudo-romantic image of the natural world that bourgeois culture had adapted, with misty eyes, from that of the aristocrats, were laid out in jarring immediacy. On the one hand there was hierarchy, a sentimental attachment to order and 'the way things were' (often strategically linked with the subjective world of an imagined childhood). All that was bolstered by heroic aspirations and a respect for the spiritual, if not the temporal, authority of the Catholic Church and its arsenal of imagery. On the other hand there was the chaotic energy of the 'lower orders' and their music – of marching bands, sentimental serenaders, dancing 'folk' and gambolling animals, humorously reflected in the egocentric wilfulness of children and potentially animated by 'Dionysian' forces that threatened the idyll in which they conventionally participated. The effect of those forces was to reveal dream landscapes, both apocalyptic and transcendent – their aural evocation sometimes terrifyingly spilling out into off-stage spaces from which horns resounded, last trumps sounded and military drums rattled.

The power of such effects prefigured the power he had now acquired in the real world. As Director of the 'Imperial and Royal' [*Kaiserliche und Königliche*] Court Opera, Mahler had attained the highest possible status as a musician. He was answerable to the Emperor's Lord Chamberlain, Prince Rudolf Liechtenstein, through his assistant and subsequent successor Prince Alfred Montenuovo. The ailing former Director Jahn and the Philharmonic's renowned Wagnerian conductor, 'honest' Hans Richter – as Mahler called him – now held no sway over him. Visits to Brahms in Bad Ischl (the last in 1896, less than a year before Brahms's death), petitions to influential friends, a letter from Count Albert Apponyi in Budapest (Mahler had seen him when he conducted a concert there as part of a March tour that had begun in Moscow and ended back in Hamburg) – all these had helped to elevate him to the position of power that he had most desired. In that closing phase of the Austro-Hungarian monarchy, in a Vienna already reverberating with the discord that was threatening the Empire in many of its regions, Mahler's music was articulating complex truths about his world before he seems quite to have grasped their full implications for his own life.

He was under no illusions about the fact that things would be difficult for him in Vienna. If the Steinbach summers, with Natalie acting as Eckermann to his Goethe, represented a miniature version of Mahler's 'small town' with its 'simple ingenuous people' and the 'select circle who can follow me', Vienna was the embodiment of the dreaded converse, with its 'traditions', its 'eternal laws of beauty' upheld by ferociously articulate critics, and 'dog-fights' a-plenty. Although many of his old friends were there to greet and support him, most of them were settled into lives that catalogue the range of possibilities that Vienna had to offer at that time: the state bureaucracy (Löhr, Lipiner), the law (Steiner, Freund), the bohemian fringe (Wolf, with madness and the asylum looming) and intellectual sub-cultures like that of mystical theosophy (Friedrich Eckstein). And then there was the world of politics.

The Vienna of 1897 was less liberal than the one he had left as a student. Its mayor, Karl Lueger, was the charismatic leader of the right-wing Christian Socialist party; he was an antisemite, though he had a number of wealthy Jewish admirers. He would later attract the interest of the young Adolf Hitler (in fact another of the old *Leseverein*/Pernerstorfer-circle, Georg von Schönerer, had long moved towards a more obviously proto-fascist form of pan-German-ism). The main political opposition to Lueger's Christian Socialists was provided by the Social Democrats, whose leader was Mahler's old friend Victor Adler. He was as significant and influential a figure as Lueger, in his way, but was not a great public speaker and came to be regarded as somewhat detached and aloof. His most theatrical impact on the public life of the Empire took the form of the great May Day parades which spread across Europe in the 1890s and which in Vienna always ended in a mass rally in the 'Prater', the popular recre-ational park north-east of the city-centre.

Mahler continued to support Adler, and would find himself moved to join the marching workers for a time on the 1905 May Day, but some of the contradictions of Adler's position would be revealed in his own in Vienna: as the philanthropist, easily moved by beggars on the street, who nevertheless instituted a far from liberal regime in the institution that he ran from October 1897 (his initial appoint-ment had been as conductor; he was rapidly promoted to Deputy Director and then Director of the Opera). Art, he believed, was some-thing different, apart; it was *worth* the draconian demands that he made on his orchestral players and singers, many of whom shared that same belief and responded accordingly. Occasionally, however, a darker truth would present itself to Mahler in ways that awakened the Adlerian socialist within him, as in the case of the wickedly underpaid stage-hands. He told Natalie Bauer-Lechner:

The working conditions of the stage hands urgently need thorough investigation and regulation, that is – improvement. But all this is too much for *one* person to look after. I used not to have the time to trouble myself about these worst-paid of my employees; I scarcely know them or anything about them. Now and again I see one of them loom up before me on the stage like a warning apparition.

But *was* art the ideally special activity that made this suffering worthwhile? Mahler's conducting career was grounded in the hope that it was, and yet the opera that he chose for his glitteringly successful début at the start of his 'trial' period as conductor (11 May 1897) was *Lohengrin* – a work he later elucidated to Arnold Schoenberg, in revealingly patrician terms, as a moral tale about gender:

> Elsa was a doubting woman, unable to trust the man who had given her an example of trust by believing her fully, without ever wondering whether she was guilty. The capacity to trust is masculine, mistrust is feminine.[6]

The opera therefore becomes emblematic of ideology masquerading as 'spirituality' (had Mahler not read Nietzsche's vituperative and devastating critique of Wagner?); its conductor is cast in the role of a cultural administrator in the worst sense. However, the work that he chose as the first new production of his period as official Director of the *Hofoper* might conversely have been chosen to demonstrate the socio-political nature of art in a bold, even inflammatory way. It was Smetana's *Dalibor*.

The first performance took place on the Emperor's name-day (4 October). In order to understand why there was a police presence we need to consider the background of growing political crisis against which it took place, a crisis that was symptomatic of the fate of liberalism in the Empire at that time. The Bohemian and Moravian Prime Minister, Count Badeni, had triggered it by granting official rights to the Czech language equal with German in Bohemia (in the so-called 'Badeni Ordinances'). The predominantly German-speaking administrative class felt outraged and threatened, for reasons that Mahler, recalling his time in Prague, would have been able to understand. The fracas that was generated by the Ordinances led to disruptive demonstrations in parliament and on the streets of Vienna; public unrest in Bohemia was sufficiently threatening for martial law to be declared in Prague in December. In the midst of all this, with a reputation as a fire-brand and with the liberal and intellectual press at his feet, the conservative and antisemitic press already at his heels, Mahler chose to stage one of the Czechs' favourite national operas. It may have been sung in German, but his care over the staging had involved direct consultation with the Czech National Theatre in Prague and he reworked the ending in a provocative manner. What Natalie Bauer-Lechner disingenuously called Smetana's 'incongruous' conclusion, where Dalibor dies in battle, was cut, leaving the heroic Czech knight and musician alive at the end.

It was a gamble, but Viennese cultural manners prevailed. Hanslick reviewed the production's brilliant first night appreciatively, with Olympian disregard for any political implications. Max Kalbeck, on the other hand, referred explicitly to official fears that the occasion might be 'used for political purposes':

> One certainly saw people who would not normally come to the first performance of a new opera . . . many Czech members of the Imperial Parliament were there.[7]

Mahler was certainly doing what he had been employed to do: to liven up the Court Opera and its narrowly standardized, often crudely edited repertoire that had come to rely too heavily on sure-fire successes (these ironically included Mascagni's *Cavalleria Rusticana*, which Mahler himself had done much to popularize during his time in Budapest).

He loved the opera-house and its velvety, 'idealizing' acoustic, admired the Vienna Philharmonic Orchestra for its responsiveness and flexibility and felt that he had sufficient support to start doing the things that Richard Specht had once doubted were possible in Vienna. Cuts in Wagner were restored for the first time; the auditorium lights were dimmed during performances; late-comers were banned until the overture had ended (or the whole first act in Wagner) and the 'claque' – a group that rented its vociferous applause and cheers to singers for a fee – given notice. Audience figures began to improve and everything ran, as Natalie Bauer-Lechner put it, 'with military precision'. The Emperor himself congratulated Mahler in a personal audience and Prince Liechtenstein enthused with vigour:

> You really are a success! All Vienna is talking about you and is full of your doings. Even the old diehards are saying 'Something's always happening at the Opera now, whether you like it or not.'

However, storm-clouds were never entirely absent from the sky above what was now Mahler's Vienna. He could shake off the jokes in the antisemitic press and the hostile attitude of supporters of the old regime at the Opera (who had been outmanoeuvred by the way in which Mahler's appointment as director had been managed), but discord and worries of a more personal kind bore the seeds of future scandals that would beset him in that gossip-ridden city. Public status there already carried with it some of the burden of press intrusion and innuendo that we cherish as a peculiar cultural problem of our own. The engagement of former flame Anna von Mildenburg, without his knowledge, by the Opera in 1897 caused him a good deal of worry. Passionate though their affair in Hamburg had been, her attempt to surprise him into marriage (inviting a Dominican monk to her rooms for the purpose) had confirmed the worst fears of his somewhat jealous female guardians. His sister Justine and Natalie Bauer-Lechner both regarded Mildenburg as a kind of 'femme fatale' before whom Mahler became helpless. He continued to write affectionately to her and recommended her in glowing terms to Cosima Wagner, who engaged her to sing Kundry at Bayreuth. But he was right to foresee what the press gossips would make of her arrival in Vienna, and wrote to her warning that for at least a year their relationship would have to remain purely 'professional'.

Matters of jealousy and rivalry that spilled over from his personal into his public life were similarly involved with the sad affair of Hugo Wolf. Wolf had initially welcomed his old friend's return to Vienna, hoping that Mahler would take on his opera *Der Corregidor*. However, ancient bitterness (he always believed that Mahler had 'stolen' from him the idea for an opera on the subject of *Rübezahl*) flooded back into Wolf's mind as he suffered his first major breakdown in that same October of 1897. Less than a week after the *Dalibor* première the newspapers were carrying stories of Wolf's deranged visit to the Court Opera singer Hermann Winkelmann, claiming that he, Wolf, had taken Mahler's place as director of the *Hofoper*. He had then become violent and had to be 'taken to a private institution'.

All such additional irritants added unpleasantly to the stress of Mahler's busy daily routine of rehearsals, administration and evening opera performances (even when he was not conducting himself he would frequently attend, sending frantic messages backstage from the director's box at every production blunder that he noticed). His life in Vienna was materially comfortable enough. By November 1898, the year in which Emma had married and gone off to Boston with the cellist brother, Eduard, of the Philharmonic's leader Arnold Rosé, Mahler had moved into a splendid apartment in a new building designed by the modernist Otto Wagner; it was within walking distance of the Opera and connected to the telephone system. But at the height of what can only be described as his triumphantly successful 'assimilation', Mahler came significantly to cherish all the more the belief, expressed in that 1894 letter to Löhr, that such 'lucrative bread-winning artistic activity' was no more than a means to the end of being able to create for himself a version of that ideal community, unfettered by tradition and external critics, in which he might develop and realize his own ideas, his own music. Was that not a close enough description of the bourgeois family in its role as a supportive environment for 'great men'? In 1894, the still unmarried Mahler had looked, a touch pessimistically, to books for company, in the bosom of Nature, with symphonies as his children.

The summer months of vacation following the end of the opera season became all the more precious. Having given up Steinbach, the vacation of 1897 had involved pleasant Alpine travels from Brenner down to Vahrn, at the other end of the 'Pustertal' from Toblach, where his last summers would be spent. There were the usual invigorating walks, cycling trips on mountain roads (more than one ravine nearly claimed Mahler) and swims in lakes. But the facilities for composition were not the same and he seems to have planned fantasy composing-huts, like the one at Steinbach, in many beautiful spots he chanced upon in walks with Natalie. The summer of 1898 was spent in Vahrn, but here he was initially convalescing from another haemorrhoid operation; just two *Wunderhorn* songs (one of them was 'Wo die schönen Trompeten blasen') were the fruit of an unsatisfactory vacation. The tensions that may have played their part in exacerbating Mahler's 'subterranean troubles' were undoubtedly opera-related. An *ad hominem* attack on him in the *Deutsche Zeitung*, prior to his taking over the Philharmonic concerts after Richter's departure (feigning 'arm pains' to cover his judicious removal to England), had assumed a crudely antisemitic tone. Purporting to come from the pen of one of the orchestral musicians, it ridiculed Mahler's lively and demonstrative gestures on the podium, noting that he was called the 'duty corporal' by the orchestra on account of his habitually peremptory tone with them.[8]

In the summer of 1899 he achieved a more successful escape from the hothouse of Viennese 'cultural' life in the countryside around Alt-Aussee. It was once a haunt of Brahms and was now much favoured by writers (Wassermann, Hofmannsthal, Schnitzler); so too, it must be said, by a host of less intellectual holidaymakers, the noise of whose entertainment – the spa orchestra of Bad Aussee, yodelling mountaineers and the like – frequently got on Mahler's nerves. But he managed to achieve a good deal there, if not entirely on new compositions. The works whose manuscripts he had long protected nervously in a special trunk were at last being published, thanks in particular to the efforts of Guido Adler, who had recently moved back to the University of Vienna. The Second Symphony and the *Lieder eines fahrenden Gesellen* had appeared in 1897, the First Symphony was going through the press and now it was the turn of *Das klagende Lied* (revised once again the previous summer in its two-part version) and the Third Symphony. These were to appear in 1902, but Mahler was already working on the proofs in Alt-Aussee. New works were also coming into his mind. A double triumph had occurred earlier that summer when Mahler rushed off to deal with the happy effects of a laxative pill and returned with a sketch for the *Wunderhorn* song 'Revelge'. More seriously preying upon his mind, however, seems to have been the hiatus in his symphonic output.

We must assume that other matters than pressures upon his time were involved here. The heroically self-trumping philosophical narratives that had facilitated his comprehension, completion and revision of the previous three symphonies had reached a point beyond which it was inevitably hard to proceed. A clue to his underlying thought-processes might be found in a letter he had written to Anna von Mildenburg three and a half years previously, in December 1895. He had been in Berlin for the first complete performance, funded by himself, of the Second Symphony. It was a remarkable experience, both for Mahler and for his audience, in spite of the usual critical confusion and the fact that much of the hall had had to be 'papered' with students and invited guests. After the first run-through of the finale, with its huge resources and 'celestial phalanxes' of singers, he told Mildenburg: 'Such grandeur and power have never been attained before.' He was undoubtedly right, but the letter written the previous day was the more revealing one. In it Mahler had described his snowy trek to find suitable bells in a Zehlendorf foundry and referred to his thankless negotiations with the Berlin Philharmonic's administrators:

> fleshless men! Every inch of their faces shows traces of that self-destructive egoism which tortures mankind! Always me, me, me, and never you, you, my brother!

He had concluded with a striking piece of self-criticism, inspired by a flattering comment he had made about Mildenburg's own simple, 'unadorned' nature:

> I remember all too well how carefully I used to prepare my letters, how concerned I was to write what are known as 'stylish letters'.
>
> But really it was all to do with the fact that I had not found *myself* and that the person I was writing to simply provided a pretext for me to set out my ideas.

Might a similarly self-critical impulse have led him to question the grand manner of the conflict-generating trajectory and concluding 'resolution' of the first three symphonies? Might the snide suggestion of that antisemitic critic in Vienna, that his elaborate gestures were more appropriate to love-making than purposeful conducting, have applied in some way to the revelatory climaxes even of the Second Symphony's Finale? Its aim had been to dispel conventional religious expectations, set up by the evocation of an apocalypse, in a celebration of utopian egalitarianism. But was it, too, more 'me, me, me' than 'you, my brother'? Was it, as the *Neue Freie Presse* had suggested after the Viennese première in April that year (1899), just a piece of 'imaginary theatre'?[9] Perhaps some such underlying train of thought led him, at the very end of that musically introspective summer, finally to hit upon the style and outline of the Fourth Symphony: reduced in scale and outward pretensions by comparison with the preceding three, yet secretly both an extension of, and a commentary upon, them. It was to be a piece of protoypical neo-classicism, in *Wunderhorn* 'Humoresque' style. Its concluding message was that divine truths and revelations are, in the most profoundly human sense, the business of children, or rather of a 'romanticized' childhood. Mahler, now even more the modernist, knew that it was really a dream animated by memories: of the sleigh-bells and fairy-tales of an Iglau winter, of Bohemian fiddlers and the smiling face of his mother, attended perhaps by those same laughing angels who had eluded Ahasuerus in that other dream that Mahler had recounted to Jospeh Steiner in 1879.

Even as he was embarking upon his 'fairy-tale symphony' (as Adorno would call it), Mahler realized that bourgeois comfort and solitude were required in which simultaneously to evoke and historicize the bourgeois dream of art.[10] At the beginning of August 1899 he had to return to Vienna, but Natalie and Justine were dispatched to find a more suitable location for what he intended to be the more productively creative summer of 1900. They made their way to the Wörthersee (Mahler hoped that Carinthia might offer a rather less unpredictable and rain-prone climate than the Salzkammergut) where they chanced to bump into Anna von Mildenburg, of all people. As was her way, she immediately took charge of the situation and found them a local architect, who not surprisingly advised them to build rather than rent; the area was just becoming a fashionable one for vacation-home development. Mahler was summoned from Vienna to spend three days in a charmingly turreted lakeside bed-and-breakfast – the 'Schwarzenfels' – on the south shore of the lake. By the end of them, they had found an almost neighbouring plot for the house and a site above, on the forested hillside, for a new composing-studio. The latter would be completed by architect Theuer, in solid style, in time for Mahler to be able to complete the Fourth Symphony in it in the summer of 1900. They lived in a rented villa since the house would not be completed until the following year. But the location of the new *Häuschen* was perfect: on a raised terrace in the midst of otherwise unspoiled forest and accessible only by a steep climb up through stately pines that soon hid the road and the lake below.

The following summer (1901) was significant for a variety of reasons, mostly linked with the preceding season. For the first time since he had taken up his duties at the *Hofoper* Mahler had begun to reduce the punishing conducting load that he had hitherto given himself. There were strong grounds for doing so, since he was now also conducting the Philharmonic Concerts. These occasioned the

usual 'dog-fights' on account of his supposedly nervous and way-
ward interpretations and his orchestral 'retouchings' of works like
Beethoven's Ninth Symphony (27 January 1901), about which he had
issued an explanatory pamphlet in 1900. Then there was the important première of *Das klagende Lied* (17 February), marred only by the
familiar critical attacks in the wake of enthusiastic public applause
and the obstructive behaviour of male members of the choir
(conflating resistance to learning difficult new music with belliger-
ent antisemitism). The physical and mental stress took its final toll
on Mahler on 24 February, on which punishing day he had conducted
an afternoon Philharmonic Concert (featuring Bruckner's Fifth
Symphony) and an evening performance of *Die Zauberflöte*. In addi-
tion to everything else, haemorrhoids were again troubling him. He
had looked ashen at the evening opera performance. That night he
suffered a major haemorrhage. His life was probably saved only by
the late, painful but effective treatment of Dr Julius Hochenegg of
the Löw Sanitorium, who inserted a tube and operated a week later.
An Easter convalescence trip to his favourite Croatian coastal resort
of Abbazia (now Opatija) – not far from Trieste where he had first
seen the sea in 1882 – brought together the usual holiday group of
Mahler and Natalie, Arnold Rosé and Justine. The last two were now
strongly, although 'secretly', committed to each other; Natalie (who
knew about Justine and Rosé) seems still to have been hoping that
her close relationship with Mahler might also turn into something
more passionate and lasting.

His absence from Vienna, brief though it was in the circumstances, inevitably gave his hostile critics ample opportunity to
praise Joseph Hellmesberger Junior and Mahler's opera colleague
Franz Schalk, both of whom had conducted Philharmonic concerts
in his place. It was in the knowledge that things would have to
change and that he would not conduct the Philharmonic Concerts
again (having now formally resigned) that he took the train south to
Klagenfurt in early June 1901 to join Justine, Natalie and Arnold Rosé
in the newly completed house at Maiernigg. For all of them, Mahler

8   Natalie Bauer-Lechner

in particular, it represented something of a dream-come-true, with its traditionally gabled roof, its terraces and balconies, its lakeside walk, its spring (in a rapidly purchased adjoining plot of land) and 'wild' garden threaded by paths. One of these led, on the other side of the road, to the carefully-cut walk that climbed up to his high forest studio. 'Would you have believed that we could ever call such a divine place our own?', Mahler had asked Natalie one night before they went upstairs to gaze, from his balcony, at the stars reflected in the lake. Natalie makes it clear that their relationship remained platonic and that they slept in separate rooms, but her account of their pleasure in the new house and its surroundings and of their closeness that summer is all the more touching since it was the last that she would spend with him. When Mahler accompanied her in the carriage to Klagenfurt station one chill night, they had huddled close together for warmth; he was already well into the Fifth Symphony and had written three of the *Kindertotenlieder*. When he completed the symphony the following summer his somewhat less willing walking partner and sharer of the lakeside villa was his new, already pregnant wife, Alma. Natalie's Mahler would become Alma's Mahler: the same person now transposed into a quite different kind of story, and one that was only half his own making.

6   Alma's Mahler

Natalie Bauer-Lechner pictured Mahler as he rather deliberately presented himself to her: a romantic, a visionary, a 'personality' at whose feet we too imagine ourselves sitting. The voice and manner that dominate the pages of her much rewritten and subsequently vandalized account are unmistakably those of a nineteenth-century 'great man'. Many of the slightly more risqué or personally revealing passages that it once contained were cut by the relatives and friends who sought to further sanitize and idealize Mahler's image after his death. Alma, too, was subjected to cautionary admonitions right up to her last published volume of autobiography (1960).[1] She, however, was able to supervise her own publications. Just as she introduced Mahler into the world of her own generation of young Viennese artists and intellectuals at the beginning of the century, so she became the journalistically 'modern' medium through which his image was transmitted into our own world: heightened, often exaggerated, but compellingly immediate in its grandeur and pathos.

The pathos arose from her often devastating critical analysis of his personality, in which she answers or corroborates some of the recurring questions and implications of this biography. In other respects her work tends to block access to his own perception of himself and of their relationship, which we can find in complicatedly mediated form in his letters to her (judiciously selected and edited by her) and, even more complicatedly, in the music he wrote in the last ten years of his life. Perhaps the story that music told did, at the end, approach the autobiographical, the 'self-indulgent'; at the same time it seemed to participate no less forcefully in the collective project of an anti-Romantic modernism. The ramifications in Mahler's public career of that long-developing paradox have a bearing on the circumstances which brought him and Alma Schindler together.

Back in 1900, the proud possessor of his autograph on an 1899 postcard from Alt-Aussee (she had first met him that summer), Alma was just one of the admiring spectators at his opera performances. She was also one of the many supposedly modern spirits who rather scornfully dismissed his music, including the First Symphony when he conducted it in Vienna on 18 November 1900. The nature of Mahler's modernity as a composer had been dealt with interestingly in the first short study of his life and work. This was published in Leipzig, at the start of 1901, as part of a series on 'Modern Musicians'; its full title was *Gustav Mahler – A Biographical-Critical Appreciation*, its author Ludwig Schiedermair. Just thirty-eight pages long, it interestingly located Mahler within the dialectical picture of modernity then current. It was dominated less by Nietzsche than by the widely read Hungarian-born physician, cultural critic and (since 1897) vice-president of Theodor Herzl's Zionist Congress, Max Nordau (*The Conventional Lies of Cultured Humanity*, 1883, *Degeneration* [*Entartung*], 1893). Nordau's critique of contemporary culture was complicated and not always consistent, but it confronted squarely art's involvement in, and reflection of, contemporary society, not least that of the Habsburg Empire into which he too had been born.

Relevant here is Schiedermair's early analysis of what Adorno would one day call Mahler's 'tone', derived from that of the Bohemian peoples, where

> Germanness [*Deutsches Wesen*] is mixed with Hungarian elements, in which echoes of the sounds of the far east could also be heard.

9   Silhouette by Benno Mahler, showing Mahler conducting Siegfried Wagner's
opera *Der Bärenhäuter* (Act I/7; première March 1899)

This multi-voicedness of Mahler's music was often held by anti-semites and conservatives to be the key to the 'analytical' or frag-mentary aspect of his vision, both as a conductor and as a composer – one that was constitutionally incapable of encompassing the unity of the 'grand form'. In his concluding peroration, however, Schie-dermair explicitly hailed Mahler as a composer who harnessed what he had earlier in the book described as a freedom-seeking 'dithyram-bic vitality' (dithyrambischen Schwung). Its goal was not anarchy but idealism:

> in our realism-orientated era, Mahler has helped to raise the
> banner of idealism, which also scorns the decadent outlook
> of music since Wagner.[2]

This point might be clarified by Nordau's definition of the pes-simistic negativity that, he believed, underlay all such 'decadence':

> As soon as one recognizes that the institutions which have been
> handed down are empty, senseless, mock forms, half scarecrows
> and half theatre scenery, one necessarily suffers the horror and
> indignation, the disheartenment and attacks of black humour,
> which might be experienced by a man living among lunatics who,
> in order not to sustain physical injuries, has to join in all the
> lunatics' crazy ideas.
>   This continuing contradiction between our views and all the
> forms of our culture, this need to live surrounded by institutions
> we consider lies, that is what makes us pessimists and sceptics . . .
> In such unbearable discord we lose all our joy in existence and
> all our desire to try.

For all that he disagreed with some of Schiedermair's interpreta-tions of individual works, we know that Mahler rather liked his book and felt that he had 'come off rather well in it'. The idealism celebrat-ed by Schiedermair subsequently found expression in Mahler's let-ters to Alma, one of which, from 1905, reads almost like a gloss on the passage from Nordau:

> When we're alone for a time we achieve a unity with ourselves and
> nature, certainly pleasanter society than the people one sees every

day. Then we become positive (instead of getting stuck fast in negation) and finally productive. The commonplace takes us farther and
farther from ourselves, but we are brought back to ourselves by
solitude, and from ourselves to God is only a step . . .

How petty our ordinary life, stuck fast in negation and criticism,
seems to us then. – You find the same thing in your reading, don't
you? Shakespeare is the positive, the productive; Ibsen merely
analysis, negation, barrenness. Now you can understand why it is I
strive to rescue the positive and productive mood from the clutches
of the commonplace and hence often take a bird's-eye view . . .
Never believe the positive is not there or is not the one reality.
Think simply that the sun has gone behind a cloud and is bound
to emerge again.

There is good cause to interpret much of Mahler's later music as
filled with horror and indignation, with black humour and pragmatic madness. In this his detractors might justifiably have discovered
elements, in Nordau's terms, of 'decadence'. By 1938 that discovery
had been adapted by many of Mahler's former friends and acquaintances, including Schiedermair, to their support of Hitler's Third
Reich and its antisemitic category of 'Entartung'. But its roots
extend back to Nordau and, indeed, the intellectual milieu of
Mahler's youth in Vienna. In that light, his concern to stress his own
anti-decadent 'idealism', not least in public, might alert us to the
increasing conservatism that marked many of his utterances and
some of his private affiliations and interests during the last years of
his life. The turning-point, perhaps, was a famous semi-public pro-
nouncement about 'programme-music', made after a successful
Munich performance of the Second Symphony on 20 October 1900 –
sponsored, as it turned out, by the local Hugo Wolf Society as its
opening event.

Mahler had been sufficiently pleased with the concert to fall into
one of his spirited, speechifying moods at the convivial gathering
afterwards in the Park Hotel. Justine, Natalie Bauer-Lechner and
Guido Adler were present; Schiedermair was also there and in-
corporated an account of the occasion into his book, thus ensuring

the wider circulation of Mahler's diatribe against descriptive 'programmes'. It had been inspired by the presence in the group that evening of the musicologist and critic Arthur Seidl (1863–1928). Without permission, Seidl had recently published, in his book *Moderner Geist in der deutschen Tonkunst*, a generous extract from a letter Mahler had written to him – it was the one in which he had explained the inspiration for the conclusion of the Second Symphony, had made the comment about the closeness of lived experience and musical composition for him (see chapter 5, p. 98) and discussed the nature of his artistic relationship to Strauss, to whom Seidl's book had been dedicated. It was there that Mahler also alluded to Schopenhauer's image of 'two miners digging a shaft from opposite ends and then meeting underground'. Now, with an appreciative and influential audience gathered round him, Mahler announced his intention to abandon all published explanations of his music:

> Away with programmes, they give a false picture! Let the public
> form its own thoughts . . . and not be forced to read someone else's
> prejudgement while they are listening.[3]

The point about leaving the audience's imagination free is important; Mahler's complicated and somewhat inconsistent statements on this subject cannot be taken literally. In Munich his dominant need seemed to be to stress the difference between himself and Strauss – already the best known and most succesful of the 'moderns'. But later comments on this subject that he prepared for Schiedermair's benefit suggest that he was also concerned to foster a more conservative, increasingly 'traditional' public profile in this respect. Schiedermair was inevitably commissioned to write programme-notes and essays after the publication of his book. Mahler responded, in December 1901, to an enquiry from him about the new Fourth Symphony by getting Bruno Walter, who had just arrived in Vienna to take up a post at the Opera, to send an elaborate double letter to him (one part of which was intended for publication). In it, tantalizing clues to the Fourth's programme had been given, but introduced with the following stern admonition:

> No programme will lead one to an understanding of this work, nor any other Mahler symphony. It is absolute music [*absolute Musik*] and non-literary from beginning to end: a four-movement symphony, each movement organic in itself.

Had Mahler sold out to the anti-modernist, anti-programmatic ideas of Hanslick? Was he attempting to establish his credentials as a true German artist in the face of frequent accusations to the contrary? In June 1900, a hot and rather thankless 'patriotic enterprise' had taken him with the Vienna Philharmonic to Paris during the World Exhibition. His performances had been generally well-received, but in the light of his expostulation – in a café conversation with Arnold Rosé and Ludwig Karpath – that 'German art is the only art!', it was typically ironic that Colette's husband 'Willy' should have found Mahler rather bad at conducting German music. In his *Tristan* Prelude Willy discerned stretches of 'rather unintelligent coldness' and he found his *Eroica* distressingly 'chopped up': 'there was a large audience in the hall, but Beethoven was absent'. If French journalistic eyes, dazzled by the Exhibition, had been more closely focused on Mahler during that visit they would have had ample reason to categorize him as something the Parisian establishment and aristocratic society would have regarded rather more subversively 'un-German', given his Jewish birth. For it was during this visit that Mahler first made the acquaintance of General Picquart and Paul Clemenceau, brother of George Clemenceau and thus no less associated than Picquart (who had been jailed for his supposed treason) with the supporters of Dreyfus, the Jewish officer whom 'decent' France had unjustly branded a traitor. It so happened that Paul Clemenceau's wife Sophie was an Austrian, whose sister Berta Szeps-Zuckerkandl was a prominent Viennese hostess. It was out of a desire to sustain his friendship with Sophie Clemenceau that Mahler was drawn into the orbit of her sister's *salon*; there, at a dinner in November 1901, he met the 22-year-old Alma Schindler.

While often presented, in first-hand accounts, as awkward and uneasy in society, Mahler was ready to comply with formal manners when required. He would straighten his back in the presence of members of the aristocracy and knew the value as well as the pleasure to be derived from keeping in with influential hostesses. Ferdinand Pfohl would recall legendary gaffes, like his tendency to lick the compote spoon before passing the dish to his neighbour; these would often as not be put down to 'artistic temperament'. He also makes it clear that then, as later, Mahler was much in demand, and made it his business to be so. Soon after Pfohl arrived in Hamburg he found himself confronted by Mahler with the question:

> Have you made any connections yet in Hamburg society? It will certainly interest as much as benefit you to get the feel of cultured circles of that sort. I will introduce you to a few families.[4]

Gregarious, charming and difficult by turns, Mahler's presence at a meal or afternoon '*Jause*' was certainly a coup for any hostess.

He seems to have been on rather good form the night he first met Alma at the Zuckerkandls'. As well as Sophie Clemenceau and his sister Justine, the company had included the painter Gustav Klimt and *Burgtheater* director Max Burckhard. Both of these had paid court to Alma, thus fanning her reputation as one of the rising stars among Vienna's 'artistic' beauties of the period. Her father, Emil Schindler, had been a well-known landscape painter and water-colourist; five years after his death, to the distress of Alma and her older sister Grete, her mother had married the painter Carl Moll, a leading figure, with Klimt, of the Vienna 'Secession'. A baby step-sister arrived in 1899. Alma had coped with her feelings to some extent by fostering the love of music which she had shared with her beloved father. By the time Mahler met her she was making promising strides with private music-teachers, not least as a composer. She was also seriously in

10 Alma Mahler with daughters Maria ('Putzi'), left, and Anna ('Gucki')

love with her composition teacher, Alexander Zemlinsky. A composer himself, with a rapidly developing reputation (his opera Es *war Einmal* had been staged by Mahler at the *Hofoper* in 1900), he was already a friend and mentor of the slightly younger Arnold Schoenberg.

Although seated at the opposite end of the Zuckerkandls' dinner-table, Alma was aware that Mahler had soon begun to scrutinize her, in his tensely energetic way, through the celebrated spectacles that had flashed lightning at so many orchestral players. After dinner he joined her group and was soon dominating an insouciant conversation about the nature of beauty, in which the notoriously unpreposessing Zemlinsky had been cited admiringly by Alma. Her celebration of his 'spiritual' beauty was conceived as an introduction, apparently, to making the most of Mahler's ear by recommending that he take on her teacher's ballet: Das gläserne Herz (with a scenario by Hofmannsthal). Mahler talked 'as though he addressed an assembled crowd', she later recalled, adding:

> He had wielded power so long, encountering only abject submission on every hand, that his isolation had become loneliness.

It is difficult to be entirely clear whether Mahler had been stricken with love at first sight that evening, or whether, aware now of the progress of the affair between Justine and Arnold Rosé, he had made a conscious decision to seek a wife himself and thus release his long-faithful sister. Did he discern in Alma an interesting and eligible candidate for the post? Love certainly developed rapidly between them: oddly, perhaps a little awkwardly and unequally; but opera invitations, anonymous poetry and further visits followed in rapid succession. Mahler's letters to her became increasingly more tender and vulnerably self-revealing. At first he cast himself as Hans Sachs to her Eva. Only slowly did he grow bold enough to try on the costume of Walther von Stolzing. At some point in the process there had come a nocturnal walk through the snow from the Molls' new home in Döbling, where Mahler had assessed Alma's freshly unpacked book-collection and been horrified to find a complete Nietzsche edition. It was on that cold night, with the street lamps casting glittering circles on the snow, that Mahler had had to get the Döbling post-office to call the Opera to get his own ex-directory phone-number so that he could call Justine and warn her that he would be late. His shoe-laces had kept coming undone, thanks, no doubt, to nervousness as much as to his notoriously impetuous and arhythmic manner of walking. And then he had suddenly blurted out

It's not so simple to marry a person like me. I am free and must be free. I cannot be bound or tied to one spot. My job at the Opera is simply from one day to the next.[5]

Not surprisingly, Alma sensed a 'feeling of suffocation' ('He laid down the law without thinking of consulting my feelings'). But within a few weeks they were engaged and the story broke in the Viennese press just after Christmas. Surviving portions of Alma's original diary of the period include references to increasingly passionate, if unconsummated, afternoon sexual encounters whose initial awkwardness was accompanied by tense anxiety on Mahler's part. While this might lend credibility to his claim to have remained sexually uninitiated up to that point, Alma makes it clear that she had herself initially resisted full intercourse. De La Grange is surely correct in assuming that that, nevertheless, was what happened on 2 January to occasion Alma's simple diary entry: 'Bliss upon bliss'. She was soon pregnant and troubled by a sense of guilt, for all her free-thinking and anti-Christian ways. Her initial fascination with the poetic idea of being 'married' to a man like Mahler became overlaid with more complex worries and emotions. Other problems had yet to be overcome. Mahler's old friends in Vienna, many of whom knew nothing about the engagement until they read about it in the *Neue Freie Presse*, were the cause of a good many of these.

While it is clear that Alma established a reasonable working relationship with Justine, Mahler's other friends appalled her. '22 years old, a dazzling beauty, the most beautiful girl in Vienna', was how Bruno Walter described her in a rather worried letter to his parents about the engagement. She was also as astute and full of life as could be, and was not for one moment prepared to be overawed by, or respectful towards, what she considered to be a dry and pedantic circle of middle-aged members of the bourgeoisie whom Mahler

invited to meet her in his apartment on 5 January 1902. Apart from
the Molls, Kolo Moser, Arnold Rosé and Justine – all of whom Alma
already knew – Mildenburg was also there along with the Spieglers.
The most important guest, in a way, was Siegfried Lipiner: for long
the unofficial leader of Mahler's circle. With him was his second wife
Clementine, the sister of Albert Spiegler, whose own wife Nanna had
once been married to Lipiner.

Alma reacted badly to the formal atmosphere of the occasion,
darkened not least by Mahler's own taciturnity that evening (did it
mask a kind of embarrassment?). Lipiner seems to have taken it
upon himself to probe her knowledge and intellectual qualities. His
pompous manner inspired her maliciously to mock not only Plato
but also, by implication, the painter Guido Reni, on whom Lipiner
had attempted to launch one of his characteristic disquisitions.
Things went from bad to worse when Mildenburg had ventured to
ask Alma's opinion of Mahler's music, to receive the reply that what
little she knew she did not like. The long, angry and hurt letter that
Lipiner wrote to Mahler about that evening is at once sad and slightly
comic in its superior attitude towards Alma: she had failed to show
'respect' for her elders and betters and had scorned some of Lipiner's most cherished 'Masters'. To read it now is to come down
wholly on Alma's side; she seems refreshingly to have acted on
behalf of the new century, in the spirit of both modernism and femi-
nism, in mocking the nineteenth-century patrician airs that Lipiner
assumed.[6]

It is small wonder that Mahler should have become withdrawn.
His ideas and values had often been argued out with Lipiner (as
Natalie records). However much he might disagree with him,
Mahler enjoyed his company and admired his now forgotten poetry,
some of which may have influenced him. He must already have envisaged the new kind of isolation that this marriage would impose upon
him. Later it would intensify his love and need of Alma, even as he
lamented not only the years but also the difference in temperament
and values that separated them. We must nevertheless be cautious in

assessing the real extent of that difference, and of the nature of Alma's 'modernism'.

One interpretation of her role in Mahler's life would picture her as having liberated him from his nineteenth-century past and turned him towards a bright, twentieth-century future. Its harbingers were the painters and designers of the new Secession (see below, p. 131) and the *Jung Wien* writers and poets: practitioners of Jugendstil and proto-avant-garde shockers of the bourgeoisie with their often explicit sensuality and eroticism. Yet one notable historian with Viennese blood, E. J. Hobsbawm, has refused to overestimate *fin-de-siècle* modernism in the city, suggesting that its protagonists were relatively ineffectual café-revolutionaries, their sphere of influence limited to

> little magazines and a few impresarios and collectors with a flair
> and a taste for new works and their creators . . . They were taken
> up by a section of high fashion. That was all.

The observation is made pertinent to Mahler by Hobsbawm's supplementary suggestion that the more important development was the onset of a democratizing (if still capitalist) popular culture. 'The plebeian arts', as Hobsbawm puts it, 'were about to conquer the world.'[7]

For all his new connections with the Secession and with artists like Gustav Klimt and Alfred Roller, Mahler's now more frequently performed early symphonies were damned as much for their supposedly banal material and plebeian effects as for their modernity. One notable cellist in the Philharmonic, the composer Franz Schmidt, liked to characterize Mahler's symphonies as 'cheap novels'. This all contrasted rather awkwardly with the somewhat rarefied character of the idealism that he and Alma were to nurture in their periodically isolated life together. Within their marriage each of them was further isolated in a more personal way: Alma from her music, the fashionable world and the friends she had left; Mahler from old acquaintances who supported the essentially conservative, Habsburg-liberal values that he had sought to explore and possibly revalidate in his music. Their relations with Richard Strauss and his wife Pauline were one of the areas in which they came together in agreement. In her account of the two couples' dealings with each other towards the end of 1902, Alma mocks the 'common' speech and *petit-bourgeois* talk about shopping which Pauline preferred to high-flown artistic conversation of the kind that Mahler and Strauss were meanwhile having. In fact Strauss was praising the traditionally popular and pleasurable beauties of 'bel canto' technique over the more cerebral singing-actor style of Mahler's favoured performers in Vienna. All the time he appeared to celebrate musical varieties of materialism in the face of Mahler's idealized 'spirituality'.

On a rainy morning in March 1902 Mahler married Alma in the ornate and echoing space of the *Karlskirche*. It was virtually empty, since they had deliberately advertised a false time for the wedding. When Justine married Arnold Rosé the following day, her brother and his new wife were already in Russia, where Mahler had planned some conducting engagements in St Petersburg as the focal point of a honeymoon trip. Alma's account of it is not particularly revealing, except for the description of their short stop-over in Warsaw on the way back to Vienna. She describes them as having been importuned by a strange man promising dubious entertainment, but Mahler had been touched to see her give what she thought to be her last remaining change to an old Jew selling matches in the railway station. Back in Vienna, Alma moved in to take Justine's place in the Auenbrugger-gasse apartment. It was she who would now manage the household and provide for Mahler's needs when he returned from the scandals and conflicts that increasingly beset him at the Opera. That year, his supposed tendency to hire and fire musicians in an unpredictable and unsettling manner was soon being discussed in the newspapers. His productive energies were meanwhile engaged in other projects.

In April 1902, not long after their return from Moscow, Mahler's new involvement with Carl Moll's artistic circle was marked in a significant way when he conducted his own arrangement for wind band of part of the finale of Beethoven's Ninth Symphony in the already famous 1898 *Secession* building on the Karlsplatz. It was fondly known as the 'golden cabbage' by the burghers of Vienna on account of the filigree dome of open-work metal leaves that topped the squat, temple-like structure. It might almost have come from a set for *Aida* but was the new gallery of the group of young artists who had, with Gustav Klimt, decided in 1897 to 'secede' from the conservative *Künstlerhaus* (the established Viennese exhibiting society) and further their aims as the *Vereinigung Bildender Künstler Österreichs* (Graphic Artists' Association of Vienna), known also simply as 'the Secession'. The occasion of Mahler's performance was the private view before its fourteenth exhibition. Interestingly enough, this took the form of a modernist celebration and appropriation of Beethoven, the iconic representative of Vienna's traditional musical culture. Its centrepiece was Max Klinger's recent monumental sculpture of the largely undraped composer – seated, an eagle at his feet, on an elaborately decorated throne made of rare varieties of stone and studded with jewels. The exhibition was planned to turn the building into an aestheticized 'spiritual' space. The central room, with the sculpture, was approached via a series of side-chambers. These contained carefully placed exhibits, special mouldings and Klimt's 'Beethoven' frieze, whose focal image was a nude couple, locked in a tenderly erotic embrace, against an idealized 'Choir of Heavenly Angels' (a phalanx of floating women, apparently humming with eyes shut and awaiting their own spiritual/physical embrace).

The implications of the whole affair were complex. Many Viennese Beethovenians were shocked, but there is no indication that Mahler was upset by the 'shamelessness' or 'immorality' of the imagery in the way that he could be upset by fleshly display on the operatic stage (Alma was to see him angrily send Marie Gutheil-Schoder – as Julietta – off the set of *Tales of Hoffmann* to have her generously side-slit dress stitched up). He would, in fact, have had every reason to be fascinated by Klinger's sculpture and the illustrative decoration on the throne, in which physical and spiritual forms of love (a naked Aphrodite beneath a crucifixion scene) confronted each other. In the same striking manner, Christ had approached an assembly of the old Greek gods in Klinger's enormous painting *Christ in Olympus*, exhibited at the Secession in 1899. That image, as much as anything that *Jugendstil*, *Jung Wien*, and the Secession might relevantly have offered, illuminates the world of Mahler's Third Symphony (completed in 1896) in a most productive way. In *Christ in Olympus* Klinger's decorative *Jugendstil* sensuality was still held in check by the photographic naturalism of the painting and the monumentality of its allegorical border: a formal and physical manifestation of its status as a piece of traditional high art. Underlying elements of conventional symphonic form, whose presence Mahler had come to cherish as the composition of the enormous first movement approached its conclusion in the summer of 1896, seem to have performed a similar function in the Third Symphony. His discovery that it had 'the same scaffolding, the same basic groundplan that you'll find in the works of Mozart and, on a grander scale, of Beethoven', was no doubt intended to be reinforced by the suppression of all the original 'programmatic' titles at its first complete peformance in 1902.

Chronologically, the first Mahler première to take place after the beginning of his relationship with Alma was that of the Fourth Symphony in Munich, less than three weeks after they had met. It was not a work with which Alma (who was not present in Munich) had any sympathy. She found it naive and archaic by turn when he attempted to explain it to her before the Vienna performance that concluded the work's disastrous initial tour in January 1901. What would later be regarded as Mahler's most modestly proportioned and approachable symphony had sparked off a furore of often explicitly anti-semitic criticism. Reviewers referred to fake naivety that masked decadent modernist irony. Worse still it was 'entertaining', with its outwardly attractive melodies, licentious orchestration and

elaborately worked-up 'Trugschlüsse' (literally 'deceptive conclu-
sions'; the term also implies sophistry, 'fallacies'). The young Swiss
art-lover William Ritter, later one of Mahler's most devoted younger
supporters, summed it all up in his description of its confusingly
polyglot music whose supposedly Viennese themes were so 'moist
and persuasive, tantalizing and seductive' that they occasioned
'lewd glances in the concert hall, the salacious dribble at the corners
of the mouths of some of the old men, and above all the ugly, whor-
ing laughs of certain respectable women!'[8] But where the Fourth
Symphony seemed exceptionally to approach the pornographic, the
Third confirmed the disreputable mass appeal of such music by
achieving a resounding public success. From this point on, audience
applause would begin to drown out critical antipathy and
incomprehension of Mahler's symphonies – a fact that led some critics to mobilize 'mass culture' arguments against him, describing
him as a manipulative, even demagogic entertainer.

The première of the Third, on 9 June 1902, was the first such occasion that Alma attended as Mahler's wife. It was a significant one,
too: the main event of the annual *Allgemeine Deutsche Musikverein* festival, held in Krefeld. In the rather provincial surroundings Alma,
uncomfortably pregnant in the hot summer weather, discovered herself to be the partner of a celebrity who, even more than in cosmopolitan Vienna, attracted attention wherever they went. His
striking appearance – hat in hand, chin pushed urgently forwards –
played its part, as did his notoriously impetuous and uneven stride.
She claimed that he much amused a group of children who would
follow behind them, on one occasion returning his hat with some
hilarity after he had left it in a tea-shop. In the fussily decorated private house in which they were forced to lodge, he typically managed
to kick a bucket of water downstairs in the direction of the lady of the
house. Such things were part of the 'theatre' of art in the popular
imagination, nourished on Hoffmannnesque tales of the eccentric-
ities of the influentially inspired. In Mahler's case they appear to
have been a perfectly natural feature of his character, marked by a

high degree of oblivious self-centredness. The music, the work, was what mattered – and that, in the case of the Third Symphony, for once pleased almost everyone.

News about the preliminary rehearsals in Cologne had raised audience expectations; a grand festival event was anticipated, and the Third provided it in style. Particularly striking was the success achieved by the first movement – an incomprehensible stumbling-block for the critics (as Mahler had foreseen). The *Allgemeine Deutsche Musikverein* was still very much an organization with modernist sympathies, by the standard of the times, and at the end of the Third's first movement its new president, Richard Strauss, had marched up to the podium, applauding demonstratively as if to indicate the official approval of an association historically aligned with the battle against an institutionalized official culture. In reality it was itself becoming increasingly institutionalized and even conservative. The fact that the Third Symphony articulated and confronted similar contradictions may even have contributed to its success as an ideal exemplar of art-as-religion, of the symphony as the *Gesamtkunstwerk* of the modern spirit. Strauss became increasingly less demonstrative in his response to the later movements of the symphony but the general applause and appreciation of the rest of the audience appeared to increase as Mahler's musical panorama of Nature, structured as an allegorical history of human consciousness, moved towards its climax in the concluding Adagio of love that even the most nonplussed traditionalists were ready to greet as 'noble', as an example of true German art.

The Third Symphony is one of the most ambitious monuments to liberalism in its specifically Austro-Hungarian form. It came as near as conceivably possible to reconciling the tensions and contradictions on which both it and the Empire were grandly and precariously based. Alma was not alone that night in finding that the experience of the work 'finally convinced me of Mahler's greatness'.[9]

Mahler would one day comment upon the ephemerality of art's power to symbolize resolution, or to achieve that 'remarkable clarity of visions, which instantly dissolve like phantoms, like things experienced in dreams'. This, he said, was 'the deepest cause of the artist's life of conflict'. He soon unwillingly (if not unwittingly) found himself participating in a catastrophic authentication of that essentially Romantic model of the tragic awareness of creative genius. To suggest that his music began in its own way to reflect that participation is to return to the problem about the relationship between life and art: about the shifting boundaries of artistic texts as opposed to the 'real' experience of life which they might reflect. We know about Mahler's experience in the last decade of his life through a variety of textual sources of which he was the author; letters as well as music. We also know (see chapter 5, p. 112) that Mahler accepted that there had been a measure of creative artifice in his own earlier letters.

One of his highest philosophical or even metaphysical aims as a composer was always both to invoke and evoke experiences of what Adorno would call moments of *Durchbruch*: moments in which some distantly apprehended Other 'breaks through' the shell of artistic illusion in revelatory fashion. Mahler's deepest inner subjective life had long been constructed and played out in the arena of art. The progressive, implicitly critical undermining of that arena within his own culture seems at times to have overtaken him as if unawares. Evidence of self-reflexive criticism in Mahler's middle-period and later works is nevertheless often seen as confirming his modernist credentials. Is the complicated 'intertextual' artifice of his passionately felt love-letters to Alma also urgently and even self-destructively explored in some of his later music? In those letters, Alma is soon cast in the role of quasi-Wagnerian 'redeemer' to a long repressed and sexually troubled man:

> Every time a woman has crossed my path, I have been tortured afresh by having to recognize the gap between dreams of happiness and the sorry truth.

Alma came to represent the *Durchbruch* incarnate, his dream of happiness. By Christmas 1901 she is figured as the spiritual partner in his sacred quest:

Now, when I am so close to the fulfilment of my highest aspirations
and feel such inward happiness, I want to lead myself and you up
into those regions where we catch a glimpse of eternity and the
divine. That is how I want to be yours and you to be mine.[10]

The scene of impending marital and artistic crisis was set.

First, however, there was the Fifth Symphony to be completed. The
reconfiguring of the narrative 'breakthrough'-symphony to accommodate something like the rondo-finale of classical convention con-
veniently traced a redemptive progression, just like the one that
Mahler seemed now to have completed in real life. At the end of the
tunnel there beckoned a 'world without burdens' (*Welt ohne Schwere*).
Mengelberg's claim to have been been told by Mahler that the Adagietto had been sent to Alma as a 'declaration of love' confirms this
reading of the symphony's inner programme. Mahler may, indeed,
have been symphonically constructing his subjective life even as he
was subjectively 'reconstructing' the symphony's traditional form.
The Fifth seems to re-use one of the discarded ground-plans of the
optimistic Third Symphony (particularly the division of the first part
into two movements, the first introductory and funereal). By contrast, the Sixth Symphony would map onto an ostensibly non-pro-
grammatic, 'traditional' symphonic model a dynamic discourse in
which ever greater tensions between stark oppositions (the spiritual
and the worldly, dream and nightmare) favoured the chaotic, dark
side of the Heaven/Hell imagery that was earlier likened to the
Traumdichtung in Jean Paul (see p. 101). The 'world without burdens'
seemed now to have been replaced by a world without hope (Mahler
himself conducted the work with the title 'Tragic' attached to it in the
programme-book). The parallel worlds of art and life had perhaps
been shadowing each other all along. If there *were* any useful distinction, it was between much more broadly defined and overlapping categories of both. Their redefinition needed quite new conceptual
tools, maybe even those employed some years later by Sigmund
Freud in the consultative walk that Mahler took with him in 1910.

The place where much of this was initially thought through was the new summer villa on the Wörthersee, built by Mahler as an escape from the city, a place where he might be 'at one' with himself, nature and his art. He took Alma to Maiernigg for the first time after the première of the Third Symphony. The joyful Fifth may have been the work in hand, but the tense polarities of the Sixth seem already to have been prefigured in the double image of those long summer mornings: with Mahler working alone in his forest studio and Alma waiting below, occasionally weeping, in the house whose folksy internal decoration she found 'philistine'. Unable even to play the piano, since the sound reached and disturbed Mahler, her diary entries bear witness to her youthful effort to will herself into the role of the selflessly faithful young wife and mother (the passages in square brackets in what follows appear to have been crossed out in the surviving typed transcript of these entries):

> He said yesterday that he's NEVER WORKED SO EASILY AND CONTINUOUSLY AS NOW and I took heart. Knowing that through my suffering I am giving him joy, how can I falter for a single moment! [From now on I shall keep my inner struggle to myself.] I want to sow the ground on which he walks with peace, contentment, equanimity. But my face and eyes betray me! [And always these tears!] I've never cried so much as now when I have everything a woman can aspire to.[11]

The later editing reminds us that diary-entries of this kind, as Mahler perceived of his own earlier letters, are themselves products of creativity that is nevertheless conditioned by the shared narratives that frame the possibilities for individual behaviour in any culture. Mahler, the schoolmaster-husband, seemed often to see Alma as a character in a bourgeois novel of patriarchal solemnity and self-regarding sentimentality. Alma must with difficulty have rejected other, different narratives in which she might have figured herself more easily: narratives owing more to Nietzsche, Ibsen or the image-world of Klimt's paintings. To make matters worse, Anna von Mildenburg took it upon herself to visit the Maiernigg villa frequent-ly, bringing a whole repertoire of operatic scenarios in which she and

11a Street-side view of Mahler's villa on the Wörthersee

Mahler would upstage the young, and pregnant, wife. In the end Alma's strength of character prevailed, but however much she might resist Mildenburg's demeaning theatricality, she was still condemned to play the part that Mahler had written for her in a long and extraordinary letter that he had sent her on 19 December 1901.

She chose not to include it amongst the letters from him that make up the second half of her 1940 memoir (*Gustav Mahler – Erinnerungen und Briefe*); indeed, she claimed to have destroyed it. Her reticence no doubt related to the many home truths about herself that it contained. Mahler had rather cruelly analysed her social set as arrogantly pseudo-intellectual:

> you all intoxicate each other with verbosity (you think yourselves
> 'enlightened', but you merely drew your curtains so that you could
> worship your beloved gaslight as though it were the sun).[12]

While essentially characterizing *her* as a pretty young girl with a lot to learn, Mahler simultaneously revealed much about himself. He was provoked in part by the concept of *Individualität* which appears to have been the subject of a conversation between Alma and Max Burckhard. He had warned her that two such strong 'individuals' as

11b Lake-side view of Mahler's villa on the Wörthersee

Mahler and she could only achieve a happy marriage at the cost of the self-denial and capitulation of one of them. Alma, Mahler suggested by way of response, had really not yet struggled and suffered enough to achieve true individuality ('personality' in Roy Macdonald Stock's translation here):

> Although you're an adorable, infinitely adorable and enchanting girl with an upright soul, and a richly talented, frank and already self-assured person, you're still not a personality. What you are to me, Alma, what you could perhaps be or become – the dearest and most sublime object in my life, the loyal and courageous companion who understands and advances me, my stronghold invulnerable to enemies from both within and without, my peace, my heaven, in which I can constantly immerse myself, find myself again and rebuild myself – is so unutterably exalted and beautiful, so much and so great, in a word, my wife. But even this will not make you a personality in the sense in which the word is applied to those supreme beings who not only shape their own existence but also that of humanity and who alone deserve to be called personalities.

Was that how Mahler pictured himself? It seems so, from what follows – much of it apparently provoked by the letter from Alma in which she had cited her conversation with Burckhard and suggested that she and Mahler did not '*agree* on several things'. This provoked a salvo from all the guns of his Nordau-like opposition to cultural 'decadence' (his scorn of Schopenhauer's misogyny and Nietzsche's élitism sits rather awkwardly in this context):

> My little Alma, we must agree *in our love* and in our hearts! But in our ideas? My Alma! What are your ideas? Schopenhauer's chapter on women, the whole deceitful and viciously shameless immorality of Nietzsche's superiority of an élite, the turbid meanderings of Maeterlinck's drunken mind, Bierbaum and company's public house humour etc., etc.?

There was also the matter of her music. Two composers in the family was something that Mahler could not countenance, although he felt just a touch embarrassed at

having, in a sense, to set my music against yours, of having to put
it into the proper perspective and defend it against you, who don't
really know it and in any case don't yet understand it. You won't
think me vain, will you, Alma? . . . Would it be possible for you,
from now on, to regard my music as yours? I prefer not to discuss
'your' music in detail just now – I'll revert to it later. In general,
however – how do you picture the married life of a husband and
wife who are both composers? Have you any idea how ridiculous
and, in time, how degrading for both of us such a peculiarly
competitive relationship would inevitably become? What will
happen if, just when you're 'in the mood', you're obliged to attend
to the house or to something I might happen to need, since, as
you wrote, you ought to relieve me of the menial details of life?
Don't misunderstand me and start imagining that I hold the
bourgeois view of the relationship between husband and wife,
which regards the latter as a sort of plaything for her husband
and, at the same time, as his housekeeper. Surely you would never
suspect me of feeling and thinking that way, would you? But one
thing is certain and that is that you must become 'what I need' if
we are to be happy together, i.e. my wife, not my colleague. Would
it mean the destruction of your life and would you feel you were
having to forego an indispensable highlight of your existence if
you were to give up your music entirely in order to possess and
also be mine instead?

The letter, continued after a rehearsal at the Opera, contained a
good deal more in the same vein and concluded with a request,
almost a demand, that Alma reply promptly and before their next
meeting. Her mother had counselled her to have done with him.
Alma nevertheless wrote back assenting to everything. Thus the die
was cast and an intense drama set in motion that would have as many
high-points, crises and collapses into darkness as the finale of the
Sixth Symphony. The correspondence between art and life remained
one of parallelism or counterpoint, however. Mahler told Alma in
1904 that he had tried to 'capture' her (the German word she recalled
him using, 'festzuhalten', might appropriately imply detention or
arrest) in the great second theme of the Sixth's first movement.[13]

That theme nevertheless seems to function more as an expression of the feeling she inspired in him, one which he tries to return to and hold onto in the midst of a work that was less of an emotional account of their relationship than a kind of musical testing-ground. Self-destructive psycho-philosophical weaponry and experimental systems for protection and counter-attack were mobilized there, as if on a symbolic stage whose actor-manager sought to outmanoeuvre the future rather than record the past.

The irreconcilability of the Sixth Symphony's oppositions, in that later Maiernigg summer, certainly echoed those underlying their marriage in 1902. The root causes of those oppositions already lay exposed in that crucial cards-on-the-table letter of December 1901, in which the anti-bourgeois modernist defined Alma's role as a strikingly bourgeois-sounding marriage-partner. The key to the evolution of their relationship lay in the split-screen image of the Maiernigg summer mornings: Mahler writing symphonies in the forest, surrounded by volumes of Goethe, Kant and Bach; Alma copying out his manuscript and, subsequently, looking after their two daughters in the lakeside villa below. Meanwhile, in Alma's account, the shadowy figures of rarely named, voiceless servants move fitfully across corners of the screen: a cook (Agnes) who had to take Mahler's breakfast up to the studio by a slippery path on which he might not catch sight of her, a faithful manservant (Anton) who would sometimes row them across the lake to Krumpendorf, a maid-servant for Alma (Kathi), a gardener. More exclusively defined than she by the role they played in Mahler's life, their very shadowiness, like that of the forgotten stage-hands at the Opera, draws one's attention to them when they appear. They too might occasionally have given him pause – 'warning apparitions' as much as the Opera stage-hands. Mahler's life, like that of many powerful and busy men in his world, had little room for such concerns. He once put it to Alma: 'I must keep on the heights. I cannot let anything irritate me or drag me down'.

12 Mahler's composing studio in the forest above his villa on the Wörthersee

7   On the heights

Buried amongst the anecdotes in Alma's 1940 memoir is one about a silly and yet touching little scene that must have occurred soon after their marriage. An afternoon excursion had taken them to the Prater, to join the other promenaders and frequenters of its cafés and amusements. Apparently oblivious of the minor sensation their presence was creating, Mahler had decided that they should take the tram back into town. He joined the queue with the somewhat taller and now painfully self-conscious Alma at his side. The tram appeared, but as it did so Mahler suddenly decided that he needed to relieve himself and accordingly disappeared into a nearby convenience. Alma had probably begun to remonstrate, realized that too many eyes were fixed on them and then given up – only to find herself standing alone, wretchedly aware of the smiles and curious sympathy of the people standing with her as she 'longed for the earth to open'.

There is anger and exasperation in the telling, perhaps also the smile of love. A year or two earlier Alma might herself have been standing in that queue as just another onlooker fascinated by 'der Mahler', as the Viennese came to know him. Now she was married to him and had discovered that behind the 'Individualität' there was an all-too-human 'Mensch' who was no less self-willed and obliviously self-centred than the easily distracted schoolboy of Iglau. Others of his friends, including his devoted critic and biographer Richard

13 Mahler, smoking, in the garden of the Molls' villa in Vienna (seated, left to right: Max Reinhardt, Carl Moll and Hans Pfitzner)

Specht, affectionately discerned in him something of the overgrown child. Specht became a family friend and on occasional visits was able to observe Mahler and Alma in some of the calmer interludes in the otherwise difficult middle years of their marriage. He noted that Mahler could at times show a touching warmth and concern towards Alma 'even when she was inwardly very far from him'. With his two daughters, Maria (known fondly as Putzi – born 3 November 1902) and Anna (nicknamed Gucki – born 15 June 1904), Mahler appeared to Specht in a revealing new light. The dictatorial conductor became an unaffectedly enthusiastic improviser of fantastic fairy stories whose colourful symbolism and precision of expression seemed, to Specht, to reflect the character of the inner movements of the Sixth and Seventh Symphonies.[1]

The double-sidedness of the couple's marriage problems is registered in the fact that by 1904 it was Alma who felt Mahler to be inwardly distant from her ('his love . . . seemed not only at its last gasp but already buried'). Her plan of the Auenbruggergasse apartment that is reproduced in two versions by de La Grange, and apparently post-dates the birth of Anna, ominously located Mahler's bedroom at one end of the main suite of rooms, her own at the other. Yet they had found a way of living together that provided Mahler, at least, with the security and attention he needed to facilitate his composition and make as bearable as possible his work at the Opera. While the Sixth Symphony (1903–5) and the Kindertotenlieder (completed in 1904), must on some level be taken as indicative of inner crisis, Mahler's external career as both conductor and, eventually, composer remained very much 'on the heights' in those years. His belief in the wider public mission of his work led inexorably towards the conception of the Eighth Symphony (1906–7), as a grandiose effort of public benefaction that would also celebrate his reawakening love for Alma in a remarkable way.

By 1903, his sixth year at the Hofoper, Mahler's idealism had temporarily won the day in Vienna. It had been, and would remain an uphill battle against the taste for a more relaxed, more sociable and hedonistic kind of theatrical entertainment which the Jahn and Richter era had provided in plenty. That more southern, Italianate and communal-performative aspect of operatic tradition Mahler tried to sweep aside in the name of a relentless German idealism rooted in Wagner's operatic reforms. Star singers who could not become 'company' performers were liable to be dispensed with by him as readily as their favoured repertoire of crude or melodramatic gestures. His concern for authenticity and the minutest details of staging infuriated to the point of violence Jahn-era stars like Theodor Reichmann, whose death in 1903 some even blamed on the demands which Mahler had made on him; it must be said that Reichmann went a considerable way towards meeting them. Other stars, like the tenor Ernst van Dyck and soprano Marie Renard survived the Mahler regime only for a year or two. Both left the Hofoper in 1900. In their place he built up a company of singers who made up in intelligence and acting ability what they may have lacked as 'voices'. Even with these, Mahler often pushed too hard or expected too much. He

14 Hostile, antisemitic cartoon of Mahler c.1902, the *Hofoper* in the background.
The caption reads: 'Reichmann goes too! / Jew Mahler as "bird-scarer" driving
away our best singers!'

must in some measure be held responsible for the hatred and antipathy that built up over time and expressed itself in the recurring
scandals that eventually brought about his departure in 1907. His
favoured singers, like Anna von Mildenburg, Leopold Demuth, Leo
Slezak and Selma Kurz, were nevertheless able to work together to
create performances of such commitment and intensity that
Mahler's opera seasons, even when he began to conduct less
frequently, came to be cherished as prolonged festivals whose
recalled glories long outlived the bitterness of the disputes that
brought them to an end.

1903 saw one of the greatest of the productions of his later Vienna
years: the Erik Schmedes/Anna von Mildenburg *Tristan und Isolde*,
with sets designed by the boldly appointed Secessionist, Alfred
Roller. Here at last Mahler found a use for a fashionably contemporary aesthetic that discarded some of the picturesque naturalism of
conventional painted sets to create a partly symbolic theatrical space

where lighting, colour and broad structural designs became ideal servants of the work's mood and character. The Viennese audience, still relatively new to uncut Wagner performances, was astonished and delighted by the first act set, with its cleverly achieved illusion of a ship sailing away from the auditorium. Isolde's heavily curtained orange-yellow tent dominated the foreground; the raised fore-deck behind it was lit only by a green light emanating from unseen hatches. In Act II, Specht describes the effect of the gold stars set in a violet sky that progressively turned to cold grey before the blood-red dawn at the end. There were problems with the production, Roller had never been backstage in a theatre before and lacked the experience to accommodate sight-lines from all parts of the house; but many regarded it as the beginning of an entirely new opera aesthetic.

The communal, company atmosphere of those years was heightened by the fact that it remained customary not to announce in advance the name of the conductor of individual performances. Of course Mahler devotees had ways of finding out, and came to anticipate which premières, and which operas, he was most likely to take on. In theory, Franz Schalk or the young Bruno Walter, later the Italian Francesco Spetrino, would be just as likely to appear on the podium, although Mahler continued to oversee the rehearsal and planning of all productions. One of the premières he did conduct that year was that of the first Vienna staging of Charpentier's *Louise*. Its charmingly eccentric composer was present, his enthusiasm helping to reinforce Mahler's special ties with Paris.

Throughout this period, however, his other life as both composer and conductor of his own music continued. The private/public dichotomy was further emphasized by the fact that the Sixth and Seventh Symphonies, with their more inward and even self-referential preoccupations, were created against a backdrop of performances of his earlier, grand 'festival' symphonies for chorus and orchestra. The 1903 *Allgemeine Deutsche Musikverein* festival in Basel, for example, capitalized on the previous year's triumph with the Third by mounting a most successful performance of the Second Symphony in the city's lofty, candle-lit cathedral. Even the jealously sceptical, and antisemitic German composer Max von Schillings was almost won over by a performance that electrified the large audience, including the composer Ernest Bloch ('an impression of supernatural grandeur'), and caused the Czech musician Oscar Nedbal publicly to kneel before Mahler and kiss his hand.[2]

In October, after the Maiernigg vacation in which the Sixth Symphony began to take shape, it was the turn of the Third Symphony again, this time in Holland, where Mahler conducted it in Amsterdam with a choir of 200 schoolchildren and over 300 women's voices. The work's enthusiastic reception, less than a week after its Dutch première in Arnhem under Martin Heuckeroth, marked the beginning of an important connection between Mahler and Holland: more specifically between Mahler and the young Amsterdam Concertgebouw conductor Willem Mengelberg. He had been present at the Third's première in Krefeld and was responsible for the Amsterdam invitation to Mahler (and subsequent ones). Mengelberg became a devoted friend and an enthusiastic interpreter of his works.

The Third, the symphony of love, children, animals and the marching bandsmen of Pan, began to overtake the Second in popularity in those years. It seemed powerfully to reflect the mood and aspirations of concert-goers at the beginning of the new century in many European cities. But the contradictions it attempted to resolve still remained unresolved in Mahler's personal and professional life; indeed that December found him dismissively resisting a claim for better working conditions by those same court-theatre stage-hands whose predicament had once troubled him. Now he was scornful and outraged in his response to their demands for improved hours and pay and for the institution of a 'joint disciplinary board', made up of equal numbers of employee and management representatives. Both court theatres were involved, the *Burgtheater* as well as the *Hofoper*. While the former reached an agreement with its stage-hands, Mahler was reported in the Viennese press as having insisted that, as far as he was concerned, everything depends on strict obedience and absolute precision. In a theatre the safety of many thousands of people is at stake. Everything must run like clockwork and interference from the out-side simply cannot be tolerated. The Director alone must have the authority to punish when orders have not been carried out.

A socialist member of parliament addressed the ensuing protest meeting, pointing out that directors were more easily dispensed with than well-trained workers. They did not succeed, although the trouble simmered on. Just over a year later Mahler summarily dis-missed a group of men whom he regarded as 'extremist' trouble-makers and whose petition for reinstatement he recommended his official superiors to reject.[3]

By that time (August 1905), the political implications of Mahler's idealistic modernity had once again been contradictorily empha-sized – not only by his spontaneous decision to join the May Day march on the Ringstrasse (shocking the German composer Hans Pfitzner, who was making clumsy advances to Alma at the time) but also by his public affiliations with Vienna's younger generation of artistic radicals. In 1904, persuaded by Guido Adler, he had accepted the honorary presidency of an association whose name signalled its intentions to become a musical equivalent of the Secession. Klimt and his friends had called their association, in the 1890s, *Die Vereini-gung Bildender Künstler Österreichs*. In 1904 Arnold Schoenberg and Alexander Zemlinsky set up a *Vereinigung Schaffender Tonkünstler in Wien* (Association of Creative Composers in Vienna) – re-using the term *Vereinigung* (suggesting a more democratic kind of 'union' or 'collective' than a more traditionally constitued 'Verein') and sub-stituting 'creative' for 'graphic'. The ironic implication was that the still existing Vienna *Tonkünstlerverein* (whose president Brahms had once been) was increasingly antipathetic to new music.

One wonders, however, what Mahler's disgruntled stage-hands would have made of the association's manifesto, possibly written by Schoenberg and announced in a leaflet published in May 1904. Fol-lowing an introductory section on the gap that had opened up

between the Viennese public and new music, it had addressed the
conservative role played by financially motivated agents and concert-
promoters in regulating the relationship between composers and
the public. What was needed, the leaflet suggested, was a more direct
relationship like the one now enjoyed by the painters and sculptors
of the Secession:

> And, just as in the latter case it took organisation, collective action,
> to achieve what no one could ever have achieved on his own –
> emancipation from the art-dealers – so, too, do composers need to
> close their ranks and act together.
>   The majority of the creative musicians in Vienna have therefore
> resolved to found a society which aims
>   *to create such a direct relationship between itself and the public; to give
>   modern music a permanent home in Vienna, where it will be fostered; and
>   to keep the public constantly informed about the current state of musical
>   composition.*

This was cultural politics in action, although precisely how it
mapped onto political affiliations of the more conventional sort
requires careful analysis. Such analysis would certainly have to
remain sensitive to the way in which Mahler's stage-hands might
have read this in the wake of the failure of their own recent collective
action. It would also have to consider the contemporary debate surrounding the institution of what was, in effect, a performing rights
society. It was prompted and supported by Richard Strauss, who persuaded Mahler to join it at the beginning of 1904. The relationship
between artistic idealism and the more material concerns of a brand
of 'real' politics was stressed by Strauss's representation to the German Reichstag in 1901. His main opponent was the freethinking
socialist leader Eugen Richter, who remained worried about the
impact of performing rights levies on those whom Strauss dismissed
(ostensibly apolitically) as '200,000 innkeepers and amateur choral
singers'. Strauss the bourgeois materialist later dreaded the
possibility that the German petty bourgeoisie might one day be able
to attend cut-price Sunday afternoon performances of *Parsifal*.[4] In

this area Mahler, the liberal idealist, came closer to Strauss than
either might have believed possible. Theoretically he should have
had more sympathy with Richter, but Mahler, too, thought that the
lower orders' access to high art should be controlled, on specifically
moral grounds. He once scolded an organizer of the workers' education movement for planning to bring a group to La Traviata rather
than to the more edifying Fidelio or Die Meistersinger. Was this where
their two mine-shafts, to recall Mahler's Schopenhauerian image,
approached each other underground? The fact that Mahler conducted Strauss's Symphonia Domestica, of all pieces, in the one full-
scale orchestral concert mounted by the Vereinigung Schaffender
Tonkünstler in November 1904 could only fan the suspicion of sceptics
that the society's audience-educating, composer-emancipating aims
were easily reducible to the reinforcement of middle-class manners
and ideals in the modishly frank language of those who were used to
keeping others in their place.

It was apparently for a chamber-concert of the Vereinigung that
Mahler had completed his cycle of five settings from Rückert's
Kindertotenlieder (the concert took place in January 1905). 1904 was
also the year in which the Sixth Symphony was completed at
Maiernigg and in which Mahler probably first met the thirty-year-old
Arnold Schoenberg when he came to the Auenbruggergasse apartment with his friend and brother-in-law Alexander Zemlinsky to discuss matters relating to the Vereinigung. Schoenberg's early songs
and the sextet Verklärte Nacht were already acquiring a reputation as
examples of the most contentious ultra-modernism in music. Anton
Webern and Alban Berg both began their studies with Schoenberg
that autumn. Mahler claimed initially not fully to understand the
score of Verklärte Nacht (championed by Arnold Rosé, whose aug-
mented quartet had given its première in 1902). He was sufficiently
impressed by the work in performance, however, to conceive a
supportively affectionate admiration for the younger composer. It
would weather a number of abrasive outbursts of the paradoxical
disputatiousness for which Schoenberg became notorious. These

15 Mahler, seated on a bomb, conducting a cacophonous performance, presumably of one of his own symphonies; the musicians include Arnold Rosé, Richard Strauss (pile-driving the 'Publikum' into the ground) and Arnold Schoenberg (playing a sewing-machine)

could certainly inflame the authoritarian side of Mahler, who was used to 'holding forth' without opposition or interruption. He seems to have restored his pride by privately casting Schoenberg and Zemlinsky in the roles of the popular comic characters Dr Eisele and Baron Beisele.[5]

What was more important in the new bond between Mahler and the youthful representatives of Vienna's musical avant-garde was the specifically educative and communicative role that was adopted by the *Vereinigung* under whose auspices their relationship developed. In 1904 new music was still attempting to court the middle-class mass audience that consumed art sufficiently voraciously to support a sizeable and lucrative industry of composers, theatres, performers, concert-agencies, publishers and journalists. The tension between traditional high culture and a more egalitarian popular art had not yet resolved itself into simplistically opposed categories of 'classical' and 'popular' music in the late twentieth-century sense, although the terms had long acquired something of their later meaning in nineteenth-century concert life. Mahler's anxiety in 1906 or 1907 that he should not be caught browsing in a score of Lehár's *The Merry Widow* in Vienna's main music shop (he got Alma to find the passage they had forgotten while he distracted the assistant) points to an institutionalized embarrassment about taking seriously music that was written for entertainment. Elements of an advancing mass-culture debate were certainly to be encountered in criticism of new music – particularly Mahler's. Each of the two key *Vereinigung* concerts with which Mahler was involved in the single season of its effective life representatively straddled the serious/popular divide as it complicatedly conditioned the development of avant-garde modernism in the early twentieth century.

First there was the inaugural concert of 23 November 1904. Although ecomonic factors required that they make do with the less than first-rate *Konzertverein* orchestra, Zemlinsky and Mahler had shared the programme in which Zemlinsky conducted three orchestral songs by Hermann Bischoff and Siegmund von Hausegger's *Dionysische Phantasie*. Mahler's contribution was Richard Strauss's brand-new *Symphonia Domestica*. Several critics alluded to the way in which humour and even a degree of coarseness were linked, in that work, to structural and orchestral techniques of the utmost 'New German' modernity. And then, in January 1905, had come the chamber concert featuring Mahler's songs, this time with an orchestra including a number of *Hofoper* musicians. A selection of *Wunderhorn* songs (from the pleasantly waltzing 'Rheinlegendchen' to the grimly reaped visions of 'Der Tamboursg'sell' and 'Revelge') was followed by the lyrically earnest *Kindertotenlieder* and four of the independent Rückert Lieder (all except 'Liebst du um Schönheit'). Large-scale works drawing on Mahler's *Wunderhorn* style, like the Third Symphony, first performed in Vienna less than a month before the song evening (14 December 1904), seemed for many to juxtapose usually segregated kinds of musical taste in a manner that was both aesthetically and socially unacceptable. The *Wiener Abendpost* critic, Robert Hirschfeld, already one of the sharpest of Mahler's opponents in Vienna, considered the work to be wrecked by Mahler's contradictory mixture of the Beethovenian with vulgarly banal 'popular tunes'.

That Mahler had anticipated a similar line of criticism in response to the Fifth Symphony, premièred in Cologne earlier in the autumn (18 October) of that pivotally 'modernist' year of 1904, is amusingly emphasized by the letter he wrote to Alma after its first rehearsal. Seeing his critics, with the public at large, as an audience of sheep, he characterized the Scherzo as beyond the comprehension of all of them precisely on account of its exuberant and transgressive diversity (here prophetically linked to a phrase – 'the singing of the rival spheres' – from Goethe's *Faust*):

> what are they to make of this chaos of which new worlds are for ever being engendered, only to crumble in ruins the moment after? What are they to say to these primeval sounds, this foaming, roaring, raging sea, to these dancing stars, to these breath-taking, iridescent and flashing breakers? What can a flock of sheep do but bleat in response to 'the singing of the rival spheres'? How blessed, how blessed a tailor to be! Oh that I had been born a commercial traveller and engaged as a baritone at the opera! Oh that I might give my symphony its first performance fifty years after my death!
>
> Now I'm going for a walk along the Rhine – the only resident of Cologne who will quietly go his way after the première without pronouncing me a monster. Oh that I were 'quite the mama, quite the papa!'[6]

The manner of this letter owed something to Nietzsche and anticipates ironic allusions made by Schoenberg and his pupils to the easier path of 'consumable' composers like Richard Strauss and to the ordinary, unimaginative members of the bourgeoisie who opposed innovation. The deeper irony is that in 1904 Schoenberg might have been as likely to cast Mahler onto the same scrap-heap. Such a move was to be curiously reinforced by the fact that the Fifth Symphony and *Symphonia Domestica* were often compared at this time (the aunts' and uncles' programmatic encounters with baby Franz in the *Symphonia* is what Mahler skittishly alludes to in the last sentence of the above quotation). In 1905 the two works shared a high-profile platform in one of the concerts of the first Alsace-Lorraine Music Festival in Strasbourg. Mahler conducted the Fifth as the first item, Strauss his *Symphonia Domestica* as the last. They were separated by Brahms's *Alto Rhapsody* and Mozart's G major ('Strasbourg') Violin Concerto.

A long essay on the festival by the French writer Romain Rolland offered a number of insights and observations that were striking for their cultural-political tone. Rolland – a Germanophile and a warm but not uncritical Strauss supporter – was particularly shocked by the third and final concert of the festival, an all-Beethoven programme conducted by Mahler, whose performance of the Ninth Symphony he found neurasthenic: 'an outrageous exhibition' of bizarre tempi (slow Scherzo, 'post haste' Adagio) and pauses (particularly in the Finale). This led him to unburden himself of a typical description of Mahler's appearance (the antisemitic coloration might not have been intended):

> He has the legendary looks of one of those German musicians of the Schubert type who have something of the schoolmaster or the minister about them: a long, clean-shaven face, dishevelled hair on a pointed skull, bald at the temples, eyes blinking behind glasses, a big nose, a large mouth with thin lips, hollow cheeks, and an ascetic, ironical and ravaged appearance. He is excessively highly strung, and in Germany silhouette caricatures of him have popularised his dumb-show antics like a scalded cat on the conductor's rostrum.

In fact Rolland found Strauss's performance of the Mozart concerto in the second concert equally lacking in idiomatic charm; he came to the conclusion that the 'new' Germans no longer understood their own tradition, only themselves. Their creative projection he found to be revealing of what in Mahler's case he deemed a 'rarely concentrated mind' so saturated with a professional knowledge of past music that his own self-expression was filtered 'through a haze of reminiscences, through a classical atmosphere'.

The works by these two composers that flanked the second concert accordingly interested him not least for their regressive tendency *away* from programmatic modernity (emphasized by Mahler's refusal to provide any narrative key to the Fifth) and towards a revival of classical symphonic form. Respectful of both composers, in differing measure, Rolland nevertheless found that revival marked by 'neurosis'. In Strauss's case the evidence was coarseness and lack of taste, in Mahler's a mixture of strictness and incoherence which reflected 'the hypnotism of force [Rolland presumably meant 'power'] which is driving all German artists crazy nowadays'. In a festival intended to celebrate both French *and* German music Rolland noted without rancour the dominance of the German but found himself obliged to draw the line at the closing scene of *Die Meistersinger*, conducted by Strauss, which had been heavy-handedly inserted into the first of the three concerts, otherwise the only one to include any French music (César Franck and Charpentier). What seems particularly to have concerned him were the implications of the Strasbourg audience's indiscriminate readiness to applaud. He therefore suspected its frivolous sentimentality of concealing an element of Germanic brutality:

> Its most striking characteristic, since Wagner, is the cult of force. While listening to the end of *Die Meistersinger* I felt how such arrogant music, that imperial march, reflected this military, middle-class nation, weighed down with health and glory.

His provocative linkage of the character of modern Germany with the European middle-class concert audience and the music that Mahler believed to be more suitable for Viennese workers than *La Traviata*, explains Rolland's disappointment with the 'striving after Wagnerian grandiosity' that he discerned in the Fifth Symphony. He also disliked its 'stale' themes, the Viennese waltz of the Scherzo, the 'sickly sentimentality' of the Adagietto and the repetitious pedantry which seemed to 'stifle' the 'whirling intoxication' of the Rondo. Just the previous month, on 14 April 1905, it happened that

Budapest had been reminded of its former opera director by a prominent performance of the Third Symphony, conducted by an enthusiastic amateur: the prosperous insurance executive Kálmán Feld. The
success of the performance aroused all the old passions both for and
against Mahler. A cutting review in the nationalist *Pesti Napló* would
have impressed Robert Hirschfeld by taking Rolland's critique of
Mahler a stage further. It characterized him not as a highly strung
neurotic, but as a kind of

> long-bearded, pot-bellied drum major who marches at the head
> of the Turkish military band, huffing and puffing in his inflated
> arrogance. Whoever heard Mahler's Third Symphony today was
> struck by its similarity to the 'Burgmusik', for there is something in
> this music that reminds one of the square, pedestrian imagination
> of the needlessly, emptily noisy style of, in particular, the uni-
> formed military band master.[7]

The spectre of Roth's Bandmaster Nechwal returns to haunt us – as a
version of him seems to have haunted Mahler's music and its
imagery. Always we have to ask: Who *were* Mahler's soldiers? Where
was he leading them? Was it a forced march into the pantheon of
Great German Art? Might its goal therefore have been applauded by a
conservative audience that would nevertheless mock the constitutional incapacity of Mahler, the musical Dreyfus, to reach it? For
some he undoubtedly remained the Jewish outsider whose real loyalties were as suspect as his skills as a leader. One wonders whether
Rolland's judiciously ambivalent respect for the Mahler of the Fifth
Symphony would have been strengthened or further weakened by
knowledge of the Sixth Symphony, which led its audience to the edge
of an emotional abyss, or of the Seventh. Its musical discourse might
indeed have seemed to be fantastically reconstructed out of that
'haze of reminiscences', at once personal and cultural, that Rolland
had criticized as hindering, rather than constituting, Mahler's personal expression.

The Seventh Symphony (1904–5) makes use of as wide a range of allusive musical imagery as any of his works, while remaining mysteriously canny about its cumulative meaning. There are certainly questions to be asked about the causes and the cultural location of the exuberance of its finale (are we in the pantheon of Great Art there, or an anarchic circus-tent on some festival fringe?). In the summers of 1906 and 1907 Mahler confronted and provided a kind of answer to such questions in the last of his symphonies to be conceived and drafted at Maiernigg. Here 'analysis, negation, barrenness' were conclusively replaced by the 'positive and productive mood' mentioned in a letter to Alma written in the summer of 1905, during which he completed the Seventh Symphony (see p. 120). Yet the Eighth Symphony, in which that new mood resounded with such overwhelming vigour, would come to be regarded even by many of Mahler's admirers as his most dubious 'official magnum opus' (Adorno's estimation in 1960). The conception of his great choral symphony as a 'gift to the nation' has fuelled the suspicion of more than one generation of Mahler critics that here their composer most fully revealed his feet of clay. Goethe and pious Catholicism seemed to be whipped together into a heady mixture that represented the conservative, authoritarian German bandmaster in Mahler at his very worst.

Alternative interpretations are certainly possible, perhaps desirable. Adorno himself experimented with a less negative one in 1930, when he described the Eighth as an '*ecclesia militans* . . . determined to call the oppressed to the true battle'. From a musical point of view, the key seems to lie in the shared discourse that the Sixth and Seventh Symphonies had established between themselves. We can follow it in the history of the initial phrase of the Sixth Symphony's opening march theme. It would play a leading role in the Seventh Symphony before achieving its last metamorphosis as the Eighth's 'Veni, veni creator spiritus'. As important, perhaps, although less often noticed, is the four-note motif – F sharp rising to B natural then falling through A sharp to G sharp – which is announced solemnly (*Sehr feierlich*) on horns and trombones, at cue 39 in the Seventh's first move-

ment. The B major epiphany which it initiates forms the focal point of
that movement: an effulgent celebration of its second subject that
grows out of a slow process of recollection. We seem to hear Mahler
gradually recapturing that naive sense of unity 'with ourselves and
nature' – in music recalling that in which the early symphonies had
oddly, sometimes ironically figured nature's 'otherness' as the sound
of distant fanfares, the deathly fiddling of 'Freund Hein' or the voices
of animals. The second subject of the Sixth Symphony's first movement, we remember, had been intended to represent Alma. The fact
that this four-note motif – the ceremonial door-keeper of the equivalent theme in the Seventh – should find its apotheosis in the melody
that introduces the Mater Gloriosa in the Eighth Symphony could
encourage a reading of it as linking the private and the public aspects
of his life and career in a remarkable fashion.

In 1905 the opening of the Seventh Symphony had announced
itself to a creatively 'blocked' Mahler in time with the oars of a boat.
He was being rowed across the Wörthersee, from Krumpendorf to
Maiernigg, after returning from one of his frequent trips to Schluderbach in the Dolomites in search of inspiration. He recalled the
occasion in a letter to Alma of 1910, noting: 'You were not at
Krumpendorf to meet me, because I had not let you know the time of
my arrival'. In the summer of 1906, barely two weeks after he had
conducted the first performance of the Sixth Symphony – a tense
reading, after which he had wept in the dressing-room – the opening
of the Eighth (he claimed) had occurred to him as if unbidden as he
entered his forest studio at Maiernigg. Had he perhaps been using
the words of the old Catholic hymn ('Come, creator spirit!') as a kind
of inner prayer or incantation? The music and structure of the symphony seem rapidly to have followed, in spite of urgently tele-
grammed communications to Fritz Löhr in Vienna, asking him to
send a full text of the 'Veni Creator Spiritus'. It is not a straightforward declaration of faith. The hymn, as other commentators have
noted, is essentially pre-dogmatic in its exuberant invocation to the
redeeming Trinity. Posited and praised, it is also explicitly *challenged*

by a great body of voices and musicians that is thoroughly imbued with the spirit of the Second Symphony's Finale. The vast *Traumdeutung* that follows in one sense affirms the conservatism that Mahler's taste for Goethe, Hölderlin, Rückert, Kant and Bach might have signalled in those years. It is not difficult to discern in it Rolland's 'hypnotism of power' linked to a notorious patriarchal celebration of the 'eternal feminine'. In another sense we might, no less relevantly, be struck by the fact that that Goethean goal – the *Schlussszene* of Goethe's *Faust*, Part II – is a celebration of the creative male subject that unvoices and dematerializes him in a metaphorical space dominated by the 'penitent' Gretchen and the Mater Gloriosa. Given the prolonged tension in Mahler's marriage, it is tempting to suggest that he was in some sense returning here, not in a rowing-boat but in his art, to an imaginatively reconstructed 'Alma'.[8]

She recalled a significant change in his attitude to her in that autumn of 1906. While describing their November visit to Brno (then Brünn), where Mahler conducted his First Symphony, Alma mentions an example of his changed behaviour that had been witnessed by Oskar Nedbal:

> in the theatre one evening Mahler put his arm under mine on the marble balustrade, so that my bare forearm should not rest on the cold stone. Nedbal often told this story afterwards with tears in his eyes. Mahler began at that time to have a new feeling for me, a conscious feeling in contrast with his earlier self-absorption.

One might almost imagine that he was making a final attempt to woo Life into imitating Art – this had always been the goal of the Wagnerian *Gesamtkunstwerk* as a quasi-religious enactment, relying on what Wagner called 'emotionalizing the intellect'. Might we construct a postmodernist reading of the Eighth as aspiring to 'feminize' the intellect rather than to intellectualize the feminine, in the more usual patriarchal manner?

Still the work must be situated on that broad, post-*Parsifal* road where a procession of massed choirs, orchestras and spiritual dramas led, via Max Reinhardt's Salzburg Festival productions of Hofmannsthal's *Jedermann*, in the direction of the proto-Fascist Munich Festivals of the 1920s and 1930s. It is in the very proximity of those alternative possibilities, in that symphony whose performance in 1910 required the musical mobilization of a good part of German-speaking Europe, that its representative significance so precariously consists. Its context in the unfolding events of Mahler's own life and of the wider arena of European culture in the period immediately preceding the First World War, heightens its significance in an extraordinary way.

Before that first performance, a grim series of events contrived to explode Mahler's subjective equilibrium with the effect of a cunningly placed time-bomb. It brought him tumbling from 'the heights' in a manner that was crucial both to the completion of his oeuvre, in the few years that remained to him, and to the critical perspective in which the whole cycle of his works was later evaluated.

After the tentative rapprochement between himself and Alma that seemed to shadow the creation of the Eighth Symphony in 1906, the following year (in which he completed it) found Mahler in bolder mood than circumstances might have led one to predict. A campaign against him at the Opera and in the press marked its beginning; but there was much else to occupy him. In spite of increasingly frequent absences to conduct his symphonies elsewhere, February saw the staging of a new Mahler–Roller production of *Die Walküre*. Outside the Opera his confidence in his own judgement and vision led him publicly and vociferously to applaud the scandal-generating performance of two recent works by Schoenberg: the Op. 7 String Quartet and the *Kammersymphonie* Op. 9. After the second, Alma had been telephoned by Guido Adler to warn her that

> Gustav made a painful exhibition of himself today. May cost him his job. You ought to stop him. I went home and shed tears when I thought of the way music is going. Yes, I shed tears.

Alma may have exaggerated the extent of Adler's concern – she seems to have relegated him to the 'Lipiner' camp of her adversaries amongst Mahler's old friends. Others would nevertheless have felt either anxious or angry about Mahler's near-involvement in public fisticuffs after the Op. 7 String Quartet performance. Mahler himself admitted that he had difficulty in understanding the *Kammersymphonie* but had been prepared to give Schoenberg the benefit of the doubt ('perhaps he's right. I am old and I dare say my ear is not sensitive enough.')[9]

In March the *Hofoper* mounted Gluck's *Iphigénie en Aulide*, the last new production on which Mahler collaborated with Roller. Specht recalled it as having come as close as anything Mahler ever did to achieving an ethical, spiritualized kind of music-theatre; its visual effect he likened to Etruscan vase-painting. Alma nevertheless suggests that Roller's increasing dominance at the Opera, during a period in which Mahler was conducting fewer performances, fuelled the ever-burning fires of intrigue and hostility against him. These contributed as much to making Mahler's position untenable as did a gradual heightening of tension in his relations with Montenuovo and the officials who managed the Court Opera. Mahler had, for example, struggled in vain with them and the censor during 1905–6 for permission to stage Strauss's *Salome*; it eventually reached Vienna in May 1907, but at the *Deutsches Volkstheater*, which was not under court jurisdiction. The whole affair depressed and annoyed him.

In April 1907 he returned from a somewhat vexatious conducting-trip to Rome (with Alma) to find various opera scandals being played up by hostile sections of the press. Each was eager to latch on to the gossip of disgruntled singers or angry orchestral musicians. Before finally making his longed-for retreat to Maiernigg at the end of June, Mahler had judiciously signed a lucrative contract with the Metropolitan Opera in New York for a four-month winter opera season, beginning in December that year. The details had been arranged in early June at a Berlin meeting with the Met's director, Heinrich

Conried; the engagement was announced in the New York press on
12 June. It was now that catastrophe struck. Their two children had
been left in the care of Miss Turner, the English governess, while
Mahler and Alma had been in Rome; on their return, Anna developed
scarlet fever. She recovered, but in Maiernigg their elder daughter,
Maria, not yet five years old, also developed scarlet fever and diph-
theria. In her memoir Alma starkly describes the short but harrow-
ing period of the child's illness and death, which came, after a
tracheotomy, on 12 July. Mahler, who had become uncommunicative
and withdrawn in his distress, now shared his tears with Alma and
Anna. Alma's mother was summoned and that night they all slept
together in his room 'like birds in a storm'.

Two days later he had sent Alma and her mother down to the lakeside to spare them having to face the removal of Maria's coffin to a
hearse on the road above the house. Frau Moll had nevertheless seen
it and collapsed. As Mahler, his face marked from weeping,
approached them, Alma had suddenly glimpsed beyond him what
her mother had already seen; she too fainted. After routinely calling
in the doctor, Mahler seems to have made an effort to lighten the
atmosphere by offering himself, supposedly the healthy one, for
examination. The guarded tone of voice which Doctor Blumenthal
adopted after listening to his heart told them immediately that
something was wrong. Within a matter of days Mahler had con-
sulted a leading heart specialist in Vienna and was diagnosed as
suffering from a valve-defect of the heart, probably inherited from
his mother. A routine of strictly limited exercise was imposed.
Mahler returned to Maiernigg only to take his remaining family
away from the now unbearable house and relocate them for the
rest of the summer in a hotel beside Lake Toblach, well south of the
town, on the road to Schluderbach, where he had so often sought
inspiration and refreshment. It was an afternoon's walk from Alt
Schluderbach, where the last three summers of his life would be
spent. The first work that he completed there in 1908, *Das Lied von der*

Erde, concluded with the same words as the Eighth Symphony – 'Ewig! Ewig!' ('For ever! For ever!'). But the music of radiant affirmation was replaced by a fading reiteration, as of one who bade farewell to life.

8 What I leave behind me . . .'

. . . art was war – an exhausting struggle, it was hard these days to
remain fit for long. A life of self-conquest and defiant resolve, an
astringent, steadfast and frugal life which he had turned into the
symbol of that heroism for delicate constitutions, that heroism so
much in keeping with the times – surely he might call this manly,
might call it courageous?   (Thomas Mann: *Death in Venice*)[1]

In Visconti's celebrated film version of *Death in Venice*, Thomas
Mann's novelist is turned into a composer whose music is obsessively Mahler's. That the story was not 'about' Mahler, but Mann himself, is well known. What is less well known is that Mann, who wrote
the novella not far from Venice in 1911 while Mahler's last illness was
being reported in the newspapers, intentionally gave Aschenbach
some of the features of the composer. Mann had most recently
encountered him in Munich at the time of the first performance of
the Eighth Symphony, in September 1910, and had been sufficiently
moved to send Mahler a copy of his latest novel, *Royal Highness*, along
with a short letter in which he hailed the man who 'embodied the
most serious and sacred artistic will of our age'. There is no evidence
that Mahler read the novel, which Mann described as 'an epic jest',
although he might have been amused and occasionally moved by it.
Its central character, Klaus Heinrich, is the heir to a fictitious, minor
south-German principality that has failed to keep pace with the

16 Mahler in 1907

modern world: he solves its problems by marrying the daughter of a
rich American businessman. Although his energetically Nietzschean tutor, Doctor Überbein, shoots himself, Klaus Heinrich
prepares to make do with an 'austere happiness' in which he will be
sustained in his lonely official duties by love. The denouement finds

him standing with his new bride at a window of the castle, beneath which 'All the municipal bands were playing at once in the brightly lit square packed with people'.

The German operetta-prince, really an artist-*manqué*, who survives the nineteenth century to acquire a sort of commodified cultural power as a model of judicious decency, is a characteristic creation of Mann's ironic imagination. No less so was Gustav von Aschenbach, the respected novelist who is destroyed by his passion for a fourteen-year-old boy – a passion whose dangerous reality he had tried to mask as aesthetic fancy. The original owner of Aschenbach's 'lofty, rugged knotty brow', his 'rimless gold spectacles' and 'aristocratically hooked nose' found himself little better equipped to deal with the reality of intimate emotional crisis, save in an art that accepted the burden of its own illusoriness. Mahler's last works were filled with the after-shocks of the shattering of artistically mediated dreams. The redemptive dream of love that he had woven into his marriage to Alma Schindler was turned into a nightmare by her affair with a man of her own age. The cultural dream of redemption by American finance was similarly soured by Mahler's direct experience of its hostility to idealism. The utopian dream of such idealism – that the people packed into the square below Klaus Heinrich's castle window might be redeemed and reconciled by music – was hardly sustained by the significant proportion of disaffected and resentful musicians who played under Mahler, or by his own increasing sense of perplexity in the presence of economically and racially disadvantaged people. He had long been devoted to helping beggars and the poor and was a willing philanthropist. Yet *en masse*, he found the disadvantaged disconcerting: 'Are these my brothers?' became a recurring question of his later years, whether in the presence of Polish Jews in Lemberg or the opium-smokers in New York's China Town.[2]

In the Toblach region of the Tyrol, where Mahler took his family in the summer of 1907 following the tragedy of Maria's death and the diagnosis of his own heart condition, things seemed more reassuringly familiar. It had been a favourite place of retreat, perhaps escape, for Mahler over many years. Not a place to stay for long, perhaps, but one which offered him that experience of the elemental in nature that he clearly needed. The railway line that once led from Toblach via Schluderbach to Misurina has gone, but the nearby road, widened and much resurfaced, still snakes through the long and sometimes rather gloomy Landro valley, whose mountainous walls periodically break to afford breathtaking views of viciously razor-edged peaks. As one approaches Schluderbach, the peaks of the Drei Zinnen form the centre-piece of a grand vista to the east. A little further on one reaches the Dürrensee: the modest but picturesque lake, through whose forest of dwarf pines (it still flourishes) Mahler had thrashed in June 1905 to work off the migraine that train journeys so often brought on. The path around the lake, where cowbells may still be heard, gives striking glimpses of jutting buttresses and towers of the cliffs that climb steeply above the road on the opposite side. Adorno must have been thinking of some such place when he characterized the juxtaposition of cultural and geographical worlds in Das Lied von der Erde:

> where a porcelain China and the artifically red cliffs of the Dolomites border on each other under a mineral sky.[3]

He goes on to suggest that the orientalism of that work, unprecedented in Mahler's earlier output, may have functioned in part as an emerging symbolic representation of his own Jewishness. It is equally clear that the passionate yet distant, intimate yet arcane world of the ancient Chinese poetry collected, in German versions, in Hans Bethge's Die chinesische Flöte, supplied both consolation and pretexts for the cathartic expression of existential anguish.

A question-mark hangs over the chronology of Das Lied von der Erde, effective though the poetic structure of Alma's account may be (she suggests that it was sketched in the weeks following Maria's death). Bethge's Die chinesische Flöte was advertised for publication by the Insel-Verlag of Leipzig at the end of July 1907 and may not have

17 The Dolomites, a view from the path around the Dürrensee, just to the north
of Schluderbach

been available until October. Had Mahler's old friend Theodor
Pollak really given him a copy in time for him to sketch the settings
that summer? The only dated manuscript movements (for voice and
piano) corroborate Roller's assertion that Mahler composed nothing more in 1907, and that 1908 was the year in which *Das Lied von der
Erde* was composed, during the first summer spent in the ancient
farmhouse of Alt-Schluderbach, a mile or two east of the town of
Toblach (now Dobbiaco) at the northern end of the Landro valley.

It was certainly there, in the last of his composing-huts, set at the
edge of a pine forest, that the finishing touches were put to that most
elaborate and specifically symphonic of all Mahler's sequences of
orchestral songs. His more recently cultivated voice of piously lyrical
Victorian sentimentality (*Kindertotenlieder*, *Um Mitternacht*) – did it
find its apotheosis in certain stretches of the Eighth Symphony? –
was conclusively replaced by one whose every artifice seemed to
serve a relentless, if humane realism. Its motive force was an impossible, almost self-destructive desire both to confront and contain a
mortal grief. The lyricism that finally evades its own self-protective
checks and balances in *Das Lied von der Erde* has as little to do with trite
consolation or 'pantheism' as one of the poems Mahler had written
long ago in Kassel, in 1884:

> . . .
> I saw in a dream my poor mute life
> – A spark that has boldly escaped the forge
> It must (I saw) float dying into space [*das All*].

The usual panacea for that sense of unavoidable oblivion was to
be subtly, if satirically, characterized by Robert Musil in the first
volume of his *Der Mann ohne Eigenschaften* (*The Man without Qualities*,
1930). Evoking Vienna just before the first World War, he adopted a
Zweigian mode:

> one day one suddenly has a wild craving: Get out! Jump clear! It is
> a nostalgic yearning to be brought to a standstill, to cease evolving,
> to get stuck, to turn back to a point that lies before the wrong fork.

And in the good old days, when there was still such a place as Imperial Austria, one could leave the train of events, get into an ordinary train on an ordinary railway-line, and travel back home.

We must nevertheless be careful to avoid the convenient construction of some *fin-de-siècle* 'Zeitgeist' of despair or sense of impending, world-historical doom. The existential crisis explored in *Das Lied von der Erde* had other, more personal determinants even than the death of a daughter and an attendant sense of individual mortality. Who is the 'friend' to whom Mahler addressed his 'Abschied' if not Alma? He frequently played parts of it on the piano to her during the last two years of his life. To Bruno Walter he posed the stark question: 'What do you think? Is it really bearable? Won't people do away with themselves afterwards?'[4]

Before the collapse of his relationship with Alma in 1910, Mahler's life regained something of its old frenetic pace. Its intensity often refutes suggestions that his heart-trouble clouded his every hour from the summer of 1907. The summers, in fact, found him at his worst, since freedom encouraged introspection about the new limits on his formerly cherished daily walks and mountain climbs. Until well into 1910, when fully occupied during the conducting season, Mahler worked and planned in a manner that suggested a strong, albeit anxious sense of his own future. To some extent, of course, that future had been mapped by the New York contract which had been arranged before the disasters of July 1907. At the end of August he duly returned to Vienna to work out his notice at the Opera (officially terminating on 31 December). His last performance there, of *Fidelio*, actually took place on 15 October. After that he left for a conducting tour of almost a month's duration, beginning and ending in St Petersburg, but including an important trip to Helsinki. There he conducted Beethoven and Wagner and met leading members of the Finnish equivalent of the Viennese Secession. They included the architect Eliel Saarinen and the painter Axel Gallén-

Kallela, to whose piercing gaze and military good looks Mahler had previously found himself drawn in Vienna. Gallén-Kallela's nocturnal oil-sketch of a pensive Mahler, his face lit by the log-fire at Saarinen's house at Hvitträsk is, in its way, as striking a product of that Finnish trip as the conversation with Sibelius, whose biographer, Karl Eckman, immortalized Mahler's response to comments about the strictness and organic 'logic' of symphonic form: 'No, the symphony must be like the world. It must embrace everything.'

Back in St Petersburg, on 9 November, Mahler impressed the young Stravinsky in a concert that included his own Fifth Symphony. His next concert was his farewell to Vienna, a Musikvereinsaal special devoted to the Second Symphony. His departure from the imperial capital in early December, 1907, was a protracted 'event' in itself – almost a preview of his funeral four years later; it was certainly characterized by some of the aspects of theatrical spectacle that Zweig describes as typical of such things in Vienna. For so long the object of fiercely polarized factions amongst orchestral players, singers and critics, Mahler now found himself caught between triumphant malice on one side and the bitterest regrets on the other. The regrets were shared not only by his long-standing friends, but by the student representatives of the so-called 'fourth gallery', that highest tier of seating in the opera-house where, as Bruno Walter was to put it, 'almost all Viennese musicians and singers as well as the general youth devoted to art received their decisive artistic impressions'. Mahler and Wolf had been up there once; now Mahler was himself the hero of an enthusiastic group of youthful musicians that included Schoenberg, Zemlinsky and Webern. They invited him to spend a last, convivial evening with them in the Schutzengel in Grinzing; he clearly rather enjoyed it.

Ranged on the opposing side were a few of the stars and many of the lesser singers at the Opera. It may have been one of these who tore to shreds the copy of Mahler's official letter of farewell to his colleagues, posted at the Opera on 7 December 1907 and printed in a number of newspapers:

> The hour has come in which our shared work comes to an end. I
> am departing from the work-place that has grown dear to me and
> here bid you farewell.
>
> Instead of something whole, completed, as I had dreamed, what
> I leave behind me is fragmentary and incomplete: such is man's lot.
>
> . . .
>
> Accept my hearty thanks, you who have helped forward my
> difficult and often thankless task, who have supported me and
> fought at my side . . .

The shredder of the letter may simply have had a personal grudge
against Mahler or been an antisemite. The gesture might also be
seen as evidence of the crushed and dispirited mentality of many of
the orchestra's 'salaried slaves' (the phrase is that of the Philharmonic cellist and composer Franz Schmidt, who had little time
for Mahler). It was a mentality and condition only fitfully, if ever,
comprehended by Mahler, who shared the then common view of his
adopted class that those of lower station, like those of different race,
were the way they were for evolutionary and cultural reasons that
might be regretted but not easily changed. Such ideas were already
being mobilized against Jews like himself, but he could at times
endorse them with unabashed conviction. During Mahler's last season in America, his views about music and race would be para-
phrased thus in a New York magazine interview:

> the music of the African savage, be he Zulu, Hottentot, Kafir or
> Abyssinian, rises but a trifle above the rhythmic basis. When these
> people, the ancestors of the present American Negroes, made their
> compulsory voyages from the jungles of the Dark Continent to the
> New World it should be remembered that they were in most cases
> savages pure and simple.
>
> While I have the greatest respect for the accomplishments of a
> few of the American Negroes who have risen above their
> surroundings to high places and to distinguished attainments, I
> cannot subscribe myself to the doctrine that all men are born equal,
> as it is inconceivable to me. It is not reasonable to expect that a race
> could arise from a savage condition to a high ethnological state in a

century or two. It took Northern Europe nearly one thousand years to fight its way from barbarism to civilization.[5]

It is less clear what his views about America and equality were on 9 December 1907, as he boarded the train for Paris with Alma, bidding farewell to their flower-laden friends on the platform (they included Klimt, Roller, Schoenberg and Zemlinsky). That his reasons for crossing the Atlantic were primarily pragmatic and financial is clear, although the irony of his thus taking a leaf out of Strauss's materialistic book seems not to have struck him. Idealism in the future was what he hoped American money would buy him. After their arrival in New York on 21 December, on board the *Kaiserin Augusta Victoria*, the power of money was immediately evident in their luxurious suite on the eleventh floor of the Hotel Majestic, furnished with two grand pianos. Christmas in New York, in spite of the efforts of Viennese acquaintances like Maurice Baumfeld, was a depressing, childless affair however. They had left Anna with Alma's mother and were still mourning the loss of Maria. The Metropolitan Opera House and its orchestra nevertheless delighted Mahler, who made his début there on 1 January with *Tristan und Isolde*.

That he performed it with the old cuts, largely restored in Vienna but still standard in New York, signalled just how significant a hostage to fortune Mahler was prepared to offer. The fact was not lost on some members of the New York press, who welcomed such flexibility in the reputedly tyrannical Vienna Court Opera Director and saw it as an additional testament to his genial qualities. Some of them excitedly anticipated that he would take over as manager of the Metropolitan from Conried, who was ailing and due to retire at the end of the season. Mahler was indeed offered the job, but resolutely declined it. He wished to remain a visitor in the New World, experiencing without embracing the lavish, if often eccentric material culture of the wealthy emigrés he came to know there. A number of them were in the medical profession. These, and others like them, were the men who financed New York's high-profile aesthetic culture which

Mahler had been imported to add lustre to; their wives frequently ran the influential committees which dispensed the money.

He did what was expected of him, including appearing at dinners in the houses of influential businessmen, where his habitually idio-syncratic behaviour (sometimes saying almost nothing, at others delivering a tirade) if anything increased his reputation as a moody European maestro, although it frayed Alma's nerves and caused her to take to her bed. Beyond all reproach were his performances, with first-rate star singers (including Caruso and Chaliapin) and a fine orchestra that had less reason to fear him than the one in Vienna. In spite of the somewhat philistine audience, for whom opera was primarily a social occasion, his *Tristan*, *Die Walküre* and *Siegfried*, his *Figaro* and *Don Giovanni* and a *Fidelio* with Roller's sets and costumes were all received with interest and enthusiasm by the critics. Some of the performances were conducted in Philadelphia, which the Metro-politan company habitually visited during the winter season (it also spent a week in Boston).

Apart from a performance of the third *Leonora* overture at Conried's annual benefit concert in March, Mahler's contract permitted him no concert conducting. Other deprivations associated with his removal from Europe almost inevitably inspired attempts to arrange for specific talents and individuals to be imported to aid his personal efforts on behalf of German Culture in America. He particularly hoped to get Roller over to do for the Metropolitan's rather hide-bound style of design what he had done in Vienna. The reproduction *Fidelio* was as far as he would get in that direction. By the same token, things that reminded him of 'home' occasionally took him back in time to the world of his childhood. One such event was the arrival of a barrel-organ down on the street beneath their hotel apartment. Alma anxiously phoned the reception desk to see if it could be moved (familiar as she was with Mahler's sensitivity to noise when working). It was, but then Mahler appeared in her room to lament the silencing of the 'lovely barrel-organ . . . it took me back to my childhood'.

With her rather deliberate sense of drama, Alma relates that story immediately after her account of the public funeral procession for Deputy Fire Chief Charles W. Kruger, who had lost his life in the course of his duties. In sight of their hotel window, a large crowd heard a brief address before the procession moved on in a silence that was broken only by the dull thud of a muffled drum. Alma claimed that she turned away from the spectacle, which she had leaned out of a window to observe, only to see Mahler leaning out from another, 'his face streaming with tears'. No doubt that was, as she suggests, the experience which would give rise to the use of the muffled drum in the finale of the Tenth Symphony. The dramatic pathos of the scene must have been made all the more poignant by his own recent loss. In April 1908 he spoke of having been tormented by homesickness in America: 'I shall never be anything but a dyed-in-the-wool Viennese.' Add to all this the painful indignity of being taken for Alma's father by an official on their return to Europe in May 1908, and we are surely close to the configuration of inner pre-occupations which must have coloured that summer's work on *Das Lied von der Erde*.

First, however, he had two conducting obligations to fulfil: a poorly attended concert in Wiesbaden on 8 May, featuring his First Symphony, and a Wagner, Smetana and Beethoven concert in Prague on 23 May, where the young Otto Klemperer recalled him as looking 'tanned and extremely fit'. By that time, it seems, Alma and her mother had succeeded in the task that would once have been entrusted to Justine and Natalie Bauer-Lechner. They had found a new summer residence to replace the now unbearable villa at Maiernigg (which Alma sold that autumn). This was an upstairs suite of rooms in the rather grand old farmhouse at Alt-Schluder-bach, a mile or two to the west of Toblach, where they had fled the previous summer. Not far away was Mahler's favourite Tyrolean valley that cut through the Dolomites to Schluderbach and Misurina. It was not altogether ideal. The Trenkers, who owned the house, made all the noise that a multi-generation Tyrolean farming family might be expected to make. But they provided for the needs of their famous summer guest and his visitors and assisted in the building of the last of Mahler's outdoor composing studios. This one was a relatively modest wooden structure, a short walk away from the house, at the edge of the pine forest that came down from the foothills of the Dolomites as far as the Trenkers' fields.

Only the absence of a visible lake (the Toblach lake is situated some distance from the town, at the head of the Landro valley) significantly distinguished the place from Mahler's previous summer vacation homes. In spite of a display of his habitually enthusiastic egoism while apportioning the rooms, choosing the largest for himself, the solitude and enforced caution about physical exercise inspired once again a rather gloomy and hypochondriac mood that could only be dispelled by work. He fails, however, to mention that the work in hand was *Das Lied von der Erde* in a letter to Bruno Walter from which comes the following:

> It is wonderful here. If only I could have enjoyed something like this once in my life after completing a work! – for that, as you know yourself, is the only time when one is really capable of enjoying things. At the same time I am noticing a strange thing. I can do nothing but work. Over the years I have forgotten how to do anything else. I am like a morphine addict, or an alcoholic, who is suddenly deprived of his drug. – I am now exerting the sole remaining virtue I have: patience! Most probably I have chosen the worst possible time to be alone.[6]

A subsequent reference to Alma makes it clear that it is of a shared loneliness that he speaks, a removal from the bustling, adrenalin-charged world of urban cultural life. Its true converse was not so much the vacation isolation with his family, the servants, their visitors and the noisy Trenkers downstairs, as the deeper, subjective isolation he found himself confronting in the new study/summer-house. There the old inspirational music of nature turned irretrievably into a song of the earth's sorrow, its most starkly opposed voices those of

18 Mahler's last composing-hut at Alt Schluderbach, near Toblach

elegiacally remembered joy and the spine-chilling, rage-inducing laughter of an ape amongst moonlit graves.

As so often in Mahler's later career, the mood of his current creative work must have been thrown into sharper relief by performances of his earlier works. At the end of the summer of 1908, less than three weeks after completing the draft of 'Der Abschied' (the final movement of *Das Lied von der Erde*), he conducted the first performance of the Seventh Symphony back in Prague, one of the cities of his youth. Curiously enough, this 1905 symphony of private renewal and reconciliation marked the end of Prague's celebratory concert season (opened by Mahler in May) marking the sixtieth Jubilee of the Emperor Franz Joseph. An autumnal celebration if ever there was, its outward festivity masked a wider unease about the fate that awaited the Empire when its fatherly leader (then aged 78) finally died. The neo-romantic chiaroscuro of the middle movements of the Seventh Symphony might have refracted something of that unease in a subtle way. A majority of the reviewers failed to find anything of great value in the work as a whole; the admiring attendance

at the many rehearsals by a youthful Mahler 'clique', including
Bruno Walter, the young Otto Klemperer and Alban Berg, may have
inflamed some critics' habitual ire. The more recently converted
Swiss Mahlerite William Ritter nevertheless recalled with relish the
first complete run-through of the finale. Sitting with his male partner, Janko Càdra, on stage beside Mahler's podium, with Alma on a
chair squeezed behind the cellos and waiters bustling about the
main body of the hall preparing for a banquet, he heard for the first
time

> the immortal sunrise of that glorious finale, opening with a
> frenetic outburst of the timpani reminiscent of the first bars of Die
> Meistersinger. Fired by the presence of the woman he idolized for her
> beauty and Makart-like Viennese gracefulness, the Master threw
> himself about like a madman, seated, standing, dancing, leaping
> like a jack-in-the-box in all directions at once . . . But what
> enthusiasm! Such delirium! And how we were carried away! And
> indomitably Czech though they were in their response to a German
> conductor, the orchestra was conquered, swept off its feet.

The idea of delirium inducing enthusiastic submission, indeed
the 'conquest' of a Czech orchestra by a 'German' conductor (Prague
would have remembered Mahler's former association with its German theatre) – all this reminds us of Rolland's response to Mahler at
the 1905 Strasbourg festival. Even his more committed friends thus
found their enthusiasm inspiring political imagery and allusions of
the kind that his enemies frequently mobilized against him. The
main arenas in which the meaning of his music had to be assessed
seemed ever more clearly defined as social, political and racial. Typically, Mahler's inherited German idealism blurred the colours and
obscured the direction of the forces he commanded (with the excep-
tion of the two 'Nachtmusik' titles, this was again a programme-less
symphony). But Ritter's notion of Mahler having 'conquered' the
Czechs was interestingly borne out in a review by the Czech nationalist Zdeněk Nejedly. His reading of the significance of the première
underlines even more explicitly how subversive a role the Seventh

might have played in Prague's celebration of the Austrian Emperor's jubilee:

> Nothing could be better than for this remarkable concert to shake us out of our slumber and mark the starting-point of a fresh, youthful, truly modern, new lease of life. Saturday's concert would then be a historic date for us, too. To be fair, Mahler's concert at the Exhibition was 'bilingual', and the Germans were perhaps also in the majority in the audience; but as things stand in Prague we are justified in speaking of this as a Czech concert. The musicians were almost all Czechs, and in the audience every important figure of our musical life was present. And it was just this that constituted the importance of Mahler's concert, that he gave his work its world première here, with and for us.[7]

Towards the end of the following month the Seventh was repeated in Munich in the first of a new 'Master-Conductors' series of concerts run by the impresario Emil Gutmann. Here its reception took the more usual German form: audience enthusiasm matched by doubts and reservations from the critics, alive as ever to the essentially 'non-German' nature of his musical style. That fact was almost wilfully emphasized by Mahler's choice of the second half of the rather longer concert on this occasion: the Prelude and Liebestod from Tristan and the third Leonora overture. Two weeks later, following a messy row with Justine (over the whereabouts of his youthful Rübezahl libretto) and a Beethoven, Tchaikovsky and Wagner concert in Hamburg, Mahler was back on board ship with Alma. This time Anna came with her English governess, Miss Turner. America relieved Mahler of the need to worry about distinctions between Germans, Austrians, Czechs and Jewish versions of all three. New York currently had a cruder interest in what specifically distinguished 'German' music – generously (and vaguely) defined – from its Italian counterpart.

There were two reasons for this. Conried's successor as Director of the Metropolitan Opera was himself an Italian: Giulio Gatti-Casazza, the former director of La Scala, Milan. And his star import was another conductor: fellow Italian Arturo Toscanini. Reports about his stature as an interpreter, not least of Wagner, were circulated in the New York press well in advance of his arrival and suggest something of a deliberate campaign to whip up a Mahler-versus-Toscanini controversy that might fill even more seats than had been sold in the previous, extremely expensive season. An Italian–German contest was now also affecting the theatre's managerial staff, given that Gatti-Casazza's chief administrator was the former German singer Andreas Dippel. The most depressing manifestation for Mahler of this stage-managed rivalry between Germany and Italy was Toscanini's insistence that he should make his début with *Tristan*. That Mahler would not agree to.

He prevailed, and was thus able, on 23 December, to take up again what he had already shaped the previous season as 'his' *Tristan*. His delayed reappearance at the Met. had been contractually arranged to allow him to do what he had not been able to do the previous season: conduct symphony concerts. Between their arrival in New York on 21 November (this year they stayed at the Savoy) and the first *Tristan* performance on 23 December, Mahler conducted three concerts with the New York Symphony Orchestra in Carnegie Hall: the first and last were mixed programmes featuring works by Beethoven and Wagner, along with Schumann, Smetana and Weber. The second concert, on 8 December, represented Mahler's first American appearance as a conductor of one of his own works. He chose the symphony with which he had bade farewell to Vienna: the Second – in fact its first performance in America. The now familiar European pattern of audience acclaim and critical reserve was repeated. German-born or German-trained critics inevitably contributed richly to the confusion. At least the success of the subsequent opera season was not dulled by it (as well as *Tristan*, Mahler conducted a series of *Bartered Bride* performances with 'authentic' dancers from Prague, and there was a particularly fine New York revival of *Figaro*). The same critics nevertheless went fully into the attack after the second of two concerts Mahler subsequently gave with the New York Philharmonic.

This orchestra had been reconstructed specifically as 'Mahler's' orchestra for the following season, funding having been arranged by a powerful group of society wives. His Beethoven Ninth on that occasion caused more than the usual outrage amongst the traditionalists but, as was the way of things in America, the sparks only served to ignite enthusiastic anticipation, shared by Mahler, for his next season in New York. At last he was able to look forward to putting opera behind him and concentrating on concert-conducting, with an orchestra that he could call his own.

The return to Europe in April 1909 did not, as in the previous summer, signal the start of a new round of engagements. Instead, he had something like a real holiday with Alma in Paris, where they were fêted by General Picquart and the Clemenceaus and where Mahler sat for Rodin, from whom a bust had been commissioned by Carl Moll and friends in Vienna. That things were already far from idyllic in Mahler's relationship with Alma is made clear in her account of what followed those April days in Paris:

> At that time I was in a highly nervous state and on returning to Vienna I was ordered to take a holiday at Levico . . . I was in a state of profound melancholy. I sat night after night on my balcony, weeping and looking out at the crowd of happy, brightly dressed people whose laughter grated on my ears. I longed to plunge myself into love or life or anything that could release me from this icy, glacial atmosphere. We corresponded daily about abstract topics; Mahler was worried about me and finally came himself.
>
> I drove to meet him at Trient; when he got out of the train I didn't recognize him. Before setting out, he had gone to the barber in Toblach, wanting to make himself look especially good, and been completely shorn while obliviously reading the newspaper. He was unrecognizably ugly, like a convict, without the thickly growing hair at the temples which gave his extraordinarily long and thin face its normal shape. I could not get used to it or overcome my sense of alienation and after two days he sadly departed.[8]

The work to which Mahler returned, alone, in Toblach (Anna was with her mother in Levico) must have been the Ninth Symphony. The draft of its first movement contains annotations which anticipate those in the Tenth: 'O Jugend En[t]schwundene! O Liebe! Verwehte!' ('Oh youth disappeared! Oh love! Obliterated!' – score p. 38, *Tempo I*) – 'Leb wol! Leb wol!' ('Farewell! Farewell!' – final page, *Wieder a tempo*). The temptation to consider this, at least, as a kind of 'autobiographical' music is strong. However, the ordering and structuring of what frequently sound like extracts from a stream of consciousness is what turned into a symphony such extreme emotion recollected in such disturbed tranquility. As in *Das Lied von der Erde*, this music consistently historicized the utopian idyll that should, in Mahler's culture, have been its highest goal. It is music that seems to be bidding farewell to all that music had signified, thus signifying all the more. Adorno speaks illuminatingly, in this context, of Mahler's acquired knowledge that 'happiness' is defined in recollection by its loss; of the impossibility of an art that grows implicitly hostile to the cultural category of 'art'. The more recently rediscovered draft of the concluding Adagio of the Ninth, with the annotations on its last two pages – 'Schönheit, Liebe' ('Beauty, Love') and 'Lebt wohl, lebt wohl / Welt!' (Farewell, farewell / world!) – confirms a reading of Mahler's late music as simultaneously lyrical elegy, symbolic representation of that which has been lost and a proto-expressionist cry of anguish at the irreconcilability of the musical and experiential 'fields' (a term from Adorno) that each category generates.

Such music casts a clarifying light, as of a low winter sun, back over his entire output, throwing into sharp relief its peaks and its darker recesses. Robert Hirschfeld showed understanding of both in his angry review of Bruno Walter's performance in Vienna of the Third Symphony in that autumn of 1909. His outraged negativity might equally have formed the basis of an appreciation of all that was subversively 'modernist' in that symphony, which in other respects seemed resonantly to affirm hierarchical difference. Hirschfeld accepted that the symphony was cathartic and Dionysian in its effect on a mass audience, but thought that such an effect liberated only anarchic and irrational enthusiasm ('explosive forces which have been pent up in quiet bourgeois duties and professions'). At once tasteless and ironic in its confusion of high and low cultural elements, it seemed to him to represent 'a cult of trifles and details' in which individual details acquired importance at the expense of the noble unity that 'great symphonists' properly sought to master. He felt obliged to 'combat the Mahler principle because it contains a danger'.

Behind Hirschfeld's hostility lay a personal sense of grievance, but also the continuing reverberation of Mahler-period controversy in Vienna. It had already spawned much newsprint and even two short books; in both the following titles, 'Erbe' could be translated as 'legacy', but also 'successor', referring specifically to Felix Weingartner as Mahler's successor at the Hofoper. First came the pro-Mahlerian Paul Stefan's *Gustav Mahlers Erbe: ein Beitrag zur neuesten Geschichte der deutschen Bühne und das Herrn Felix Weingartner (. . . A Contribution to the Most Recent History of the German Theatre and Herr Felix Weingartner,* 1908); then came a pro-Hirschfeld response by Paul Stauber: *Vom Kriegsschauplatz der 'Wiener Hofoper': das wahre Erbe Mahlers, Kleine Beitrag zur Geschichte der Wiener Hofoper nebst einem Anhang: Dokument zum Fall Hirschfeld (On the Battlefield of the 'Vienna Opera': Mahler's True Legacy. A Brief Contribution to the History of the Vienna Court Opera with an Appendix: Documentation of the Hirschfeld Case,* 1909). Understandably, Mahler now kept his distance from Vienna. He moved out of the Auenbruggergasse apartment that autumn, after accepting an offer from the Molls for him and Alma to use their house on the Hohe Warte as a base in the city. Yet Hirschfeld's long-evolved and peculiarly German-Viennese reading of his music seemed to be acting like a long-distance curse: the loss of utopian 'unity' became the tragically thematized subject of Mahler's works as it began ever more insidiously to threaten his personal life. Perhaps it was at this time that he first showed the score of *Das Lied von der Erde* to Bruno Walter, posing that strikingly Hirschfeldian and only half humorous question about whether it might actually cause people to kill themselves; hardly the effect sought by a traditional musical idealist of the kind into which Mahler had apparently attempted to mould himself. His marriage to Alma was certainly in a poor state during that summer, marked by a long period of separation. When she returned to Toblach he clearly put himself out to please and pamper her in ways that he had rarely done before, even taking her on a short holiday to Salzburg which Alma, mistakenly locating it in 1907, later described as a kind of second honeymoon, although she took time off to visit her old admirer, the now terminally ill Max Burckhard.

The dark musical discourse of the Ninth Symphony continued to unfold that summer. He almost certainly took it (and not *Das Lied von der Erde*, as Alma suggests) to Göding with him at the end of September, where he stayed for a few days with the Fritz Redlich family on their estate in Moravia – a kind of 'return' that was paralleled by re-established contact with Siegfried Lipiner, brought about through the good offices of Bruno Walter. All these things only emphasize the extent to which Mahler seems now to have sought elsewhere the sense of security that Alma had formerly inspired in him, however loving his letters to her from Holland during his early-October trip to conduct the Seventh Symphony in The Hague and Amsterdam. While she was packing up their belongings in the Auenbruggergasse apartment, Mahler wrote to say that he was 'feeling very anxious. Your silence means, in any case, that your liver is not in good order.' He must have known well enough that it was more than her liver that was disordered at that time.

Back in America on 19 October, for the concert season with 'his' New York Philharmonic, Mahler seems typically to have been rejuvenated by the task of training the players for what was to be an ambitious and eclectic performance schedule. It featured a great deal of modern music by Strauss, Pfitzner, Bruckner, Rachmaninov (the Third Piano Concerto, with the composer as pianist) and Debussy (the *Nocturnes*). Alma, too, seems no less typically to have recovered some of her former *joie de vivre* in the brilliant social milieu in which she played her role as Mahler's much-admired wife. Mahler seems to have thrown himself more willingly than usual into the round of New York dinner parties to which they were invited. Had he resolved to give Alma more of the kind of life she clearly longed for? In her memoir she records visits with Mahler to houses owned by the Roosevelt family on the coast, where they were taken to the home of the future President Theodore Roosevelt (he was away big-game hunting at the time). They were entertained by grand society hostesses, visited a bizarre séance presided over by Eusepia Palladino (Alma was already beginning to acquire a fashionable taste for mysticism and theosophy) and toured the opium dens of China Town with Schirmer, the publisher; this is where Mahler was troubled by his disbelief 'that these are my brothers', and again in the Jewish quarter they visited afterwards.

It was a busy, at times frenetic season. Its climax was a tour with the orchestra (in February 1910), after which Mahler fulfilled his only Metropolitan Opera commitment of that visit by conducting four performances in March of Tchaikovsky's *The Queen of Spades*, the first in America. The critical responses to his concerts had been as mixed as the sympathies and backgrounds of the critics, with the usual outrage at Mahler's 'tampering' with Beethoven and deafening way with violent modern music. In the latter category were works by Strauss, and his own still wildly misunderstood First Symphony. It was about that performance of the First, on 16 December 1909, that he had written to Bruno Walter, associating the work's youthful anger with that of the romantic, god-defying hero of Mickiewicz's *Todtenfeier* (see above, p. 101). What followed was prophetic indeed:

> This remarkable clarity of visions, which instantly dissolve like phantoms, like things experienced in dreams, is the deepest cause of the artist's life of conflict. He is condemned to lead a double life and woe betide him if for a moment life and dream mix for him – so that he has dreadfully to suffer in the one world for the laws of the other.[9]

The New York pace continued during another stay in Paris, in April 1910. Mahler conducted his Second Symphony in the echoing Tro-cadéro – to the evident incomprehension and displeasure of Debussy, who nevertheless attended a dinner party for Mahler given by the composer Gabriel Pierné (the Clemenceaus, Debussy, Fauré and Bruneau had been present). Following a rather unsatisfactory season of concerts in Rome, with a sub-standard orchestra that Mahler had harangued in his most peremptory manner, he returned with Alma to Vienna, where he settled the purchase of a plot of land on which to build a new holiday- or perhaps retirement-home high on the Sem-mering, an hour or so south of the capital and accessible by a spectac-ular railway. They then proceeded to Toblach for the last and perhaps most troubled summer of Mahler's life. During it, both he and Alma were to find themselves leading 'double lives' of an extreme and dis-tressingly conflict-laden kind.

It had not been intended to be a normal working summer. Mahler had long been planning the première of the Eighth Symphony with his Munich agent, Emil Gutmann. This was to form the climactic fes-tival event associated with that autumn's Munich Exhibition and would take place in a newly built Festival Hall seating over 3,000 people. Mahler had been directing the arrangements for hiring instrumentalists and singers, for the rehearsals and for the co-ordi-nation of choirs from a wide area of Austria and Germany (specifical-ly Vienna, Leipzig and Munich). It was to be the grand finale of his career as one of the supreme, quasi-military tacticians of idealism for the masses: an event whose 'Barnum and Bailey' aspect he affected to loathe, along with Gutmann's elaborate advertising campaign and its subsequently immortalized reference to '1,000 performers' ('I detest all that and feel myself *prostituted* by such nonsense'). At the same time he was overseeing the staging of the event with all his old skills as an opera-director: banning the distribution of analytical guides in the Festival Hall, silencing the bells of the trams on the street outside and having Roller plan the grouping and lighting of the

performers. In fact Mahler spent nearly two weeks in Munich, conducting preliminary rehearsals towards the end of June, with a view
to achieving what Gutmann remembered him repeatedly describing
as a 'homogeneous whole', sceptical though he remained about its
realization ('it's quite beyond you', he would shout at the struggling
performers).

Alma, meanwhile, had been recovering from another medically
prescribed post-American rest-cure – this time at a sanatorium in
Tobelbad, just south of Graz. Once again she took Anna with her,
leaving the servants to look after Mahler in Toblach. This summer,
however, she did more than gaze sadly at other people enjoying themselves. The sanatorium was run by a blithe-spirited German doctor
who would not have been out of place in Mann's The Magic Mountain.
He prescribed lettuce, buttermilk and . . . dancing. It was thus, on a
therapeutic dance-floor in Tobelbad that Alma probably first
glimpsed the handsome young architect, Walter Gropius. They
became lovers and her agony of the preceding year, at being isolated
from love and life, gave way to joy and a great sense of sensual release.
There followed, however, another kind of agony: her realization that
her marriage was a complicated obstacle to the long-term continuation of the affair with Gropius. There are indications that she was herself not quite ready to overcome it. Back in Toblach, Mahler had
probably already found himself recapturing, albeit unwillingly, the
isolated and elegiac mood that had given birth to the Ninth Symphony
the previous year. It may have been after the completion in draft of the
first and even second movements of the new, Tenth Symphony that,
following Alma's return with little Gucki, his two worlds of life and
art met with devastating effect in an event that set off a chain reaction
of melodramatic occurrences.

Gropius sent love-letters to Alma. Accidentally (might it unconsciously have been on purpose?) he addressed one to Mahler, who
took it as a request for Alma's hand. Her account of the events that followed must be treated with caution, but it appears that a major scene
ensued in which she poured out her heart to Mahler in a way that she

had never done before. Home truths, from both sides, left them mutually devastated. Alma's mother, of whom Mahler was exceptionally fond, was summoned to help them and at some point Alma seems to have reassured him that she could not, in fact, face leaving him. She suggests that this brought about a complete transformation of the despairing mood in which he had become guiltily aware of how inconsiderate he had been of her real needs. Now he was possessed by an ecstatically reawakened love for her. There is clear evidence of this in the poems and notes he wrote to Alma that summer; but there is no less evidence that he had seen the crisis coming, with dread, and was shattered by it.

The lyrical expressions of love which he was reduced to leaving by her bedside are filled with a desperate urgency that seems born of an awareness that all may already have been lost. One such poem speaks of 'my being flowing into yours in the bridal chamber', but Alma's account makes it clear that their 'reunion' did not involve their sleeping together. She would wake in the night to find him standing by her bed; on one occasion he had collapsed on the landing and had to be revived, as if from a heart-attack. Going to fetch him from his composing studio, she would find him lying on the floor, weeping (where he felt 'nearer to the earth'). And then, to make matters worse, she suddenly spotted Gropius in Toblach one day; confused and fearful, she had told Mahler. He went to find the young man, walking him back to the farm at Alt Schluderbach, carrying a lantern, as night was falling. The two remained silent, Mahler keeping a few paces ahead of his unwanted guest. When they arrived, he left Gropius with Alma (whom he expected to decide between them) and went to read the Bible by candlelight in his room. Eventually, she sent the young man on his way, but only after having arranged for the clandestine continuation of their affair (he later became her second husband; her passionate correspondence with him continued throughout the remaining months of Mahler's life). Naively, a little coldly, she observes in her memoir:

I knew that my marriage was no marriage and that my own life was utterly unfulfilled. I concealed all this from him, and although he knew it as well as I did we played out the comedy to the end, to spare his feelings.[10]

The depth to which Mahler had been wounded is demonstrated by his visit to Sigmund Freud at the end of August (it was arranged by the family friend and Freud pupil Dr Richard Nepallek). That someone so protective of his own inner life decided to consult Freud at all is surprising; that he should, after breaking a number of appointments, have travelled all the way to Leyden in Holland to do so, less than a week before he was due to begin the final rehearsals for the Eighth Symphony in Munich, is remarkable indeed. Reliable accounts of their conversation, in the course of a single afternoon's walk together, are probably not to be found, although evidence from Alma and Freud himself suggests that Oedipal conflict was discussed and that Mahler was in some way reprimanded for harbouring unreasonable expectations of his considerably younger wife. Alma tells us that he was 'resistant' to the idea of a mother-fixation. But he clearly told Freud a great deal, resurrecting childhood memories like the one about being confronted by a barrel-organ after a scene between his parents. According to Freud's biographer, Ernest Jones, Mahler then volunteered a disparaging self-analysis of his music's failure to achieve the highest rank of 'nobility' on account of that formative conjunction of 'high tragedy and light amusement'. While thus disappointingly encouraging the diagnostic zeal of future critics and amateur psychoanalysts, Mahler seems generally to have impressed Freud with his responsiveness.

The effect of that conversation seems to have been considerable. Alma notes that it was during this period of 'emotional upsets' that she one day heard Mahler playing her songs. Blaming himself for selfishness and blindness, he now encouraged her to complete and revise them for publication, which he organized that year with Universal Edition. And then, on one of his last nocturnal visits to her bedside before travelling to Munich (was it in the wake of his taking her

and Oskar Fried to say confession in Toblach?), Mahler announced
that he had arranged for her name to appear on the title page of the
Eighth Symphony, as its dedicatee. It was against this background of
crisis and profound inner distress that the climax of Mahler's public
career took place in Munich on 12 September, with the triumphantly
successful première of his mighty celebration of the transforming
potential of the creative spirit and, via Goethe, the redemptive power
of both maternal and erotic love.

No irony conceived by Thomas Mann, who attended the performance along with a host of Mahler's friends and relatives and
diverse representatives of Europe's intellectual élite, could have
been greater than the actual irony of the fact that Mahler's life was in
one sense running counter to the message of that work. Its distance
from musical autobiography is greater by far than either the Ninth
Symphony or the emerging Tenth. Both of those works construct
death-defying arches of lyrical expression that are constantly threatened by reversals and mockery. There are few threats in the Eighth.
Again the performance of one of his works simultaneously with the
composition of others opens a complex historical vista. The last two
symphonies certainly provide an awesome backdrop to the achieve-
ment of that première in the year of his fiftieth birthday, with his
fame at its height. Munich was the city in which Paul Stefan had published his new biography of Mahler and the anthology of congratula-
tory pieces on him by his friends and admirers. Alma tells us that the
audience in the great Festival Hall rose to its feet when Mahler
arrived on the podium. In what we might regard as the last grand
symphonic première of the nineteenth century, the composer whose
disruptive voice had first been heard in the Iglau synagogue nearly
fifty years earlier now achieved his apotheosis as bandmaster-hero
of a culture on the edge of an abyss. Emil Gutmann captured something of the communal 'aura' of the occasion in pertinently fanciful
language:

At that moment there were no singers, no audience, no instruments; there was no sounding-board, just a single body with many, many veins and nerves, waiting for the blood and breath of art to flow through them.

   . . .

Mahler brought his baton down – life-giving blood pounded rhythmically through the body. For the first time the mouth of humanity, gathered on the holy mountain, opened for the fervent cry. 'Veni Creator Spiritus!'[11]

As the tumultuous applause that greeted that performance and its repetition the following night died away, the problems in Mahler's marriage continued to manifest themselves in ways that could be confusing to those who knew the couple. Alma, caught between loyalty to her husband and love for Gropius (whom she met in Munich and would meet again in Paris before joining Mahler on the boat to America in October) was now the dominant partner, by virtue of Mahler's guilt and desperate attempts to win back her love. These induced a renewed jealous volatility in his dealings with friends and family, particularly his sister Justine and his old friend Arnold Berliner. His occasional hostility to Justine, long encouraged by Alma, must have been painful both for her and for her husband Arnold Rosé. Mahler continued to be supportive of him and had attempted to install him as leader of the expanded Munich Konzertverein orchestra for the Eighth – but the musicians refused to accept him. Then Arnold Berliner inadvertently aroused Mahler's jealousy by making Alma a present of some pearls. Mahler was gradually discovering that he had, in Alma's words, 'no notion of what gave a girl pleasure'.

He tried to make amends. That Christmas in New York he excitedly enlisted his daughter Anna in an effort to surprise her mother with a table laden with presents beneath a white cloth, topped with roses. Alma claims to have been seized by a 'pang of icy dread' at the sight and to have reduced Mahler to silence by snatching off the cloth (was there anger in the gesture, too?). We must be careful not to demonize

Alma. If, indeed, the root of the trouble had been, as Freud was later to suggest in a letter to Theodor Reik, Mahler's sexual unresponsiveness ('he withdrew his libido from her') then that, along with the other privations of her life with him, reinforces an interpretation of their troubles as a shared tragedy in which neither partner was without blame. What is clear is that Alma had indeed finally acquired the upper hand in those painful closing months of their marriage. A letter Mahler had written to her on 5 September from Munich, following a rehearsal of the Eighth's final movement, touchingly suggests the tenor of their relationship (it was his last extended letter to her):

> . . . every note addressed to you! I was so madly excited by it, just as though I was sitting by your bed again, as it used to be in those old, delightful days, telling you all about it! Oh, how lovely it is to love! And only now do I know what it is! Pain has lost its power and death its thorn. How truly does Tristan sing 'I am immortal, for how could Tristan's love die?' . . .
>
> . . . Do write a word to say whether you would like me to sleep in the adjoining room and you have Gucki with you, or *what*? I would like to have our little nest in order before you arrive.
>
> . . .
>
> Your letter of today was so dear, and for the first time in eight weeks – in my whole life for that matter – I feel the blissful happiness love gives to one who, loving with all his soul, knows that he is loved in return. So my dream has come true: 'I died to the world, I have reached my harbour!' But, Almschi, you must tell me over and over again – for by tomorrow I know I shall no longer believe it! For it is 'a happiness without rest' [*Glück ohne Ruh*]. Now good night, my darling, my sweet – perhaps today you laugh at your schoolboy . . .[12]

For all the earnest sponaneity of these words, we must remember that the work whose draft he took with him to New York, in its black portfolio, monumentalized his confrontation of the agony of those preceding eight weeks. The apparently hasty and yet deliberately placed marginal annotations in the Tenth Symphony establish a close link between its music and the subjective world of the notes and poems he had written to Alma that summer in Toblach. The radiant euphony that is the dominant mode in both of its outer Adagios, most remarkably in the transfigured theme announced by solo flute in the finale, might easily be related to the following extract from a poem to Alma of 17 August:

> I would draw together all the thrilling of my joy,
> of the eternity of holy bliss upon your breast,
> into a single melody that, as the sun's bow the
> heavens, would boldly span your sweetness.

Yet in both poetry and music the imagery of light is motivated by, and defined against, another image-world of darkness and despair. One of the notes found in the morning by Alma on her bedside table at Toblach, presumably after Mahler had left for his composing studio, reads as follows:

> My darling,
>   my lyre,
> Come and exorcize the dark spirits, they cling about me, they throw me to the ground. Stay with me, my staff, come soon today so that I can rise up. I lie there and wait and mutely ask if I can still be redeemed [erlöst] or whether I am damned.

The title page of the Tenth Symphony's second Scherzo bears witness, in still more tormented fashion, to the meaning of that wild dance whose end is marked by the first stroke of the muffled drum, recalled from their first New York winter (and annotated: 'You alone know what it means! . . . Ah! Farewell my lyre!'). The inscription tails off with an incomplete word (*dass ich ver . . .*):

> The Devil dances it with me
> Madness take me, cursed one!
> Destroy me, that I forget that I am!
> that I cease to be, that I de . . .[13]

19a

19b

19a & b From the 1924 facsimile of the draft score of the Tenth Symphony; the
title page of the fourth movement and the final page of the fifth movement (the closing section of the latter was written out again, ending in
F-sharp major, with the same annotations)

These annotations, far from demonstrating some mysterious and fatal apprehension of death (as the popular myth of the Tenth usually runs), confirm that, as in the Sixth Symphony, Mahler was engaging in a kind of symbolic musical suicide-attempt. The words, and the music, are addressed, in extremis, to Alma herself, the woman who represented light and life to him. Even the Purgatorio's anguished, annotated cry 'Oh God, Oh God, why hast thou forsaken me?' is preceded by a precisely placed 'Erbarmen!' ('Have mercy!') on the descending figure beginning at the end of bar 106. The following 'Dein Wille geschehe' ('Thy will be done!') seems already to conflate the image of the Judaic God of the Second Symphony with Goethe's Mater Gloriosa as hymned in the Eighth. That her face was that of Alma is reinforced by the similarly strategic annotation of the finale's last, searing enunciation of that same phrase: 'Almschi!' The preceding passage had been headed 'To live for you! To die for you!' That no published score of any part of the Tenth Symphony, nor even the transcription of the sketches in the performing version by Deryck Cooke, has included these annotations is a striking testament to the cultural embarrassment that underlies the doctrine of non-referentiality in German symphonic music. Mahler himself clearly did not share it, whatever his public utterances might appear to indicate.

The 1910–11 American season was paradoxically to find him given not only to further public utterances of the patricianly-traditional variety – the already cited interview published in The Etude is a case in point (see p. 174) – but also to launching himself into a busy round of concerts, both in New York and on tour. These seem in part to have been designed to consolidate his reputation as a world-famous representative of European high culture, though one with a challenging devotion to unfamiliar and demanding new music. In spite of a persistent problem with tonsillitis, he seems to have found strength in the belief that things, somehow, either were or would again be right in his relationship with Alma (was his motive in regularly playing parts of Das Lied von der Erde to her to encourage her sympathetically to hear and understand its message?). That optimism sustained a renewed vigour that enabled him not only to weather his demanding travel- and rehearsal-schedule with the New York Philharmonic, but also to begin to wax dictatorial and demanding again, in something of his former Viennese manner. A violinist called Johner acted as his 'spy' amongst the orchestral players; Mahler also became high-handed with the ladies and gentlemen of the Philharmonic Committee, into whose presence he was summoned in February 1911 to have his powers strictly defined in the presence of a lawyer.

There is little in all this to support the romantic notion that he was obsessed with 'premonitions of death'. If anything, he seems to have found a way of exorcizing his private demons through renewed commitment to his public career as an authoritative and occasionally authoritarian conductor in the grand manner. It was almost as if, in those last months and weeks of active life, he had shaken off the memory of his emotional humiliation in order to relaunch his artistic mission. Mahler's music still had much to tell in its aspect as a reflection of the world as he saw and heard it – certainly as an expression of those multiple and collective voices which so disconcerted Hirschfeld by their anarchic clarity in the Third Symphony. Even the Bach Suite that he had arranged for his 'historical' series in the previous season, playing the continuo part on harpsichord or piano like an authentic eighteenth-century *Kapellmeister*, came over in performance as something energetically personal and at the same time culturally and expressively plural. The *Cleveland Plain Dealer* said it all on 7 December 1910:

> His strength, his mastery over his instrument, were obvious from the first measure of the Bach Suite. There was no getting ready, no working up, no preliminary warming process before the orchestra found itself . . .
>
> And this from little Gustav Mahler, that mere wisp of a man, with the slight frame, the long slender hands, the loose shock of black hair standing away in all directions from the delicate, ascetic face. Little Mahler the giant!

. . .

And how that suite did dance along! For Bach was not only the Wagner and Puccini and Richard Strauss of his time. He was the Sousa as well, a fact not always appreciated. He had the merry rhythmic swing, the gay melody. And Mahler got them in his mind, and just poured them out of that orchestra in a torrent.[14]

Mahler seems not to have gone very far down the occultist path with Alma, yet he often enough, and not only in the latter part of his life, gave expression to a form of mystical belief in a 'coming life', a 'here-after' or even some sort of Nietzschean eternal recurrence. He once set the glasses jumping on a table in Richard Specht's presence, so emphatic was his conviction that an ethical life depended upon a belief that 'everything returns'. It was to Specht that he had defined his belief in another way, in terms of his art: 'I am a musician. Every-thing else is covered by that.' Behind it all lay the works of mystical philosophers like Angelus Silesius or his old friend Siegfried Lip-iner's mentor, G. T. Fechner, who had written:

I believe that this fleeting life is a preparatory stage to eternal life, and that everyone in his good or evil intentions, his good or evil deeds, produces the conditions of his future life, that his works shall follow him and that he will reap what he has sown.

In a letter to Alma of June 1909, Mahler himself had expanded upon the essentially 'productive' nature of all life, which to 'higher mor-tals' (höhere Menschen) expressed itself as a challenging and potential-ly conflict-laden act of self-consciousness:

In between the brief moments in the life of the genius, where these challenges are answered, lie the long barren stretches of existence which impose such tests and unfulfilled longings upon his aware-ness. Precisely this ceaseless and really painful struggle defines the life of these few. – Now you will already guess, or know, what I think of the 'works' of such persons. They are what is in fact ephemeral and mortal; but what the individual makes of himself – what through untiring striving and longing he becomes, that is what lasts.

Perhaps one lesson of Mahler's extraordinary life, oddly, is that it was not quite so. What he became, in human terms, was thoroughly 'grounded' in his culture. We do not, however, need to re-embrace a form of nineteenth-century aesthetic idealism to follow Adorno's lead and interpret his works, to however limited a degree, as having both expressed and transcended the historical life that he lived. This they did not by being coldly separate or 'above' it, but by pointing beyond the solitary voice of the 'higher man' to the collective hubbub out of which it had arisen and thus speaking for the unstable plurality of the mass audience which would still be listening to his symphonies a century later. Meaning was all-important to the 'articulate art' that Mahler, following a visit to Niagara Falls, claimed to prefer to 'inarticulate nature'. Such articulacy depended upon the collective as much as the individual. While the composition of the Tenth Symphony was in progress, an informal moment in a rehearsal of the Eighth found the woodwind section of the orchestra improvising a popular 'Schuhplatter' dance; Mahler called over to them: 'That's just the atmosphere that fits my symphony!'[15]

The Tenth Symphony represented a struggle to preserve the integrity and persuasive power of the subjective voice in the face of all that threatened it for reasons that have implications beyond self-interest. The symphonic form that had represented one of the great cultural arenas in and by which such subjectivity was defined – the 'form' that was celebrated in differing ways in grand public works like Mahler's Third and Eighth Symphonies – was itself beginning to fail. The dispersal of the aesthetic mythology that had sustained it was, paradoxically, the last goal of his striving for consciousness and knowledge through music, even though that knowledge was not what he had hoped.

His end came more rapidly and unexpectedly than many of his early biographers, even Alma herself, fully understood. Although a recurrence of tonsillitis seemed to play a part, along with fever and accumulated fatigue, he had by February 1911 contracted the bacterial endocarditis that was to kill him. It was thanks to their old emigré friend Dr Joseph Fraenkel that blood samples were taken for analysis by George Baehr, then assistant to Dr Emanuel Libman, the leading expert on endocarditis. Once Libman and Baehr had discovered the rich growth of streptococci in their cultures they knew that there was little to be done. David Levy has suggested that it remains uncertain whether Mahler's life could, in fact, have been saved with penicillin, had it even been available at that time. It seems likely that he soon became aware of the gravity of his condition and asked to be taken back to Europe. Perhaps he latched on to the possibility of help from either a Parisian or Viennese specialist for the sake of Alma, Anna and Frau Moll, who had hastened across the Atlantic to help nurse him as soon as news of his illness reached her.

For the story of his removal to the ship, the voyage to Paris and thence to Vienna we have Alma alone to thank; she tells it in a series of carefully selected scenes and shorter vignettes. There is the lift-boy who hid his tears as Mahler was helped out of the specially cleared hotel-foyer to Mrs Untermeyer's car; there are the efforts of Busoni – who was on the same ship – to amuse Mahler as his condition veered between extremes of fever and chill; there is Alma's experience of being almost mugged by two drunken railway porters as she tried to find the carriage in which he had been placed on the train from Cherbourg; and then her exasperation with the young Stefan Zweig, who was prepared to tell Anna a story but not to help her with their voluminous luggage. Later, in Paris, came the drive round the city which Mahler had requested, in a sudden access of recovered energy and hope for the future, only to return in the throes of a serious relapse. From that point on he clearly accepted that he would not recover and, weeping, requested of Frau Moll that he be buried with his eldest daughter in Grinzing 'in a simple grave, with no pomp and ceremony, and a plain headstone with nothing but "Mahler" on it. "Any who come to look for me will know who I was, and the rest do not need to know."'

Dr Fraenkel had given them a list of specialists, but as Easter was approaching it proved difficult to find one. Eventually André

Chantemesse of the University of Paris was contacted; he supervised Mahler's removal to a nursing home where he was able to do little more than make his own culture of impressive streptococci from Mahler's blood. For a while he rallied and even talked of going to Egypt with Alma, but then his condition worsened and, as if in a last attempt to seek a miracle cure from a fellow countryman, Professor Franz Chvostek was contacted in Vienna. He arrived the next morning to tend the celebrated invalid, whose illness was now the subject of considerable press interest in Vienna. A no doubt fanciful drawing of 'Gustav Mahler in Paris Sanatorium' had even appeared on the front page of the *Illustrirtes Wiener Extrablatt* on 18 April. Chvostek needed no time to assess the terminal state of Mahler's illness, but managed to revivify him somewhat with spirited promises of recovery and convalescence. Thus it became possible to help him make the otherwise almost unthinkable journey back to Vienna, on a stretcher.

Somehow they made it, after a journey that was attended at every station, once they entered Germany, by newspapermen eager for reports on his condition. At the tragically early age of fifty, Mahler was already the subject of one of those majestic funeral processions, even if not quite yet a 'lovely corpse', of the kind that Stefan Zweig was to describe as 'the ambition of every true Viennese': the kind of procession which some of Mahler's own most theatrical music had evoked as an image to inspire both horror and the anger out of which vision-teeming epics might grow. Alma's account puts it quite simply: 'his last journey was like that of a dying king'. But the king himself, now fêted as a cultural hero, was conceivably responding to the fact of his own impending death in ways not dissimilar to those in which he had responded to its image in his music. The last book he read, finally tearing the pages out, one by one, as his hand grew too weak to hold it, was *The Problem of Life* by Eduard von Hartmann – a philosopher scorned by Stefan Zweig as one of the 'good, solid masters of our fathers' time', and likened by him to such outmoded figures as Brahms, Ibsen and Gottfried Keller.

Perhaps at the last one needs such things. As Mahler lay dying in Vienna a surprising number of his former enemies, as well as his friends, were suddenly realizing that he had, in his way, fought for cultural values that were equally 'good' and 'solid', even if his own music seemed inexorably to threaten them. Their curiosity became ever more intrusive. On the day before he died an elaborate, if inept, piece of artwork in one Viennese paper achieved what even the most persistent news-photographer of our own times might recoil from: a picture of Mahler on his death-bed, attended by a doctor with Alma bending over him and a Sister of Mercy in attendance at the head of his bed. It was the last indignity that he suffered, while alive, at the hands of the Viennese. The following day, 18 May 1911, he died during a thunderstorm, just after eleven o'clock at night. He had become delirious at the last and failed to recognize his sister Justine. Glimpses into what was going on in his mind were afforded only by frequently repeated cries of 'My Almschi!' and then, his last word, 'Mozartl' ('little Mozart'). When he was buried in the Grinzing cemetary, four days later, the elements contrived a remarkable closing scene. Paul Stefan described it in 1913, in *Das Grab in Wien*. The crowd of mourners had waited in the rain outside a cemetary-chapel too small to hold them, until the coffin was carried out. And then:

> The rain ceases. A nightingale sings, the clods of earth fall.
> A rainbow. And the hundreds present are silent.[16]

The allusion to the Last Trump episode in the Second Symphony suggests transfiguration, a kind of redemption. It was a rhetorical move in the narrative game of happy endings which the Second Symphony had long ago superceded, replacing dogmatic myth with an energetic expressive act – staking everything on a more dangerous existential game of hope-against-hope. From the perspective of articulate art, the nightingale and the rainbow were clichés of inarticulate nature. Mahler, whose last music kept faith with such devices in the knowledge that they were powerless over life and death, would have appreciated the irony.

NOTES

Where possible, accessible English-language sources of information
and quoted material are given priority here. Translations from the
German may have been emended. Short forms of frequently cited
works are used in these notes, indicated in square brackets following
their first appearance. Textual material quoted from Blaukopf's 1976
Mahler. A Documentary Study will in most instances be found also in the
more recent, but generally less rich, *Mahler: His Life, Work and World*
(Kurt and Herta Blaukopf, London, Thames and Hudson, 1991).

Introduction

1 Alma Mahler[-Werfel]: *Mein Leben* (Frankfurt-am-Main, Fischer,
  1963 (first published 1960)) p. 186 (my translation) and *Gustav
  Mahler. Memories and Letters* (trans. Basil Creighton, ed. Donald
  Mitchell and Knud Martner, 4th edn, London, Sphere Books,1991
  [henceforth Alma Mahler: *Memories*], p.240.

2 References for many of the books referred to will be found in
  these notes; see also the note on further reading, below.

3 See Edward Reilly: *Gustav Mahler and Guido Adler. Record of a
  Friendship* (Cambridge, Cambridge University Press, 1982), p. 15.
  The book by Hans Lenneberg is *Witnesses and Scholars, Studies in
  Musical Biography* (New York and London, Gordon and Breach,
  1988).

4 Kris, Ernst and Otto Kurz: *Legend, Myth and Magic in the Image of the
  Artist: A Historical Experiment* (originally *Die Legende vom Künstler: Ein
  historischer Versuch*, Vienna, Krystall Verlag, 1934) (New Haven and
  London, Yale University Press,1979); the references that follow are
  from pp. 10–12, 52, 90 and 126.

5 Theodor Adorno: *Mahler. A Musical Physiognomy*, trans. Edmund
  Jephcott (Chicago and London, University of Chicago Press, 1992)
  [Theodor Adorno: *Mahler*]; the Boulez material quoted will all be
  found in Pierre Boulez: *Orientations* (London, Faber, 1986) in
  'Mahler: Our Contemporary?', p. 300 and in 'Gustav Mahler:

Why Biography?' (the preface to de La Grange), pp. 292–3. The
reference below to Mahler's July 1908 letter to Bruno Walter will be
found in Knud Martner (ed.): *Selected Letters of Gustav Mahler*, trans.
Eithne Wilkins, Ernst Kaiser and Bill Hopkins (London, Faber,
1979) [Knud Martner: *Selected Letters*], p. 324.

1 *Mahler's world*

1 This translation was first printed in Jiří Rychetsky: 'Mahler's
Favourite Song', in *The Musical Times*, CXXX/1762 (December 1989),
729.
2 Like many of the contemporary reports and accounts cited in this
biography, the immediate source is Kurt Blaukopf's 1976 *Mahler.
A Documentary Study* (London, Thames and Hudson, 1976) [Kurt
Blaukopf: *Documentary*], p. 150.
3 I rely in particular, here, on the account of the Prussian/Austrian
war in John Gooch: *Armies in Europe* (London, Routledge and Kegan
Paul, 1980), pp. 90–3. In a BBC Radio 3 programme of 2
September 1995, Karel Janovicky provided additional information
about Mahler's youth in Moravia and 'Ať se pinkl házi', noting that
Prussian military bands in Moravia were specifically directed to
include it in their repertoire, following the victory of 1866, to
improve the morale of the local people.
4 Alma Mahler's characterization of Bernhard Mahler will be found
in Alma Mahler: *Memories*, p. 7; the new mobility of Jews in the
Empire, which Bernhard took advantage of when he moved to
Iglau, was brought about by the Emperor's 1860 Manifesto
heralding partial decentralization and a more liberal,
parliamentary style of government. Bernhard almost conformed
for a time to the image of the 'wayfarer' or travelling journeyman
(*fahrender Gesell*) invoked in his son's song-cycle *Lieder eines fahrenden
Gesellen*. For the 1886 letter from Mahler's mother referred to below,
see Knud Martner: *Selected Letters*, p. 382.
5 Kurt Blaukopf: *Documentary*, p. 148. Another source of recollections
by Theodor Fischer is quoted in translation by Norman Lebrecht in
his *Mahler Remembered* (London, Faber, 1987), pp. 15–20.
6 The year of Ernst's death is given both as 1874 and 1875 by Henry-
Louis de La Grange; even in the recent English vol. 2 of his

biography, Ernst's dates are given in the Index as 1861–74, whereas in the Chronology he contributed to Donald Mitchell's 1995 *Gustav Mahler: The World Listens* (Haarlem, TEMA Uitgevers, 1995) Ernst's date of death is clearly given as 13 April 1875. For Mahler's account of Beeethoven's Op. 121a, see Norman Lebrecht: *Mahler Remembered*, p. 14. The account of the dream recorded in the following paragraph appears in the extended, 1984 German version of Natalie Bauer-Lechner's recollections, edited by Herbert Killian: *Gustav Mahler in die Erinnerungen von Natalie Bauer-Lechner* (Hamburg, Karl Dieter Wagner, 1984), p. 185. It is important to remember that the *Ewige Jude*, better known in English as 'the Wandering Jew', had dishonoured Christ on the way to The Crucifixion. He was a mythical figure frequently alluded to by Christian antisemites.

7 The two quotations here are from Josef Roth: *The Radetzky March*, trans. Eva Tucker (based on an earlier translation by Geoffrey Dunlop), Harmondsworth, Penguin Books, 1974, pp. 18–19 (a further new translation by Joachim Neugroschel has now been published). Kettle-drums would not generally have been found in military bands, although Roth's German text clearly uses the word 'Pauke'. (The quotation in the first paragraph of chapter 2 comes from p. 26).

2   Becoming a musician in Vienna

1 Stefan Zweig: *The World of Yesterday. An Autobiography*, 3rd edn (London, Cassell, 1944) [Stefan Zweig: *Yesterday*], p. 25; the foregoing references are to pp. 21–2. Mahler himself once commented on the clarity with which social class was defined in imperial Vienna, and inscribed in the mind of the 'immaculately ceremonious' doorkeeper of the Emperor's Lord Chamberlain; he often had to help Mahler into a coat whose lining was tattered and torn: 'Imagine how the social order [*Weltordnung*] must be all drawn up inside a head like that, and which rung of the ladder I have been assigned to!' – see Alfred Roller: *Die Bildnisse von Gustav Mahler* (Leipzig, E. P. Tal and Co., 1922) p. 11, as translated by Norman Lebrecht, in Gilbert Kaplan (ed.): *The Mahler Album* (New York and London, The Kaplan Foundation, 1995), p. 16.

2 W. H. Wackenroder and L. Tieck: *Outpourings of an Art-Loving Friar*, trans. Edward Mornin (New York, Frederick Ungar, 1975), p. 123.

3 Mahler's most negative view of Wagner's writings was apparently expressed to Frau Ida Dehmel in 1905; see *Alma Mahler: Memories*, p. 92. On the question of 'Jewish self-hatred' in this period, see Allan Janik, 'Viennese Culture and the Jewish Self-hatred Hypothesis: A Critique' in Ivar Oxaal, Michael Pollak and Gerhard Botz (eds.): *Jews, Antisemitism and Culture in Vienna* (London, Routledge and Kegan Paul, 1987), pp. 75–88.

4 *Max Graf: Composer and Critic. Two Hundred Years of Music Criticism* (London, Chapman and Hall, 1947) , p. 21.

5 The essay-fragments were first published by Hans Holländer in 1929. They are printed, in a translation by Bill Hopkins, in Paul Banks's and David Matthews's Appendix to Donald Mitchell: *Gustav Mahler. The Early Years*, revised and edited by Paul Banks and David Matthews (London, Faber, 1980), pp. 287–90; the quotations here come from pp. 288–9.

6 Much of the preceding is derived from William J. McGrath's invaluable book: *Dionysian Art and Populist Politics in Austria* (New Haven and London, Yale University Press, 1974); the information about the Binzer song and the closure of the *Leseverein* comes from the same author's 'Mahler and Freud: The Dream of the Stately House', in *Gustav Mahler Kolloquium 1979* (ed. Rudolf Klein); *Band 7 der 'Beiträge' der Österreichischen Gesellschaft für Musik* (Kassel/Basel/London, Bärenreiter, 1981), pp. 41–51.

3 Playing the artist – the beginnings of a career

1 Arthur Schnitzler: *My Youth in Vienna*, trans. Catherine Hutter (London, Weidenfeld and Nicolson, 1971), p. 59.

2 This and the preceding quotation from the letter to Joseph Steiner are from the translated version in Knud Martner: *Selected Letters*, pp. 54–7. The source of the foregoing quotation from Wackenroder is as cited in chapter 2, note 2 (p. 119).

3 Knud Martner: *Selected Letters*, p. 58. A different translation will be found in Kurt Blaukopf: *Documentary*, p. 158.

4 Stefan Zweig: *Yesterday*, p. 37.

5 The previous pages rely in particular on Henry-Louis de La Grange:

Mahler vol. 1 (London, Gollancz, 1974) [de La Grange: *Mahler* 1]
pp. 78–9. Rott's Symphony in E major was rediscovered and
transcribed for performance by Paul Banks; see his article 'Hans
Rott and the New Symphony', *The Musical Times* CXXX/1753 (March
1989), 142–7. The work is recorded on Hyperion (CDA66366) by
Gerhard Samual with the Cincinnati Philharmonic Orchestra.

6 The letter to Fritz Löhr will be found in Knud Martner: *Selected
Letters*, p. 68; the translation, as in some of the other letters quoted
in this book, has been slightly emended. Before that, the quotation
about Hanslick comes from Max Graf: *Composer and Critic. Two
Hundred Years of Music Criticism* (London, Chapman and Hall, 1947),
pp. 246–7. The recollection of Mahler in Olmütz comes from a
letter by Jacques Manheit, originally published by Ludwig Karpath;
it is printed in translation in Norman Lebrecht: *Mahler Remembered*,
pp. 29–32. The passages quoted will be found on p. 31.

7 The passage from Alma Mahler comes from *Memories*, p. 109, the
Schnitzler passage from *My Youth in Vienna*, p. 69.

8 Kurt Blaukopf: *Documentary*, p. 172. The stanzas of Mahler's 'Im
Lenz' are quoted in Paul Banks's translation, from his notes to
the Hyperion recording *Mahler's Songs of Youth* (Dame Janet Baker
accompanied by Geoffrey Parsons), CDA66100, p. 6. Before that,
Mahler's 1880 letter to Josephine Poisl will be found in de La
Grange: *Mahler* 1, p. 65.

4 The 'devil' in the wings

1 This translation, though emended, is based on that in Kurt
Blaukopf: *Documentary*, p. 172. An alternative translation appears
in Knud Martner: *Selected Letters*, pp. 82–3.

2 The article cited here was by Heinrich Tewele ('Die nationale
Bedeutung des deutschen Theaters in Prag') and appeared in
the *Dramaturgische Blätter und Bühnen-Rundschau* on 15 January 1888.
My source is Kurt Blaukopf: *Documentary*, p. 174.

3 Kurt Blaukopf: *Documentary*, p. 178; the subsequent quotation
from Steinitzer will be found in Blaukopf on p. 180.

4 This comes from one of Löhr's notes to the first edition of
Mahler's letters: see Knud Martner: *Selected Letters*, pp. 401–2
(n. 71). The Karpath quotation comes form Kurt Blaukopf:

Documentary, p. 182, although my main source of information on
Mahler's Budapest period has been Zoltan Roman: *Gustav Mahler
and Hungary* (Budapest, Akadémiai Kiadó, 1991) [Zoltan Roman:
Hungary]; information about the Budapest opera audience will be
found on p. 33, the material quoted later about Mahler's November
1889 song recital with Bianca Bianchi on pp. 77–8.

5 Zoltan Roman: *Hungary*, p. 78; material on the following pages
comes from the same source, pp. 78–80.

6 De La Grange: *Mahler* 1, p. 206. Fritz Löhr's comment about
Herzfeld will be found in Knud Martner: *Selected Letters*, p. 404
(n. 79).

7 Kurt Blaukopf: *Documentary*, p. 192. The preceding quotation from
a Budapest newspaper comes from Zoltan Roman: *Hungary*, p. 182.

8 Alma Mahler: *Memories*, p. 109.

9 Richard Specht: *Gustav Mahler* (Berlin, Schuster and Loeffler, 1913),
pp. 73–4 (n. 1).

10 The passages quoted here, in my own translation, are from
Ferdinand Pfohl: *Gustav Mahler. Eindrücke und Erinnerungen aus den
Hamburger Jahren*, ed. Knud Martner (Hamburg, Karl Dieter
Wagner, 1973); the first (and what precedes it) from p. 15, the
second (and the subsequent description of Mahler) from p. 16. The
Hamburg 'programme' for the First Symphony that follows, also in
my own translation, has often been cited, but the relevant page of
the original programme-book is printed in de La Grange: *Mahler* 1,
plate 47 (following p. 582).

11 See Leonard J. Kent and Elizabeth C. Knight (eds. and trs.): *Selected
Writings of E. T. A. Hoffmann* (Chicago and London, University of
Chicago Press, 1969), *The Tales* (vol. 1), Introduction, p. 17.

12 Herta Blaukopf (ed.): *Gustav Mahler and Richard Strauss.
Correspondence 1888–1911* trans. Edmund Jephcott (London, Faber,
1984), p. 37.

5 *Imperial and royal (Nature and the city)*

1 Knud Martner: *Selected Letters*, pp. 152–3 (translation slightly
emended).

2 See Alma Mahler: *Memories*, p. 213. Mahler's comment about
composition and experience comes from his letter of 17 February

1897 to Arthur Seidl; see Knud Martner: *Selected Letters*, p. 212
(translation emended). Stephen Hefling's interpretation of the
first movement of the Second Symphony will be found in Stephen
E. Hefling: 'Mahler's "Todtenfeier" and the Problem of Program
Music', *19th Century Music* XII/I (1988), 27–53.

3 On the Binzer song, see William J. McGrath: 'Mahler and Freud:
The Dream of the Stately House', in *Gustav Mahler Kolloquium 1979*
(ed. Rudolf Klein); *Band 7 der 'Beiträge' der Österreichischen Gesellschaft
für Musik* (Kassel/Basel/London, Bärenreiter, 1981), pp. 41–51.
Mahler's statement about the first movement of the Third
Symphony occurs in Natalie Bauer-Lechner: *Recollections of Gustav
Mahler*, trans. Dika Newlin, ed. Peter Franklin (London, Faber,
1980) [Natalie Bauer-Lechner: *Recollections*], p. 62.

4 Mahler's statement about 'Jean Paul' Richter will be found in
Bruno Walter: *Gustav Mahler*, trans. James Galston, with a
biographical essay by Ernst Krenek (New York, Viennese House,
1973), p. 138. See also J. W. Smeed: *Jean Paul's Dreams* (London,
Oxford University Press, 1966).

5 See J. W. Smeed: *Jean Paul's Dreams*, p. 8. Mahler's reference to
Mickiewicz will be found in a December 1909 letter to Bruno
Walter; see Knud Martner: *Selected Letters*, p. 346. The *Siebenkäs*
passages quoted below are taken from Jean Paul Friedrich Richter:
*Flower, Fruit, and Thorn Pieces; or the Wedded Life, Death and Marriage
of Firmian Stanislaus Siebenkäs, Parish Advocate in the Burgh of
Kuschnappel (A Genuine Thorn Piece)*, trans. Alexander Ewing (London,
George Bell and Sons, 1886), pp. 262–3 and p. 260.

6 Henry-Louis de La Grange: *Gustav Mahler. Vol. 2. Vienna: The Years
of Challenge (1897–1904)* (Oxford, Oxford University Press, 1995)
[de La Grange: *Mahler 2*], p. 691. Mahler's comment about the
stage-hands at the Opera will be found in Natalie Bauer-Lechner:
Recollections, p. 117.

7 Kurt Blaukopf: *Documentary*, p. 214. The references below to
Natalie Bauer-Lechner: *Recollections of Gustav Mahler* are to p. 107.

8 De La Grange: *Mahler 1*, p. 487.

9 De La Grange: *Mahler 1*, p. 507. My comment on the aim of the
Second Symphony's Finale relies on Natalie Bauer-Lechner:
Recollections, p. 44. The full texts of the letters to Anna von
Mildenburg (see de La Grange: *Mahler 1*, pp. 343–4) are included

in Herta Blaukopf (ed.): *Gustav Mahler Briefe. Neuausgabe erweitert und revidiert . . .* (Vienna, Paul Zsolnay, 1982), pp.135–9. The quoted sections are in an emended translation from that of de La Grange.

10 See Theodor Adorno: *Mahler*, p. 57. The concluding pages of this chapter rely on Natalie Bauer-Lechner's account (see Natalie Bauer-Lechner: *Recollections*, pp. 167–74) in the fuller version printed in Herbert Killian (ed.): *Gustav Mahler in den Erinnerungen von Natalie Bauer-Lechner*, pp. 187–94.

6 *Alma's Mahler*

1 See Introduction by Willy Haas to Alma Mahler-Werfel: *Mein Leben* (first published in 1960), p. 10.

2 This and the preceding two quotations are from Ludwig Schiedermair: *Gustav Mahler. Eine biographisch-kritische Würdigung* (Leipzig, Hermann Seemann, 1901), pp. 5, 11 and 38 (my own translation). The information on Nordau is derived in particular from Robert Pynsent's 'Conclusory Essay: Decadence, Decay and Innovation' in Robert Pynsent (ed.): *Decadence and Innovation. Austro-Hungarian Life and Art at the Turn of the Century* (London, Weidenfeld and Nicolson, 1989), pp. 128–40; the following quotation is from pp. 130–1. For Mahler's reaction to Schiedermair's book, see Kurt Blaukopf: *Documentary*, p. 225. The source of the subsequently quoted letter from Mahler to Alma is Alma Mahler: *Memories*, pp. 235–6.

3 See Ludwig Schiedermair: *Gustav Mahler. Eine biographisch-kritische Würdigung* (Leipzig, Hermann Seemann, 1901), pp. 13–14; the translation quoted is from Norman Lebrecht: *Mahler Remembered*, p. 126. The letter from Mahler that Seidl had published was that of 17 February 1897, see Knud Martner: *Selected Letters*, pp. 212–14 (the statement about Strauss will be found on p. 213). An account of the post-concert gathering in Munich will be found in Herbert Killian (ed.): *Gustav Mahler in den Erinnerungen von Natalie Bauer-Lechner*, pp. 170–1. The extract from Bruno Walter's 1901 letter to Schiedermair is in my own translation, from Bruno Walter: *Briefe 1894–1962* (Frankfurt-am-Main, S. Fischer, 1969), p.50. The material on Mahler's June 1900 trip to Paris is derived from de La Grange: *Mahler 2*, pp. 256–65.

4 Ferdinand Pfohl: *Gustav Mahler. Eindrücke und Erinnerungen aus den Hamburger Jahren*, p. 37; Mahler's dealings with the compote spoon are described on pp. 27–8.

5 This and the previous quotation are from Alma Mahler: *Memories*, pp. 5 and 19 (the quotation that follows is also from p. 19).

6 For Alma's account of that evening, see Alma Mahler: *Memories*, pp. 25–6; see also de La Grange: *Mahler 2*, pp. 462–3 (Alma's 'Bliss upon bliss' diary entry is cited on p. 461). The full German text of Lipiner's letter to Mahler (in fact the second he wrote) appears in Eveline Nikkels: *'O Mensch! Gib Acht!' Friedrich Nietzsche's Bedeutung für Gustav Mahler* (Amsterdam, Rodopi, 1989), pp. 108–12. Bruno Walter's letter to his parents is quoted in the translation to be found in Kurt Blaukopf: *Documentary*, p. 231.

7 This and the previous quotation are from E. J. Hobsbawm: *The Age of Empire 1875–1914* (London, Weidenfeld and Nicolson, 1987), p. 236. For Schmidt's estimation of Mahler's symphonies, see Harold Truscott: *The Music of Franz Schmidt. Vol. 1 The Orchestral Music* (London, Toccata Press, 1984), p. 16.

8 De La Grange: *Mahler 2*, p. 404; the review referring to 'Trugschlüsse' is quoted there on p. 411. Mahler's comment about the traditional form underlying the Third Symphony will be found in Natalie Bauer-Lechner: *Recollections*, p. 66.

9 Alma Mahler: *Memories*, p. 41. For a full account of the Third Symphony's première, see de La Grange: *Mahler 2*, pp. 527–32.

10 This and the preceding quotation are from Alma Mahler: *Memories*, pp. 210 and 219. The earlier references are to Mahler's letter to Bruno Walter (December 1909) which will be found in Knud Martner: *Selected Letters*, pp. 345–7 (translation emended, see here chapter 8). The title 'Die Welt ohne Schwere' derives from an early plan for a 'Sinfonie Nr. 4 (Humoreske)', which included a D major scherzo so titled; see Paul Bekker: *Gustav Mahlers Sinfonien (1921)* (reprinted Tutzing, Hans Schneider, 1969), p. 145.
Mengelberg's story about the Adagietto of the Fifth Symphony was noted in one of his conducting-scores of the work (see Paul Banks: 'Aspects of Mahler's Fifth Symphony: Performance Practice and Interpretation', *The Musical Times*, CXXX/1755) (May 1989), 262–3.

11 De La Grange: *Mahler 2*, p. 537.

12 All quotations are from the complete letter as printed in translation in de La Grange: *Mahler 2*, pp. 448–52.

13 Alma Mahler: *Memories*, p. 70, although the translation is inadequate. The original will be found in Alma Mahler: *Gustav Mahler. Erinnerungen und Briefe* (Amsterdam, Allert de Lange, 1949), p. 92.

7 *On the heights*

1 See Richard Specht: *Gustav Mahler* (Berlin 1913), pp. 13–14. The two versions of Alma's plan of the Auenbruggergasse apartment will be found in Henry-Louis de La Grange: *Gustav Mahler. Chronique d'une Vie. II. L'Age d'Or de Vienne* (Paris, Fayard, 1983), p. 1075 and de La Grange: *Mahler 2*, p. xix. The following quotation from Alma Mahler comes from *Memories*, p. 71.

2 The foregoing account of the 1903 Basel Festival draws in particular upon the more extended one in de La Grange: *Mahler 2*, pp. 605–14; the following account of Mahler's Amsterdam visit that autumn draws on pp. 639–47.

3 For this and the quotation above see de La Grange: *Mahler 2*, pp. 632–4.

4 Richard Strauss: *Recollections and Reflections*, ed. Willi Schuh, trans. L. J. Lawrence (London, Boosey and Hawkes, 1953), p. 67; for the previous quotation see Richard Strauss: *Briefe an die Eltern, 1882–1906*, ed. Willi Schuh (Zürich/Freiburg, Atlantis, 1954), p. 245. The extract from the manifesto of the *Vereinigung schaffender Tonkünstler* is from Willi Reich: *Schoenberg. A Critical Biography*, trans. Leo Black (London, Longman, 1971), p. 19. The May Day story involving Mahler and Pfitzner appears in Alma Mahler: *Memories*, p. 82. For the following story about the workers' education movement, see Richard Specht: *Gustav Mahler* (1913), p. 27 (note).

5 See de La Grange: *Mahler 2*, p. 691, n. 156. The following story about *The Merry Widow* comes from Alma Mahler: *Memories*, pp. 119–20.

6 See Alma Mahler: *Memories*, p. 243 (translation emended). For Robert Hirschfeld's 1904 review of the Third Symphony, see de La Grange: *Mahler 2*, p. 533.

7 Zoltan Roman: *Hungary*, p. 177. The two Rolland quotations above come from Rollo Myers (ed.): *Richard Strauss and Romain Rolland. Correspondence* (London, Calder and Boyars, 1968), pp. 204–5; Rolland's essay 'French Music and German Music' is translated in full there, pp. 197–215.

8 The above suggestions owe a great deal to Alexander von
Bohrmann: 'Metaphysik der Unmöglichkeit? Zum Text von
Mahlers VIII Symphonie' in Eveline Nikkels and Robert Becqué
(eds.): *A Mass for the Masses. Proceedings of the Mahler VIII Symposium
Amsterdam 1988*, Rijswijk, Universitaire Pers Rotterdam, 1992,
pp. 92–9. For Adorno's 1960 reading of the Eighth, see Theodor
Adorno: *Mahler*, pp. 138–9; for his 1930 reading of it see 'Mahler
Heute' in Theodor Adorno: *Gesammelte Schriften* vol. 18 (Frankfurt-
am-Main, Suhrkamp, 1984), p. 229. Mahler's description of the
Eighth as a 'gift to the nation' (*ein Geschenk an die Nation*) is recorded
in Richard Specht: *Gustav Mahler* (1913), p. 304. For Mahler's
account of the inspiration for the opening of the Seventh
Symphony, see Alma Mahler: *Memories*, p. 328; the following
quotation comes from the same source, p. 106.

9 This and the above passage about Guido Adler are from Alma
Mahler: *Memories*, p. 112. For the following reference to Specht's
recollection of *Iphigénie en Aulide*, see Richard Specht: *Gustav
Mahler* (1913), p. 143.

8 *'What I leave behind me…'*

1 From Thomas Mann: *Selected Stories*, translated and with an
introduction by David Luke (Harmondsworth, Penguin Books,
1993), p. 249. With respect to what follows: Mann's comments
about Aschenbach's resemblance to Mahler come in a letter of
18 March 1921, to Wolfgang Born, see *The Letters of Thomas Mann
1889–1955*, vol. 1 (1889–1942), (London, Secker and Warburg,
1970), p. 110; his 1910 letter to Mahler will be found in Alma
Mahler: *Gustav Mahler. Memories and Letters*, p. 342 (translation
emended); passages from *Königliche Hoheit* are quoted from
Thomas Mann: *Royal Highness* , trans. A Cecil Curtis, rev.
Constance McNab (Harmondsworth, Penguin Books, 1975),
p. 308.

2 See Alma Mahler: *Memories*, pp. 162 and 226.

3 Theodor Adorno: *Mahler*, p. 149. For Mahler's 1905 walk around
the Dürrensee, see Alma Mahler: *Memories*, p. 262.

4 See Bruno Walter: *Gustav Mahler*, p. 59 (translation emended). The
Musil passage comes from Robert Musil: *The Man Without Qualities*,

vol. I, trans. Eithne Wilkins and Ernst Kaiser (London, Pan Books, 1979 etc.), p. 31.

5 The interview was entitled 'The influence of the folk-song on German musical art'; see Norman Lebrecht: *Mahler Remembered*, p. 292. Franz Schmidt's phrase 'salaried slaves' about the Vienna Philharmonic players: source as chapter 6, note 7. Complete translations of Mahler's farewell letter to the Opera will be found in Knud Martner: *Selected Letters*, pp. 304–5 and Kurt Blaukopf: *Documentary*, pp. 250–1; elements of both are used in my emended translation here. For Walter's comment on the 'fourth gallery', see Bruno Walter: *Theme and Variations*, trans. James A. Galston (London, Hamish Hamilton, 1947), p. 155. For an account of Mahler's 1907 conversation with Sibelius see Karl Eckman: *Jean Sibelius. His Life and Personality*, trans. Edward Birse (New York, Tudor, 1938), pp. 190–2.

6 Knud Martner: *Selected Letters*, p. 322. Klemperer's description of Mahler's appearance in Prague in 1908 is from Otto Klemperer: *Minor Recollections*, trans. J. Maxwell Brownjohn (London, Dennis Dobson, 1964), p. 17. For Mahler's statement about homesickness, see Knud Martner: *Selected Letters*, p. 319. The accounts of the 1908 New York fireman's funeral and the street barrel-organ come from Alma Mahler: *Memories*, p. 135.

7 Kurt Blaukopf: *Documentary*, p. 257. For Ritter's description of the Seventh Symphony rehearsal, see Norman Lebrecht: *Mahler Remembered*, p. 198; Hans Makart was the leading academic painter of Vienna's so-called 'Ringstrasse-era'.

8 Alma Mahler: *Memories*, p. 151 (translation emended). In what follows: for Hirschfeld's 1909 review of the Third Symphony, see Peter Franklin: *Mahler Symphony no. 3* (Cambridge, Cambridge University Press, 1991), pp. 31–3.

9 Knud Martner: *Selected Letters*, p. 346, translation emended. For Mahler's 1 October 1909 letter to Alma from Holland, see Alma Mahler: *Memories*, p. 308.

10 Alma Mahler: *Memories*, p. 173. References above to a March 1910 letter from Mahler to Emil Gutmann and to the latter's recollection of rehearsals for the Eighth Symphony are from Herta Blaukopf (ed.): *Mahler's Unknown Letters*, trans. Richard Stokes (London, Gollancz, 1986), pp. 74 and 85. In what follows: concerning

Mahler's 1910 visit to Freud, see Donald Mitchell's Introduction to
the 1968 British edition of Alma Mahler: *Memories*, reprinted in the
most recent, 1991, edition pp. xvii–xviii; for Alma's account of the
visit and Mahler's rediscovery of her songs, see ibid., pp. 175–6.

11 Herta Blaukopf (ed.): *Mahler's Unknown Letters*, p. 88. The two books
published by Paul Stefan in Munich in 1910 were *Gustav Mahler: eine
Studie über Persönlichkeit und Werk* (Munich, R. Piper, 1910) and *Gustav
Mahler: ein Bild seiner Persönlichkeit in Widmungen* (Munich, R. Piper,
1910). With respect to the following: on the continuing
relationship between Alma and Gropius see Henry-Louis de La
Grange: *Gustav Mahler. Chronique d'une Vie. III. Le génie foudroyé
1907–1911* (Paris, Fayard, 1984), pp. 774ff and pp. 848ff. For
Alma's observation about Mahler's having 'no notion what gave a
girl pleasure' see Alma Mahler: *Memories*, p. 181; for her account of
their New York Christmas of 1910 see ibid., pp. 186ff. On Freud's
letter to Reik (and an indication of Mahler's formerly dismissive
attitude towards Freud) see Kurt Blaukopf: *Documentary*, p. 266.
The conclusion that Mahler's marriage was very much a 'shared'
tragedy was drawn by de La Grange in a BBC Radio interview
('Tippling with Alma') with James Woodall, of 20 August 1995.

12 Alma Mahler: *Memories*, p. 338. The quotation is from Goethe's
poem 'Rastlose Liebe' ('Restless Love').

13 The apparently hasty inscription breaks off mid-word: 'Der Teufel
tanzt es mit mir / Wahnsinn, fass mich an, Verfluchten! / vernichte
mich/ dass ich vergesse, das ich bin! / dass ich aufhöre, zu sein /
dass ich ver'. See Gustav Mahler: *Zehnte Symphonie*, Faksimile-
Ausgabe (Berlin etc., Paul Zsolnay, 1924), pages unnumbered (the
facsimile having been published in the form in which the sketches
were left: loose or double sheets of 20- and 22-stave manuscript
paper). The foregoing note from Mahler to Alma ('My darling / my
lyre . . .') appears in Alma Mahler: *Memories*, p. 333 (translation
emended); the poem from which the preceding lines are quoted, in
my own translation, is found only in the German edition of Alma's
book. See Alma Mahler: *Gustav Mahler. Erinnerungen und Briefe*, 2nd
edn, p. 462.

14 Zoltan Roman: *Gustav Mahler's American Years 1907–1911. A
Documentary History* (New York, Pendragon, 1989), p. 418.

15 Henry-Louis de La Grange: *Gustav Mahler. Chronique d'une Vie. III.*

Le génie foudroyé 1907–1911 (Paris, Fayard, 1984), p. 796 (my
translation). Before that: for Mahler's comment about nature
and art, following a visit to the Niagara Falls, see Alma Mahler:
Memories, p. 184; for the June 1909 letter to Alma see Alma Mahler:
Memories, p. 322 (translation emended); the Fechner quotation is
from Gustav Theodor Fechner: *On Life after Death* (originally *Das
Büchlein von Leben nach dem Tod*, 1835), trans. Dr Hugo Wernekke
(Chicago and London, The Open Court Publishing Co., 1914),
p. 24; for both of the references to Specht, see Richard Specht:
Gustav Mahler (1913), pp. 38–9.

16 Paul Stefan: *Das Grab in Wien* (Berlin, Erich Reiss, 1913), p. 142.
Concerning the above: Alma's account of Mahler's dying moments
is found in Alma Mahler: *Memories*, pp. 200–1 – his last word in the
German edition is printed as Mozartl, with the affectionate,
diminutive 'l'; for Zweig's comment about Hartmann, see Stefan
Zweig: *Yesterday*, p. 44. For information concerning Mahler's final
illness, I have relied in particular on the very clear account in David
Levy: 'Gustav Mahler and Emanuel Libman: Bacterial Endocarditis
in 1911', in *The British Medical Journal*, 293, 20–27 December 1986,
1628–31. For a full bibliography of relevant material, see Henry-
Louis de La Grange: *Gustav Mahler. Chronique d'une Vie. III. Le génie
foudroyé 1907–1911* (Paris, Fayard, 1984).

Recent biographical and documentary research has been particularly
productive of new or revised collections of Mahler's letters. The
earliest published collection had been brought out by Alma Mahler in
1924; that volume (an extended English edition of which was edited by
Knud Martner as *Selected Letters of Gustav Mahler*, London, Faber, 1979)
appeared in its fullest version to date, with previously omitted material
reinserted, in a German edition by Herta Blaukopf in 1982. It was
followed by an edition of Mahler's correspondence with Richard
Strauss (English version: *Gustav Mahler. Richard Strauss. Correspondence
1888–1911*, ed. Herta Blaukopf, trans. Edmund Jephcott, London,
Faber, 1984) and then *Mahler's Unknown Letters*, ed. Herta Blaukopf,
trans. Richard Stokes, London, Gollancz, 1986. To these must now
be added a major new publication which came out as this biography
was nearing its completion; its editors, Henry-Louis de La Grange
and Günther Weiss, include full texts of all the surviving letters from
Mahler to Alma in *Ein Glück ohne Ruh', Die Briefe Gustav Mahlers an Alma.
Erste Gesamtausgabe*, Berlin, Siedler, 1995. Cuts and omissions made by
Alma in her *Gustav Mahler. Memories and Letters*, referred to but still not
restored in the 4th edition of its abridged English translation
(London, Sphere Books, 1991), are fully restored, along with
extensive, hitherto unpublished material from her original diaries.
Also included is material from Mahler's letters to his sister Justine
and from Alma's to Walter Gropius. Much of this material had been
utilized in de La Grange's Mahler biography (now appearing in
a four-volume English edition, starting with vol. 2, *Vienna: The Years
of Challenge*, Oxford, Oxford University Press, 1995); nevertheless,
the publication of the original German texts is to be welcomed.
An English translation of this important book is planned.

Other significant sources of documentary and pictorial material
relevant to Mahler's life include the present author's edition of Dika
Newlin's translation of the abridged version of Natalie Bauer-Lechner:
Recollections of Gustav Mahler, London, Faber, 1980, Kurt Blaukopf's

Mahler. A Documentary Study, London, Thames and Hudson, 1976 (the
textual portion of which was republished as Kurt Blaukopf and Herta
Blaukopf: Mahler: His Life, Work and World, London, Thames and
Hudson, 1991), Norman Lebrecht's Mahler Remembered, London, Faber,
1987, and the two books by Zoltan Roman: Gustav Mahler's American
Years 1907–1911, New York, Pendragon, 1989, and Gustav Mahler and
Hungary, Budapest, Akadémiai Kiadó, 1991. A fine collection of
pictures and photographs has been published by Gilbert Kaplan
in The Mahler Album, New York and London, Kaplan Foundation, 1995,
to which must be added a similarly lavish book, edited by Donald
Mitchell, commemorating the 1995 Amsterdam Mahler Festival:
Gustav Mahler: The World Listens, Haarlem, TEMA Uitgevers, 1995.

While de La Grange's enormous multi-volume biography of Mahler
inevitably dominates the field, a number of earlier one-volume
biographies in English are still worth reading, particularly those by
Kurt Blaukopf (Gustav Mahler, London, Allen Lane, 1973) and Michael
Kennedy (Mahler, London, Dent, 1974). Those interested in Alma
Mahler's various accounts of her life with Mahler should also seek out
her autobiography And the Bridge is Love. Memories of a Lifetime, with E. B.
Ashton, London, Hutchinson, 1958 (not to be confused with her
rather different and more extensive German autobiography Mein Leben,
Frankfurt-am-Main, Fischer, 1960). Alma has herself now become the
subject of biographies by Karen Monson (Alma Mahler, Muse to Genius,
London, Collins, 1984), Françoise Giroud (Alma Mahler or The Art of
Being Loved, trans. Richard Stock, London, Oxford University Press,
1991) and Susanne Keegan (The Bride of the Wind. The Life of Alma Mahler,
London, Secker and Warburg, 1991).

The vast scope of the books and articles dealing with Mahler and
his music that is now available to specialists in the field is indicated
by Simon Michael Namenwirth's three-volume Gustav Mahler. A Critical
Bibliography (Wiesbaden, Otto Harrassowitz, 1987). A useful shorter
reference book is Susan Filler's Gustav and Alma Mahler. A Guide to
Research, New York and London, Garland, 1989.

INDEX